DESIGN AND SECURITY IN THE BUILT ENVIRONMENT

DESIGN AND SECURITY IN THE BUILT ENVIRONMENT

LINDA S. O'SHEA

KEAN UNIVERSITY

RULA AWWAD-RAFFERTY

UNIVERSITY OF IDAHO

FAIRCHILD BOOKS, INC.

NEW YORK

Director of Sales and Acquisitions: Dana Meltzer-Berkowitz
Executive Editor: Olga T. Kontzias
Senior Development Editor: Jennifer Crane
Development Editor: Joseph Miranda
Assistant Development Editor: Blake Royer
Art Director: Adam B. Bohannon
Production Director: Ginger Hillman
Senior Production Editor: Elizabeth Marotta
Associate Art Director: Erin Fitzsimmons
Copy Editor: Nancy Reinhardt
Interior Design: Tom Helleberg
Cover Design: Adam B. Bohannon

Library of Congress Catalog Card Number: 2007943511

ISBN: 978-1-56367-497-6

GST R 133004424

Printed in the United States of America

TP09

From the heart, Linda O'Shea would like to dedicate this book to her husband and best friend, Bob O'Shea; in memory of her beloved mother and stepfather, Barbara and Paul Christensen; and to her nephew, Jeffrey Manning, a fine young man fighting in the armed forces for safety and security for us all.

Rula Awwad-Rafferty would like to dedicate this book to her husband, Daniel P. Rafferty; sister, Bayan Awwad; brother, Eyas Awwad; and brother-in-law, David G. Rafferty; and to all the nieces and nephews in Jordan, Palestine, Italy, the USA, and in the great diaspora—together we have a responsibility to safety and security with sensitivity, respect, and dignity.

CONTENTS

10729658З

EXTENDED CONTENTS

1072965 83

INTRODUCTION

We travel together, passengers on a little spaceship, dependent on its vulnerable reserves of air and soil, all committed, for our safety, to its security and peace. Preserved from annihilation only by the care, the work and the love we give our fragile craft.

—Adlai E. Stevenson II (1900–1965)

The words of Adlai E. Stevenson II, although spoken a half century ago, resonate a profound relationship between us as human beings and our environment—one of interdependence and responsibility. The notions of protection and care communicated in those words echo a mantra that can be used effectively by designers as they explore the complex and interrelated facets of design problems and solutions, among which is the behemoth that is design and security in the built environment.

In the twenty-first century, security has become a paramount concern within the built-environment professions due to heightened awareness of risks, building industry standards, and stakeholders' demands. The federal government and some security agencies and personnel have attempted to address this urgent security concern by establishing a dialogue on security, providing security guidelines and mandates, and offering an array of security-related products. Simultaneously, as the dialogue evolves, we find a wide array of approaches to addressing security, both from disciplinary expertise and interdisciplinary efforts. We also find discrepancies between theory and application; disconnection between problem and solution; and misconception about terminologies, and security solutions and their impacts.

Security and safety are ubiquitous and simultaneously loaded terms; they are not a matter of temporal headlines during periods of fear and uncertainty, nor are they reserved for external threats. They are among the most basic and central of human needs and rights. Affording safe and secure environments ought not to be a means of increasing fear among stakeholders. The interior designer's commitment to protect the health, safety, and welfare of the public through her or his professional work demands that we become effective leaders and contributors in the creation and implementation of environments that embrace an integrated approach to safety and security. This approach must meet the psychological and physical needs of the built environments' users, while respecting the values, civics, and ethos of the context. The design professionals' commitment to protect the health, safety, and welfare of the public can be merged with proactive safety and security perspectives to provide opportunities for fresh and innovative design solutions to the built environments of the twenty-first century.

The pedagogical framework of *Design and Security in the Built Environment* is that when security is considered from the onset of a design problem, the outcome is a more sustainable and effective design solution, with a seamless connection between security and other functional, social, aesthetic, and economic considerations. Conceptually and programmatically, this book deconstructs concepts of safety and security in the built environment while paying attention to contextual forces and the use of a systems approach. One of the initial steps to take, as students of design, and design professionals, is to become more familiar with the security concerns at hand and to proactively initiate the security dialogue with clients and professional peers.

In addition, it is critical that designers understand the realities and effects of increased threats of terrorism, crime, and workplace violence on the built environment, as these issues have become areas of paramount ethical and liability concern for building owners and occupants. Events from our history are chronicled in the timeline on the inside covers. Refer to this for examples of benchmark events that relate to security.

Enhanced by interdisciplinary exploration, this book is intended primarily for intermediate to advanced interior design students, as well as design educators, design professionals, and all those who are interested in the ways that issues of security affect people and the built environment. This book explores design and security in the built environment in nine chapters. You should come away from this text understanding the following:

- Complexity of meaning, parameters, need for, and selected approaches to design and security in the built environment.
- Human need for safety and security from various paradigms.
- Basic psychological aspects of security as it relates to the built environment.
- Foundational studies related to security in the built environment and conceptually integrate security solutions into the built environment.
- How the built environment has changed as societies deal with acts of terrorism, violence, acts of aggression, natural and manufactured hazards and risks, and criminal behavior.

- The complexity and interrelatedness of safety and security in the built environment from a systems thinking approach.
- Basic security design programming issues, a variety of security-related materials and products, and interdisciplinary best practices.
- The impact of security on design, perception, use, and management of the built environment.
- The impact of the designer's role in security design, perception, use, and management of the built environment.
- Challenges faced in providing security for a diversity of interior environments, while balancing seemingly dichotomous goals.
- Reasoned and globally aware perspectives on how the concerns of the twenty-first century have impacted the built environment.
- Security concerns and mitigation strategies in the twenty-first century and their impact on the built environment.

Chapter 1 provides an overview of safety and security constructs and the connections to the built environment. Chapters 2 and 3 provide a foundational perspective that relays an interdisciplinary body of scholarship on security and safety in the environment and suggests a framework for analysis. Chapters 4 through 8 address security in various building types and environments including educational settings, health-care facilities, public environments, retail, workplace, and historic interiors, and these chapters provide references for best practices. Specifically, these chapters afford an opportunity to:

- Develop an awareness of conducting security assessments that identify existing and potential risk factors and hazards within the workplace, educational facilities, health-care settings, public environments, historic interiors, and other types of environments.
- Increase awareness of the variety of prevention strategies that are important security design considerations within selected interior environments.
- Review the principals of Crime Prevention through Environmental Design (CPTED) and their relationship to safety and security within identified types of interior environments.
- Increase awareness of the role of the interior designer, architect, landscape architect, facility manager, and building owner as they relate to the design of safe and secure environments.
- Reinforce an understanding of the security concerns of the twenty-first century and their impact on and interdependence with the design and management of the built environment.
- Understand the reciprocal relationship between the public environment, security solutions, experience, and behavior.

Chapter 9 reinforces the importance of the designer's role in, and relationship to, security perspectives and emerging issues. It simultaneously nudges a paradigm shift in how design and security in the built environment are viewed and addressed. Design security emphasizes the critical need to explore interdisciplinary lessons and paradigms, as well as foster innovative connections among found parallels between security in the built environment and other fields, such as connections with psychology, sociology, physiology, ethics, and forms of social commentary. Chapter 9 centrally outlines an integrative systems approach model to understanding the interconnections and implications related to design and security in the built environment. Throughout the book, the premise of interdisciplinary integration, systems thinking, and the simultaneous centrality of a design and security dialogue has been stressed.

The universal need for security and safety is not in question, rather, the question is how can designers define and conceptualize the parameters of this need, and address it in the built environment? A transformational approach to security consideration in the built environment has been in the making for over six decades. It is a prime window of opportunity for designers to become actively involved in the formation and emergence of a new era of security consciousness. Interior environments are primarily "people's places and spaces," they are designed and managed to facilitate certain types of actions and interactions. As designers, we give careful consideration to how the physical, psychological, and social environments we create support or hinder intended activities. Similarly, we should also recognize and anticipate the design and management features of the settings that influence the safety and security of stakeholders, either by facilitating or inhibiting actions. One of our responsibilities as designers is affording safety and security for people in the built environment, so it is imperative that we are well educated in matters of global worldview when addressing safety and security. In addition to cultural differences related to private and public domains, significant issues directly impact safety and security; including from the simplest of terminologies regarding labeling of floors, to signage and wayfinding, to taboos and spatial imperatives. For the built environment to be effectively safe and secure, it has to communicate with a global voice, User-Centered Design, and contextual sensitivity.

The design community must be cognizant of the leadership role it plays in facilitating and advancing a security plan that is seamless and integrated into the design, construction, and management of the environment. Achieving a positive relationship and integrated solutions for security concerns greatly depends on our ability to find ways to bring together those who design spaces, those who secure them, and those who use them. Active participation in the security dialogue, learning from past experiences dealing with security design issues, and the willingness to educate others about the value of the built environment, all partnered with an understanding of the security measures that can make a significant impact on the health, safety, and welfare of the public, will assist the design profession in defining, articulating, and creating appropriate design solutions for the twenty-first century—solutions that create a seamless connection between security and other functional, social, aesthetic, and economic considerations.

ACKNOWLEDGMENTS

We learn by watching, we learn by doing, and for many, we learn by reflecting and dialoguing. This book is about personal and group learning; it is both a reflection on tragic phenomena and a deliberate study and investigation of possibilities and solutions. But the most driving force is the hope that this book provides an opportunity to learn, investigate, reflect, and create.

We wish to acknowledge all who made our journey of exploration, reflection, and learning on the issues involved in the design of safe and secure environments meaningful and fruitful. The impetus for this book began as a reaction to horrific events and consequences, but with the guidance and perspective of many, it has evolved into a proactive dynamic and systematic perspective that addresses important issues surrounding the design profession in the twenty-first century. This investigation of design and security in the built environment has taken an integrative approach in which pushing the limits and moving beyond the comfort zones became necessary. Such an endeavor would not have been successful without the support, encouragement, inspiration, and intellectual challenges offered by many.

Many thanks go to our colleagues who actively listened to our evolving presentations at the Interior Design Educators Council (IDEC) and Environmental Design Research Association (EDRA) Conferences, while offering their knowledge, unique perspectives, and encouragement. Special thanks go to Dr. Rand Lewis, founder of Transnational Strategic Solutions, Inc. (TS2 Corp) and Ms. Ronni Whitman, interior designer and design educator, for their expert opinions and application expertise. Recognition also goes to Mr. Thierry Rosenheck, Office of Overseas Buildings Operations, US Department of State, for his ideas and perspective on Crime Prevention through Environmental Design (CPTED) and scenario planning; as well as to Peter Hecht for sharing his analysis of security at the Atlanta Olympics. Special thanks go to Professor Stephen Drown, great colleague and Chair of the Landscape Architecture Department at the University of Idaho and his student Jordan Wu, Senior in Landscape Architecture, for their contribution of examples from outreach Senior Studio Project, illustrating seamless integration of security in the master plan for the University of Idaho Sandpoint Campus. Special thanks go to the safety officers in both of our universities for their dedication and for the many conversations held related to approaches on security. Thanks to Mrs. Kaufman, the retired Boise Sheriff who spoke of CPTED from "days back when," she certainly added to the idea that some issues will be revisited and reevaluated over time, but one thing remains: we need to be safe and secure.

Our students have been a significant force in helping us see; their reactions to readings, situations, and events, along with the design journals and project solutions in which they began to identify safety and security goals and approaches, have been refreshing. The list of contributions is extensive: a special acknowledgement to the students enrolled in the Special Topics: Design Security in the Built Environment course, offered at Kean University in 2006, in which many of the preliminary ideas and scenarios for this textbook were initially developed. Many hands-on learning and application strategies emerged as students engaged in their own exploration of safety and security in various design projects at the University of Idaho. Katie Studer designed a women's shelter in Kirkuk, Iraq, for her capstone interior design project after returning from her tour of duty there; Heather Evan investigated the complexity of safety and security in a mixed-use complex in Vancouver, British Columbia, during a project site visit; Kori Arthur, double major in architecture and interior design, and the 2005/2006 interior design senior class explored ideas of community participation and intersecting safety and security cultural paradigms and worldviews when they worked with the Shoshone-Bannock tribes of Fort Hall, Idaho. Many thanks to Hanna Persson for her bioregional planning and community design solution that seamlessly addressed security for the town of Stites, Idaho. In all these examples, design and security in the built environment became personal, rich, and transformational. Our students deserve many thanks for keeping us grounded and focused, and providing us with much encouragement and perspective, especially when we faced doubts and deadlines!

Watching a nephew play and fall asleep in one of the most public of spaces sparked a question about psychological sense of safety and security, and made us wonder about those basic needs and how they may be acknowledged in our work as designers and educators. Meeting with a variety of manufacturers' representatives explaining products designed to meet safety and security needs within the workplace, viewing video documentaries of residential safe rooms, personal parachutes to evacuate tall buildings, and products for biochemical warfare, led us to believe that interior design and planning must play an important role in this new security-conscious world.

Of course, our interests would never have come to fruition if not for the energetic and professional faith that our editors at Fairchild Books had in us and in the importance of our topic for a book. Many thanks to Olga T. Kontzias, Joseph Miranda, Dana Berkowitz, and the entire staff at Fairchild for the vision, the feedback, and the great lessons learned in the process of writing a book. A special thanks for making it possible for two design educators and authors, one on the

East Coast, and one on the West Coast, to spend valuable time together in the summer of 2007, in one place, with one time zone, to solidify the work.

We would both like to acknowledge our husbands, Daniel P. Rafferty and Robert G. O'Shea, for their continued support and encouragement. Writing a book, while meeting the responsibilities of teaching, service, outreach, and other scholarship as faculty members in public institutions was a challenge, and we truly appreciate their continued patience and belief in our efforts. We would also like to thank our families and special friends, in the United States, Jordan, and across the globe. You were in our minds and hearts as we looked at examples and solutions of security in an often complex world.

Coauthoring is not always easy, working with a friend and a colleague as coauthors sometimes adds additional challenges. In many ways, we have come to this project from two opposite directions in location, writing styles, and life experiences. Through the research and writing process, we have enjoyed the coming together of minds on an important issue, the seeing of another's perspective, and the wonderful collegiality that a focus on learning brings about. That being said, we are grateful for this collaboration and its outcome, and hope that you will find value in addressing these important issues from our perspective.

DESIGN AND SECURITY IN THE BUILT ENVIRONMENT

1 WHY STUDY DESIGN AND SECURITY?

Designers are trained to balance risk with protection and to mediate between disruptive change and normalcy; good design goes hand in hand with personal needs, providing protection and security without sacrificing innovation and invention.

—SAFE: Design Takes on Risk Exhibit,
Museum of Modern Art, Fall 2005

OBJECTIVES

- Develop an understanding of the human need for safety and security
- Develop an awareness of the impact of security on design, perception, use, and management of the built environment
- Articulate the complexity of the meaning and parameters of, need for, and selected approaches to design and security in the built environment
- Increase awareness of the complexity and interrelatedness of safety and security in the built environment
- Formulate reasoned and globally aware perspectives on how the concerns of the twenty-first century have impacted the built environment

It was a beautiful wedding celebration at the Radisson Hotel in Amman, Jordan on November 9, 2005, with 300 guests in attendance; the happy newlyweds were being serenaded into the ballroom, when the horrific event occurred. Three simultaneous explosions shocked the structures of three hotels in downtown Amman, causing loss of life, property damage, horror, and an overall assault on the community's sense of security and safety. Might this have been avoided if there were appropriate security measures subtly integrated into the architecture of the hotel lobby as guests arrived for this important celebration?

In a courthouse in Atlanta, Georgia, with court in session for what should have been a normal business day, an inmate was able to retrieve a loaded weapon from a security guard, and fatally injure the guard and several bystanders as he escaped. The inadequacy of building and personal security, the maze of corridors, and the resulting shock and chaos all hindered his immediate capture and facilitated more damage and loss of life in this 2004 incident. Might this have been avoided if the inmate had been unable to hide in corridors and escape through a back door into a public area?

An employee at a Kansas City, Kansas, meat packing plant shot eight fellow employees before committing suicide in 2004; in 2003, an employee of a defense contractor in Mississippi shot 14 employees, killing six before taking his own life; and in 2000, a software engineer in Wakefield, Massachusetts, seeking revenge for a recent IRS wage garnishment, used a semi-automatic military rifle to take the lives of seven innocent employees. Might some of these tragedies have been avoided if the lobby areas of these places of work had created an architectural barrier between entering the building and access to employees?

In April 2001, a deadly shooting rampage on a high school campus in Columbine, Colorado, killed 12 students and a teacher and wounded 24 others. Might this loss have been avoided if the corridors of schools were designed for total visibility, or the building designed to prevent direct access into a classroom to help keep students safe and secure? (See Figure 1.1.) In 2005, a father tried, unsuccessfully, to

1.1 The bombing of the Alfred P. Murrah Federal Building office complex in downtown Oklahoma City, Oklahoma, claimed 168 lives and left more than 800 people injured.

abduct his three-year-old from a day-care center in suburban Chicago. What were the interior design attributes that may have contributed to outcomes of all these and other incidents? How can design professionals learn from such examples? The authors do not advocate that occurrences of such crimes or terrorist acts be taken out of context (both macro and micro) when analyzed, or that they are treated as isolated events facilitated only by inadequately designed environments. However, it is necessary to investigate the role of the designed environment as a mediator or moderator in an effort to **mitigate**—intervene in the consequences of an event—the likelihood of these occurrences and their impact.

FYI: "I'm standing in a small cell on a pair of large footprints traced on carpet. Transparent doors slam shut behind me as I stare through the locked doors in front of me. I wait. A few moments pass, and as I look around the phone-booth-size space I start feeling claustrophobic. To counter this sense of entrapment, I take deep breaths and count, inhaling and exhaling. Suddenly blasts of cool air come at me from all directions, mussing my hair and rippling my clothing—it sounds as if six tires are deflating in rapid succession. I wait for the doors to open for what seems like an eternity."

—Susan Szenasy, *Metropolis*, April 2006
Description of security at Miami International Airport

The description in the FYI box of a typical airport screening at an international airport would make anyone feel anxious and fearful. The very system that has been put in place to protect us feels clumsy and dehumanizing. Air transportation is just one example of the unprecedented global change that is occurring due to evolving security requirements, technological developments, and economic resources. Interior designers, as observers of human behavior, need to use their knowledge and expertise to provide solutions and suggestions for how people can interact with the physical world, while keeping their emotional well-being and dignity intact. If security is a twenty-first-century necessity, it needs the attention of experts in design and human behavior, those who understand individuals and their complex natures.

Addressing safety and security in the built environment has been and continues to be complex and highly charged. To whom does the responsibility for maintaining a dynamic, contextual, and appropriate system of safety and security in the built environment fall? When, and in what paradigm? Undoubtedly, the most significant benchmark event related to security in the United States in the current mindset is September 11, 2001—tragic events that have since galvanized much of the security discussion and subsequent actions and design innovations in the United States and around the world. But how can design professionals, working from the standpoint that design contributes to the overall quality of life, safety, and well-being, and simultaneously accepting that it is not possible to design all aspects of the built environment to ensure 100 percent safety and security, design places of work, play, and worship that maximize safety and security and yet afford full functionality and meaningful experience of the designed place, without a bunker mentality? Stemming from the ethos of design problem solving, this book introduces a systems approach to design and security in the built environment that can provide design professionals with a philosophy, coupled with a dynamic set of possibilities that may be appropriated for various environmental settings by the designer.

A breach of security often refocuses our attention to vulnerabilities and stimulates our actions. The previously cited events have permanently changed the way in which government and private commercial clients locate, plan, and design buildings. As a result, security has become and will continue to be an essential criterion for planning buildings in the future. The horrific examples cited earlier of terrorist acts, criminal behavior, and **workplace violence** sadly illustrate our susceptibility to violence in the places where we play and work, while heightening our awareness of the vulnerability of the built environment. Applying any number of environmental psychology theories or environment behavior theories and perspectives, they might have been avoided if more rigorous security measures were adapted within the design and planning stages as deterrents to violence.

Historic reflection is necessary to capture the progression of thinking and action, as well as the reiteration of specific guidelines related to security in the built environment. Site selection, clustering, fortifications, sentries, and space-planning concerns have been put in use throughout the ages to afford various degrees of safety and security.

An example of vernacular architecture, as shown in Figure 1.2, demonstrates an integrated sense of culture, design, use of space, and security in the built environment. However, our intuitive attention to matters of security has become more complex and specialized with the increased complexity of the built environment. Benchmarks and historical precedent related to security in the built environment in the context of this book will focus on those in the twentieth and twenty-first centuries. (See Figure 1.2.)

In addition to the threat of **terrorism** and crime, many types of emergencies do occur during the day-to-day operation and management of facilities that could potentially affect the building's inhabitants with life-and-death consequences. For example, the city-wide electrical blackout in New York City in 2004 that affected building occupants' ability to safely evacuate high-rise apartments, skyscraper-type offices, and crowded public spaces.

Although the realities of increased threats of terrorism, crime, and workplace violence are not disputed, liability concerns over the security of interior spaces and places have also become of greater importance. The design professionals' commitment to protect the health, safety, and welfare of the public can be merged with

1.2 An example of integrated sense of design, culture, and security in the built environment.

proactive safety and security perspectives to provide opportunities for fresh and innovative design solutions to the built environments of the twenty-first century.

BEST PRACTICES—ALLIED PROFESSIONS: ARCHITECTURE AND LANDSCAPE ARCHITECTURE

Design and Security in the Built Environment addresses safety and security design issues within the built environment from the perspective of the interior design and interior architecture professions. The American Institute of Architects (AIA), through its committee on Architecture for Justice and the Security Design Coalition of the American Institute of Landscape Architects (ILA) have developed valuable standards and guidelines that address designing for security from site considerations, vehicular and pedestrian access, blast-resistant building materials, and other aspects of the built environment. When appropriate, selected examples of **Best Practices**—practices that have produced outstanding results in one situation and could be adapted to another situation—of the AIA and the ILA professions are summarized in this text to provide useful examples of suggestions and/or recommendations for safety and security as it relates to specific project solutions.

> **FYI:** "Every project situation is different. Each presents a different set of requirements and limitations. Each presents a unique set of cultural, environmental, technological, and aesthetic contexts to be considered. Each presents its own set of challenges and opportunities. Design brings to the surface the major considerations inherent in a situation. It is a process that is both problem-seeking and problem-solving."
>
> —American Institute of Architects (AIA), excerpted and adapted from the *Architects Handbook of Professional Practice*, 13th edition

The Design Team

There is a significant and critical need for a systematic and ongoing dialogue among the design team members from the first stages of any project, including those who are trained experts in design, security, psychology, and other related fields (See Figure 1.3). "The first step in security planning is to assemble a multidisciplinary team," says Barbara A. Nadel, FAIA, author of *Building Security: Handbook for Architectural Planning and Design* (2004). Designers should work with a team consisting of clients, engineers, architects, landscape architects, facility managers, on-site security staff, and perhaps professional security consultants if the project is complex. The design team, working with clients, should assess potential threats, define assets that need protection (with people being the first priority), determine vulnerabilities, and develop a security plan that encompasses design, security, and operations.

WHAT IS SAFETY? WHAT IS SECURITY?

Are safety and security tangible and measurable concepts? Are they physical? Are they psychological? How do we assess humans' needs for safety and security? How can we design environments that satisfy a diversity of basic, as well as situational, safety and security needs? What are the characteristics of safe environments? When is it that we feel and are secure?

1.3 There is a significant need for security dialogue among coalitions because innovations in one field can hold great benefits in other areas.

As researchers investigate the various aspects related to safety and security from a wide range of disciplines and paradigms (e.g., psychology, sociology, and physiology), it is important that the interior designer, in partnership with related design disciplines, investigates the relationship between these varied perspectives and their potential for integration and innovation as they relate to the built environment.

Interior design as a profession deals with the health, safety, and welfare of the public through the understanding of accessibility, ergonomics, and building codes to improve quality of life. The security component becomes another layer of professional responsibility to minimize **risk**, therefore increasing safety, in the planning and integration of security features into the design solutions of the interior environment.

The commitment to protect the health, safety, and welfare of the public through their professional work demands that interior designers become effective leaders and contributors in the creation and implementation of new security guidelines and measures as they relate to the built environment in general, and the interior domain in particular. As designers grapple with the new heightened risk awareness, and the importance of considering new and safer design alternatives, our responsibility is to assure our clients that security is an integral part of the programming process just like accessibility or fire safety. As humans spend the majority of their lives indoors, it is expected that the design and management of these environments respond to the needs, fears, anxieties, and desires of their users.

Safety, Security, and the Human Spirit

Linguistically, **safe/safety**—according to the Merriam-Webster Dictionary—is "the condition of being safe from undergoing or causing hurt, injury, or loss; free from harm or risk, secure from threat of danger, harm, or loss, affording safety or security from danger, risk, or difficulty." Whereas **security** is defined as "the quality or state of being secure and affording safety; and free from risk of loss, and free from danger, fear or anxiety." It is apparent that security is both a feeling and a physical condition—both are significant sides of the coin—and that the discussion regarding security and feeling safe must acknowledge that perception is an important aspect in assessing risks and mitigating them.

Security is an inalienable right for every human being, according to Article 3 of the United Nations Universal Declaration of Human Rights, signed by all member nations in 1948. This document states that "everyone has the right to life, liberty, and security of person." Actually, this is not the only article that mentions security of the person or society as one of the human rights; Article 22 focuses on economic, social, and cultural security, and other articles embed notions of security throughout. The preamble of the Universal Declaration of Human Rights begins by stating, "Whereas recognition of the inherent dignity and of the equal and inalienable rights of all members of the human family is the foundation of freedom, justice, and peace in the world. Whereas disregard and contempt for human rights have resulted in barbarous acts which have outraged the conscience of mankind, and the advent of a world in which human beings shall enjoy freedom of speech and belief and freedom from fear and want." The connection between various facets of human rights and that of security is inescapable, as it is the foundation of what fosters a sense of community and humanity.

It is intriguing, and most appropriate, to find that theories dealing with security span several social science areas, such as psychology, political science, criminology, and sociology. Built environment literature related to security has been most concentrated in overall planning, gated communities, and low income neighborhood design. The specialized foundation for this body of knowledge, however, echoes back to the early part of the twentieth century and is highlighted in Chapter 2.

The Hierarchy of Human Needs—Maslow and Beyond

Humanistic psychologist Abraham Maslow developed a theory of personality that has influenced a number of different fields including design, education, and the social sciences. This wide influence is due in part to the high level of practicality of Maslow's theory, which accurately describes many realities of personal experiences. Maslow articulated a **hierarchy of needs** based on what he called deficiency needs, growth needs, and self actualization needs. Within the deficiency needs, each lower need must be met before moving to the next higher level. Once each of these needs has been satisfied, if at some future time a deficiency is detected, the individual will act to remove the deficiency. The first four levels included in deficiency needs are:

1. Physiological: hunger, thirst, bodily comforts, etc.
2. Safety/security: out of danger
3. Belonging-ness and love: affiliate with others, to be accepted
4. Esteem: to achieve, be competent, gain approval and recognition

According to Maslow, an individual is ready to act upon the growth needs if and only if the deficiency needs are met. Maslow in his later work differentiated between growth needs and self actualization (Maslow & Lowery, 1998). The growth and self-actualization needs are:

1. Cognitive: to know, to understand, and explore
2. Aesthetic: symmetry, order, and beauty
3. Self actualization: to find self-fulfillment and realize one's potential
4. Self-transcendence: to connect to something beyond the ego or to help others find self-fulfillment and realize their potential (see Figure 1.4)

1.4
Maslow's hierarchy of needs.

1.5
Children often display signs of security and insecurity in their degree of adaptation, orientation, and use of space. Sense of security also affects cognitive, emotional, and physical development.

When all physiological needs are satisfied and are no longer controlling thoughts and behaviors, the need for security can become active. The safety and security needs operate mainly on a psychological level. Once we manage a certain level of physical comfort and safety, we will seek to establish stability and consistency in a chaotic world.

Adults usually have little awareness of their security needs except in times of emergency or periods of disorganization in the social structure (such as widespread rioting, a major catastrophic event, or personal condition that highlights insecurity). Some adults however manifest their stationary position regarding security as if they expect a catastrophe to happen any moment, be it in relation to their overall lives, or to a particular place in the environment. Children on the other hand, often display the signs of insecurity and the need to be safe and often strive for predictability and certainty (see Figure 1.5).

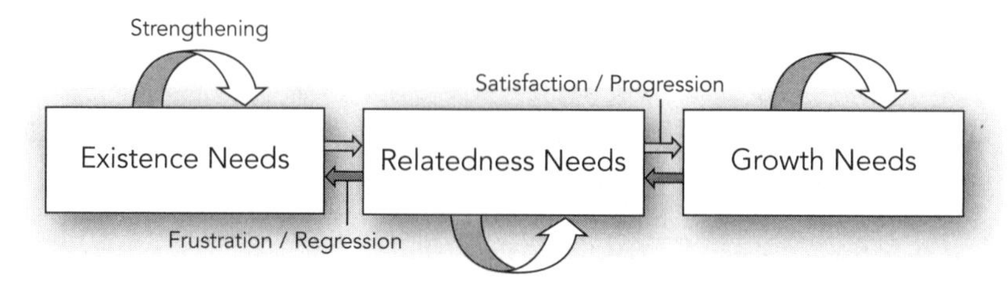

1.6 The most important contribution of the ERG model is the addition of the frustration-regression hypothesis: When individuals are frustrated in meeting higher level needs, the next lower needs reemerge.

In 1969, Clayton P. Alderfer proposed the ERG (Existence, Relatedness, and Growth) theory in a *Psychological Review* article entitled "An Empirical Test of a New Theory of Human Need." The ERG theory is similar to Maslow's Hierarchy of Human Needs in articulating various layers of needs, but differs in that all the three ERG areas are not hierarchically ordered, and can and do occur simultaneously. The three needs categories according to ERG theory are:

1. *Existence Needs:* physiological and safety needs (such as hunger, thirst, and sex), which corresponds to Maslow's first two levels
2. *Relatedness Needs:* social and external esteem (involvement with family, friends, coworkers, and employers), corresponding to Maslow's third and fourth levels
3. *Growth Needs:* internal esteem and self actualization (desires to be creative, productive, and to complete meaningful tasks), corresponding to Maslow's fourth and fifth levels

ERG theory recognizes that the order of importance of the three categories may vary for each individual. The most important contribution of the ERG model is the addition of the frustration-regression hypothesis: when individuals are frustrated in meeting higher level needs, the next lower level needs reemerge. ERG theory, used as a business model, suggests that managers recognize that employees have multiple needs to satisfy simultaneously. According to the ERG theory, focusing exclusively on one need at a time will neither effectively motivate employees, nor will it reflect the overall outcome of the interrelatedness of these needs (see Figure 1.6). Security needs in this sense are not reserved only for a lower-level type of need, but in reality and as we see in various examples from around the world, safety and security emerge as a reaction to various internal and external factors regardless of the level of self actualization a person or a group may have achieved.

Designers should note that as a human right, and as a need, researchers have identified the need for safety and security among the most basic for existence and survival. The safety and security needs can become very urgent on the social scene whenever there are real threats to the basic law and order, to cultural institutions, or to the authority of society. The threat of chaos or of nihilism can be expected to produce a regression from any higher needs to the more prepotent safety needs in most human beings. This tends to be true for all human beings, including healthy ones, because they too tend to respond to danger with realistic regression to the safety need level and will prepare to defend themselves in whatever means perceived as available to them.

When all physiological needs are satisfied and are no longer controlling thoughts and behaviors, the need for security can become active. The safety and security needs operate mainly on a psychological level. Once we manage a certain level of physical comfort and safety, we will seek to establish stability and consistency in a chaotic world.

The AIA's booklet *Building Security through Design—A Primer for Architects, Design Professionals, and Their Clients* (2001) provides four frameworks of analysis to identify security needs. These frameworks are: **asset analysis, threat analysis, vulnerability analysis**, and risk analysis (pp. 8–10). These frameworks take an economics approach as they focus primarily on the likelihood that a structure may be targeted, and the value of the assets that may be affected. Such frameworks are widely used by various government and public agencies, which negatively impact the human experience of place and certainly affect the core of what an interior designer does. As designers primarily focus on the creation of spaces and places for people's activities, aspirations, and growth, a component that addresses human factors, human capital, and value-rich experiences must be included in risk assessment frameworks.

General building security involves technical, physical, and operational solutions. Design strategies proposed by security professionals, architects, landscape architects, and facility managers revolve around several themes or strategies. Some of these strategies are applicable in interior design settings; however, it is in the collaborative interdisciplinary approach from the inception of the idea to its conclusion—and even beyond—that the full potential of these strategies will be realized. Security in this sense is similar to accessibility, if a designer approaches the problem from only a "meet the code" perspective or as an afterthought, the resulting solution often is costly, lacks cohesion and flexibility, and does not meet the spirit of universal access. Interior designers, facility managers, fire, security, and code officials, other design professionals, and building occupants should be

1.7A

As shown in this thirteenth-century Romanesque Landstejn Castle in Slavonice, Czech Republic, hardening targets may be appropriate in specific situations and environments.

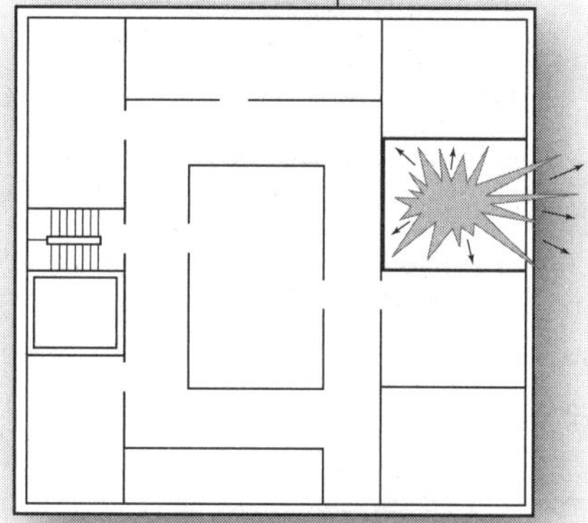

1.7B

Isolation and hardening of vulnerable areas, such as lobbies, can protect other parts of the building from an attack.

involved from the onset in the planning and design process. This allows the project team to look at issues holistically and remain flexible to the challenges of potential risks and security concerns.

The tendency to **harden targets**—to modify a building element, such as walls, doors, and windows—as a strategy to meet security needs becomes ineffective and most likely obtrusive to the experience of public space. The need to balance the needs for life-safety, openness, and enhanced security while maintaining high levels of preparedness demands project-specific transparent design solutions (see Figures 1.7 through 1.9). **Transparent design solutions** integrate security and design in ways that most people don't even notice. They are the creative solutions that provide security that is unobtrusive to the public eye, minimizes obvious barriers, and maximizes design excellence. This design choice should be considered on a case-by-case basis.

1.8 Utilizing transparent design solutions may be appropriate, as exemplified by the U.S. Federal Courthouse in Seattle, Washington. This design by NBBJ features a transparent wall by the secure area of the courthouse and allows a clear view of the reflecting pool.

1.9 This mini Plexiglas system is unobtrusive to the public eye, minimizes obvious barriers, and maximizes functionality and users' comfort.

FYI: According to a survey conducted by the American Institute of Architects (AIA), 55 percent of AIA architects say their clients have made building security a higher priority in the last year. Forty-six percent say at least one client has ordered implementation of security features in existing buildings or in a building design.

—*Architectural Record;* September 10, 2002

VULNERABILITY, RISK, AND SYSTEMS THINKING

Vulnerability is sensitive to external and internal factors that vary across time, either seasonally (e.g., for farmers), instantly (e.g., with a rapid onset disaster such as a volcanic eruption), or progressively (e.g., associated with past and present development issues such as structural adjustment, globalization, or HIV). Vulnerability

OPEN SYSTEMS CONCEPTS

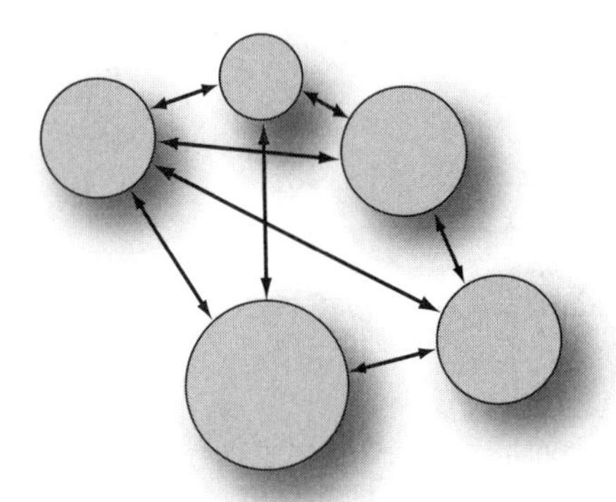

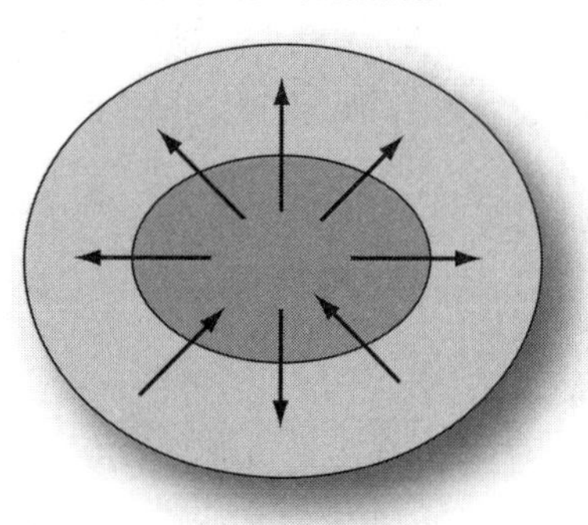

1.10 A system's thinking approach, using an open system.

also relates to situation, context, and people. Usually the underlying, longer-term factors coupled with development and other socioeconomic variables contribute to vulnerability. When addressing security, we attempt to view a situation or an entity based on our particular understanding of vulnerability and risks.

Risk perception and management, although firmly tied to context, are often terms relegated to protocols and procedures that may become obsolete or compromised. Risk is a conflicted construct and defining risk impacts how it is managed. Consider variations of age, gender, ethnicity, income, and how those may impact both risk definition and management. Regrettably, risk is often defined and managed from an economics perspective only, which impacts the sustainability of solutions.

Design and security involve much more than addressing risks and vulnerabilities and physical parameters of protection, or measuring assets and vulnerabilities. Designing for security lies in the intersection of physical, social, economic, political, cultural, and physiological paradigms. **Systems thinking** or systems approach—viewing problems as part of an overall system—is central to the discussion of design and security. Systems thinking affords an integrative, interdisciplinary, holistic perspective that builds on parallel, complementary, and interdependent aspects relative to security in the built environment. A system is a dynamic network of interconnecting elements, and as all systems tend to lean toward equilibrium, a change in only one of the elements produces a change in all the others (see Figure 1.10).

The systems framework outlines several characteristics or tenets that describe and predict the character and functionality of a system, as well as highlight the interrelatedness of subsystems and systems to their larger context. Within this approach, it is understood that complex systems must be disassembled into subsystems to analyze and understand the components before being reassembled into a whole. Affording safety and security, protection, and mitigation continues to be an increasingly complex situation, thus necessitating an integrative holistic approach. This approach helps us understand not only the appropriateness and results of design strategies or security management components in the overall security and safety of a building and its occupants for example, but also helps us predict various related scenarios and address them proactively. Regardless of the cause, we find ourselves needing to be more prepared for disaster recovery planning, trauma and crisis mitigation, new health and safety regulations, and preventive technologies, combined with a focus on design, place making, and professional responsiveness.

FYI: Fear Factor—Designing in a Post-9/11 World

"Concern for security in a suddenly uncertain age has certainly reshaped psychology, politics, and design in America, but it has undoubtedly had the most direct impact on architecture. For any public space, security has become a complex, layered concept that covers detailed blast specifications of window glass as well as issues of controlled access, electronic passkey systems, street-level vehicle barriers, and exterior **surveillance.** Open spaces have become either suspect urban no-man's lands or bleak accommodations to street setback requirements, bristling with barriers and cameras that anticipate visiting trucks packed with C4 explosives, not bubbly tourists packed with cameras and guidebooks. In an era of suicide bombers, places without checkpoints seem almost naked, like windowless buildings or unfenced playgrounds."

—John Hockenberry, *Metropolis,* April 17, 2006
www.metroploicmag.com/cda/stroy.artid=1920

THE ROLE OF SECURITY ORGANIZATIONS

Most recently, we are familiar with the variety of coalitions and interest groups that have formed or reactivated following the collapse of the World Trade Center, and other recent tragedies that have occurred around the world to study, advocate, and propose ways to address security in the built environment. Security in the built environment, and professional groups focused on studying risks, crimes, terrorism incidents, and general environmental threats have been in existence further back than current events.

Crime Prevention through Environmental Design (CPTED)

The umbrella paradigm is what's known as **Crime Prevention through Environmental Design,** or **CPTED.** The CPTED mission is "to create safer environments and improve the quality of life through the use of CPTED principles and strategies."

The CPTED also states that "the proper design and effective use of the built environment can lead to a reduction in the fear and incidence of crime." Its goal is to reduce opportunities for crime that may be inherent in the design of structures or in the design of neighborhoods, and to that goal, they have proposed several guidelines that have been adopted by law enforcement, planners, architects, and policy makers internationally. CPTED chapters and its advocates continue to explore various venues for integrating security into the design and management of the built environment.

For example, the Vancouver CPTED design principles are "contextually based." The design principles are based upon the typical building form of development and the specific crime environment within the Vancouver metropolitan area and as such, "application of these design principles should take place in conjunction with a full understanding of the local building forms and crime environment" (The Vancouver CPTED Web site, www.designcentreforcpted.org, 2007).

Learning from the Vancouver CPTED design principles, one can glean a myriad of considerations that are intended to be integrated into the built environment. It is interesting to note that one problem encountered in public spaces such as restaurants, malls, and airports—usually referred to as **soft targets**—is that of anonymity. People expect to see strangers in public spaces; similarly, many security strategies do not differentiate between individuals harboring criminal intentions from innocent citizens. A few of the design principles introduced in CPTED and implemented by skilled design professionals in the Vancouver metropolitan area used to reduce opportunities for crime are: creating a sense of ownership, use of adequate lighting, and avoiding areas of concealment.

FYI: Vancouver BC CPTED Strategies: See a full outline and explanation of the Vancouver CPTED security design principles at: www.designcentreforcpted.org/Pages/Principles.html.

The Skyscraper Safety Campaign (SSC)

The Skyscraper Safety Campaign's (SSC) goal is to encourage improved compliance with building and fire codes in New York City and nationwide to safeguard firefighters and people who must live and work in skyscrapers. SSC also seeks to educate "codes groups" to allow the fire service to have more input into writing building codes. Chapter 3 provides an in-depth review of security design-related building codes.

The Security Design Coalition (SDC)

The Security Design Coalition (SDC) formed in 2002, with design experts joining security experts to address security of public places, holds a series of briefings with federal agencies, including the US Department of Homeland Security (DHS). The Security Design Coalition's aim is to "advocate for the implementation of security measures in public places that incorporate good design principles." Members of this coalition include the American Planning Association, the American Society of Landscape Architects, American Institute of Architects, Scenic America, and the National Trust for Historic Preservation.

The Building Owners and Managers Association (BOMA)

The Building Owners and Managers Association (BOMA) takes steps to safeguard the nation's office buildings and tenants and is committed to keeping tenants safe and secure through emergency and evacuation planning. As an organization heavily involved in the building and occupancy of the built environment, a major focus of BOMA is to develop and implement policies and procedures to ensure occupant safety.

General Services Administration (GSA)

In the United States, the General Services Administration (GSA) and its division, GSA Homeland Security Solutions, along with the Department of Homeland Security (DHS), provide numerous products and services, from installing surveillance and security system, to increasing preparedness for a biological attack. The Transportation Security Administration (TSA), a division of DHS, deals with issues of safety and security through its mission of providing secure travel.

These and other coalitions and groups have made significant contributions to preparing safe and secure environments. However, as Dennis R. Smith states, "The protection of the public's safety has mainly involved attention to fire safety and structural integrity. To broaden this area of responsibility, interior designers, in particular, and design professionals in general, need to explore design approaches and solutions that offer occupants further protection from many other types of hazards, both natural and man-made. Such designs will need to take into account possible threats to security as well as safety in the traditional sense, whether in public spaces, the workplace, or the home" (Smith, 2003).

Codes, Regulations, and Design-related Issues

With each passing year, regulatory constraints on design have increased steadily. There are numerous standards, codes, and industry guidelines for various types of buildings and government agencies. Beginning with simple safety requirements, building codes and regulations have grown into a major force in design that affects every aspect of architecture, interior design, and building construction and renovation.

The collapse of the World Trade Center and damage to the Pentagon on 9/11, the Columbine school shootings, and acts of violence within the workplace, courthouses, and retail settings have raised issues related to building evacuation, places of refuge, and unsecured building accessibility. These events created an increased awareness and concern by architects, designers, engineers, government officials, and building code experts around the world about the impact that terrorist attacks,

1.11 Engineers say they want to "harden" the construction of high-rise buildings, since the second terrorist attack on the World Trade Center.

fires, or other disasters can have on public safety–related professional risk liability issues for buildings in urban centers (see Figure 1.11).

The challenge of making safer structures is just starting to reflect lessons learned from the collapse of the World Trade Center in 2001. The National Institute of Standards and Technology (NIST) is in the process of compiling data to serve as a foundation for building high-rises with improved structural integrity, better fireproofing, and enhanced evacuation capabilities.

Safer buildings, especially tall buildings that are more fire resistant and less easily evacuated, are the goal of the first comprehensive set of building code changes approved by the International Code Council (ICC), based on the recommendations of the National Institute of Standards and Technology (NIST). These changes were adapted into the 2007 supplement of the ICC's International Building Code (IBC), which offers the option to local and regional code agency's to adopt some of or all of the code's provisions. Among the recommendations that should be considered by the interior design professional include; photoluminescent markings on exit paths in buildings more than 75-feet high to facilitate rapid egress and building evacuation, use of appropriate exit **signage,** emergency evacuation signage, and wayfinding information, and the use of equipment to house light sticks and other emergency evacuation products.

FYI: The full list of recommendations made by the National Institute of Standards and Technology (NIST) may be found at http://wtc.nist.gov/.

An overriding design principle, when integrating security into the built environment, is the principle goal of maintaining a setting that is welcoming to visitors and users of the facility. Opportunities to create security amenities that are *transparent,* that is, seamlessly integrated with the character of the space, not only enhances the experience for the users, but provides the necessary security layering that is needed. The significance of the many acts of violence previously discussed is the characterization of those targets as soft targets, which essentially describes the majority of the everyday built environments in which we live, work, and play.

Design Programming and Planning

The interior design professional, as a member of the design team, should understand, appreciate, and address security and safety concerns within interior environments. Their goal should be to create more secure spaces and places for people through an awareness of the variety of issues in the programming and planning stages that influence the safety and security design solutions for individual project types.

Selected examples of safety and security design solutions that can and should be addressed by the interior design professional are identified in the following sections.

Architectural Components

- Integrate security design to minimize visual and other impacts on the interior surfaces and finishes.
- Doors are generally required to open outward, and blast-resistant doors may be required in some situations.

Space-planning Concerns

- Minimize public entrances into a building.
- Consider placement for checkpoints for delivery people, and mailroom sites.
- Internal layout of space(s) is important to provide entry control and protection.
- Consider a means of egress allowing for compartmentalization and direct exit to the outside.

Materials, Finishes, and Products

- Use of wallcovering that increases the security and confidentiality of telecommunications
- Mitigate ballistic threat by providing visual shielding or screening devices on fenestration
- Use of ER evacuation kits mounted underneath desk top surfaces
- Use of thumb scanner on keypads for access into authorized or restricted areas

- Use of overall body scanners that are unobtrusive and part of the design
- Addition of blast-resistant interior window or blast curtains to prevent glass fragmentation hazards
- Use of new interior materials with flame-retardant composite materials to slow the spread of fire

Wayfinding/Signage

- Use of systematic, well-defined **wayfinding**—ways for people to navigate from place to place—and signage programs

Life Safety

- Occupant evacuation
- Stairwells on opposite sides of buildings
- Installation of photoluminescence markings on exit signs and stairs
- Stairwells marked to identify floor number and the site of reentry locations
- Prohibit locking of reentry doors in stairwells
- Wider emergency stairwells and separate exits
- Light sticks, masks, and other survival products housed visibly and accessibly along side fire extinguishers

Building Systems

- Heating, ventilation, and air conditioning (HVAC) systems installed and protected to prevent the entry of external contaminants
- Strategic placement of HVAC systems to prevent tampering

Design Ethics and Professional Responsibility

Among the professionals most central to the security dialogue are those who are responsible for creating healthy, safe, functional, and beautiful environments. As designers, it is our responsibility to protect the health, safety, and welfare of the public, and as such, we must all be informed and educated on the safety and security issues that have become integral components of the built environment. As designers, we need to explore and highlight venues for seamless integration of security into consistent, coherent, and welcoming environments that can afford a sense of safety and security to all users.

The significance of assessing not only what security measures need to be taken into consideration, but the impact of those measures on the functionality, meaning, and user perception of the built environment needs to be addressed. An integrative dialogue among design professionals including landscape architects, architects, and interior designers must take place at a level that promotes future-oriented design thinking from all those involved in the creation of the built environment. Members of the design community can encourage clients to make ethically responsible decisions concerning safety and security by themselves staying informed about emerging security technology (see Chapter 9) and by devising ways in which that technology can be creatively and unobtrusively incorporated into the built environment.

Consider security from the onset of the design and it becomes an integrated and transparent component of the problem definition and criteria used to solve design problems. The outcome of such an integrated approach is a more sustainable and effective design solution, where a seamless connection between security and other functional, social, aesthetic, and economic considerations is achieved. As we aspire to represent people's needs and wants in our designs, we continually strive to positively affect their quality of life and experience of the spaces and places that we create. Threats to either the quality of life or to the environment is filtered through risk perception first and mediated by the modifications or changes to the built environment. In this sense, as designers we are involved in this web of intricate dialogue between environment, people, and security.

CONCLUSION

Safety and security are complex and multilayered constructs, combining physiological, physical, psychological, social, political, economic, and cultural dimensions. Similarly, general building security involves technical, physical, and operational solutions. Design strategies that have been proposed by security professionals, architects, landscape architects, and facility managers revolve around several themes and strategies. Some of these strategies are applicable in interior design settings; however, it is in the collaborative interdisciplinary approach from the inception of the idea to its conclusion—and even beyond—that the full potential of these strategies are realized. Interior designers, facility managers, fire, security, and code officials, other design professionals, and building occupants should be involved at the onset of the planning and design process. This allows the project team to look at issues holistically and remain flexible to the challenges of potential risks and security concerns. Security, in this sense, is similar to accessibility, if a designer approached the problem from only a "meet the code" perspective or as an afterthought, the resulting solution often is costly, lacks cohesion and flexibility, and does not meet the spirit of universal access.

The tendency to harden targets—to modify building elements, such as walls, doors, and windows—as a strategy to meet security needs become ineffective, and most likely obtrusive to the experience of public space. The need to balance the needs for life safety, openness, and enhanced security while maintaining high levels of preparedness demands project-specific transparent design solutions. Transparent design solutions integrate security and design in ways that most people do not even notice. They are the creative solutions that provide security that is unobtrusive to the public eye, minimizes obvious barriers, and maximizes design excellence.

KEY CONCEPTS

- Safe/safety is the condition of being safe from undergoing or causing hurt, injury, or loss; free from harm or risk, secure from threat of danger, harm, or loss, affording safety or security from danger, risk, or difficulty.
- Whereas security is defined as the quality or state of being secure and affording safety; and free from risk of loss, and free from danger, fear or anxiety, it is apparent that security is both a feeling and a physical condition.
- According to Maslow, safety and security are the most basic and central of human needs and rights.
- Security for the purposes of design and security consultants is the protection of assets, both physical and psychological, from unauthorized access, theft, or damage. The goal is to detect, deter, and detain, focusing on the prevention of unauthorized access and minimizing the aftermath of a breach to security.
- Terrorism, crime, biohazards, workplace violence, and accidents have heightened public awareness regarding security in the built environment, requiring design and construction professionals, facility managers, building owners, and public officials to address security concerns.
- Liability concerns over the security of interior spaces and places have become important as society addresses the threats and situations that have become part of the landscape of life in the twenty-first century.
- Several coalitions and interest groups have been formed since 2001 in the United States and other countries to study, advocate, and propose means of addressing security in the built environment from a variety of perspectives.
- As we investigate the impact of security concerns, innovations, and needs of the interior environment, new code requirements have come into place.
- Members of the design community can encourage clients to make ethically responsible decisions concerning safety and security by devising ways in which that security design solutions and related technology can be creatively and unobtrusively incorporated into the built environment.

ASSIGNMENTS

1. Develop an understanding of the human need for safety and security.
2. Formulate concepts regarding the safety and security concerns of the twenty-first century.
3. Formulate ideas on how the concerns of the twenty-first century have impacted the built environment.

ACTIVITIES

1. Divide into teams of three to four students. Discuss your interpretation and/or definitions of the words safety and security. Each group should then share their team's definitions with the entire class. Discuss the similarities and differences between the lists. As a class, determine the favored definition(s) and discuss why. If students are multicultural, or varied in age, discuss cultural and age differences and possible links of experiences to perceptions.
2. Using September 11, 2001, brainstorm and generate a list of the many ways in which the world, as they know it, has changed, for example, getting a drivers license, travel, profiling, taking photographs, and so on. Discuss each team's list as a class. Repeat the exercise using other security breach incidents from a "closer to home" perspective, with which the students are more intimately familiar, in terms of scale and impact. Compare the two outcomes (lists) in as many comparison points, reflections, and approaches as possible and appropriate.
3. Using the above generated "ways in which the world has changed" lists, identify and discuss how these changes have had, or can have, an effect on the built environment, for example, airport screening equipment, access to public spaces, or use of new equipment.

0 7 2 9 6 5 8 3 4 1

2 THE CONCEPT OF SECURITY AND ITS ROLE IN OUR LIVES

Think of where you feel most secure. Lying fully prone on a warm beach or snuggled in your own bed? Lost in swirling crowds during a lunchtime break or hiking in the high country? Few would answer, "Behind locked doors and high walls." As psychologist Richard Farson has observed, the term "security" is bound in paradox: Where security systems assert themselves most forcefully—in prisons, for example—fear, discomfort, and even danger often flourish; conversely, the absence of visible protection can promote the feeling of well-being.

—Robert Ivy, Editor, *Architectural Record*, 2002

OBJECTIVES

- Further develop an understanding of the human need for safety and security.
- Develop familiarity and an understanding of the foundational studies related to security in the built environment and conceptually integrate security solutions into the built environment.
- Reinforce an understanding of security concerns and mitigation strategies in the twenty-first century and their impact on the built environment.

"The scars left by Timothy McVeigh's anger bite deeply through this southern Plains city where, six years after the worst act of terrorism on U.S. soil, survivors occasionally still pluck shards of glass from their skin. The 1995 bombing of the Alfred P. Murrah Federal Building caused the deaths of 168 men, women and children and injured more than 800 others. In a flash, it challenged notions about the innocence and security of the nation's heartland" (Horne, 2001). The Oklahoma City bombing tragedy, in more ways than one, exemplifies a breach of access and consequently, a catastrophic breach of security in the built environment, causing major loss of life.

But on the other side of the coin, some of the means we have attempted to use to rectify possible security breaches are seen as playing on one's sense of fear and insecurity; "I feel like I'm working in a building marked with a bull's-eye," says a worker. "I suppose these security measures should assure me, but they actually make me worry. The metal detectors, security guards, blast-proof glass—they're all messages telling us that nobody's safe" (Clay).

The changing nature of the beast as we address security in our everyday environments is not a static and one-dimensional task. "Communities in New York have been changed enormously over the years because of gun crimes. In the 1970s and 1980s, many parents feared sending their children outside; even cops were outgunned by thugs carrying military-style assault weapons. Then, on December 7, 1993, Colin Ferguson opened fire with a 9mm pistol equipped with a high capacity magazine on a 5:33 P.M. rush hour eastbound LIRR train traveling between New Hyde Park and Garden City. Ferguson's shooting rampage killed six and injured more than a dozen others" (Schumer, 2005).

The continuous drama of our interactions with the built environment in times of safety and comfort, as well as in times of insecurity and fear, reveal complex themes, lessons, and implications of the impact of safety and security on the psychological, physiological, physical, and social dimensions that define our daily lives. Crime reduction involves a range of activities, including improving the physical security of vulnerable targets, improving the environment in an area, and working to provide a better quality of life.

SECURITY, FEAR, AND CRIME

Serious crimes against people and property generate considerable fear within the community. Crimes like theft, break-in, rape, and murder are serious threats to public safety. The resulting fear of crime itself can restrict people's freedom of movement and prevent them from fully participating in the community (see Figure 2.1). According to Mark Warr (2000), "Much of the confusion over the meaning of fear seems to arise from a failure to recognize elementary distinctions between perception, cognition, and emotion. Notwithstanding the claims of some, fear is not a perception of the environment (an awareness or experience of sensory stimuli), but rather a reaction to the perceived environment. Although fear may result from the cognitive processing or evaluation of perceptual information (e.g., a judgment that an approaching male is armed, or that a sound

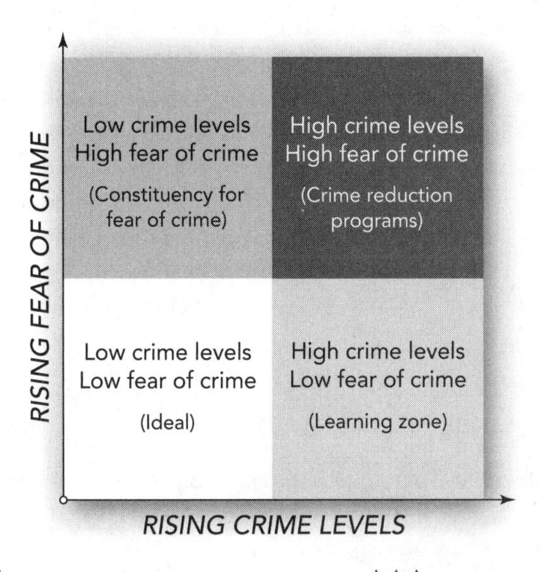

2.1 Fear of crime matrix.

signals danger), fear is not itself a belief, attitude, or evaluation. On the contrary, fear is an emotion, a feeling of alarm or dread caused by an awareness or expectation of danger."

Criminologists and sociologists indicate that fear of being victimized has been found to be prevalent among the most isolated and vulnerable, such as the elderly and individuals who are unable to express territorial control over their environments. Conversely, physical characteristics of the built environment have been identified as possible cues to danger by their influence on social interactions. Warr (2000) and others identified several cues to danger that affect people in public places, including darkness (which obscures potential threats), novelty of an environment (unfamiliar environments are more frightening than familiar ones), and the presence of bystanders or companions (both as a calming effect and as a source of threat). Signs of "incivility" that can provoke fear are physical features of neighborhoods and environments such as graffiti, signs of disuse, and social cues like the presence of unauthorized users of a space.

Manipulating environmental cues to danger, for example painting over graffiti, improving lighting, enhancing potential for active surveillance, and other place-specific strategies offer tangible and possibly powerful means for regulating public fear of crime. Neighborhood Watch groups, for example, attempt to tackle fear of crime in the community in addition to reducing crime. The aims of such groups are often manifested in a twofold scenario that on the one hand, reduces fear of crime by removing or minimizing physical vulnerabilities, and on the other, empowers the residents of the communities with a sense of control over their environments.

FYI: Bruce Schneier, writer and security expert, stated that "Safety and security are different. . . . The difference is random versus directed action. Safety is being secure against random faults; against Murphy's Law. . . . Security is much harder in that you are dealing with a malicious and intelligent adversary creating failures at the most inopportune times. . . . Security is a complex system that needs to be addressed dynamically, by building into it several 'security valves' and especially by allowing for human discretion and intervention."

—SAFE: Design Takes on Risk Exhibit, p. 15

SECURITY, CRIME, AND THE BUILT ENVIRONMENT RESEARCH

Robert E. Keib, Vice President of Operations at Gregg Protection Services and who served in the federal law enforcement and security community since 1971, stated, "The public expects a safe and secure workplace. The public expects an environment where there is not a concern of a purse being stolen, an assault in the hallway, or a rape in the restroom. The corporate clients that occupy the facility expect to be safe and secure from thefts of property, industrial espionage, and acts of sabotage. These are expectations, but are they realistic, an achievable goal or wishful thinking?" (2000). In this labyrinth of design and security, will interior design and interior designers rise to the challenge?

As designers explore the spectrum of their possible involvement in designing with security in mind, they become more aware of their dynamic, organic, and complex roles. They make critical decisions about openness and security and the physical and psychological dimensions of security and fear, and address threats and perceptions of threats of a continuously evolving and changing nature, best described by Robert Ivy (2002) as "The **Security Paradox**."

Oscar Newman and Other Pioneers of Defensible Space

The seeds for systematically addressing and integrating security into the built environment in the modern era were sown in the early 1960s by Oscar Newman (architect), Jane Jacobs (editor, *Architectural Forum* magazine), and C. Ray Jeffery (psychologist and criminologist), all of whom developed much of their work in reaction to various studies of violence, crime, behavior, and the urban landscape.

The Initial Years

The social reformer Elizabeth Wood was the first executive secretary for the Chicago Housing Authority (CHA), serving with distinction until 1954. She was one of the prime advocates of the centrality of the physical environment as means to achieving social objectives. Through her work for the CHA, she

2.2 Interactions within the built environment, such as in outdoor cafes, exemplify an active "eyes on the street" behavior that is a cornerstone in studies of safety and security.

attempted to bring about design changes aimed at enhancing quality of life for residents and increasing the aesthetic qualities of the residential environment. She also developed a series of guidelines for improving security conditions of these environments that include improved visibility of apartment units by residents, as well as the need for spaces where residents could gather, thereby increasing the potential for resident surveillance and social control of their environments. A similar approach is used widely in group residential settings where a main hall, or lobby, becomes a place for gathering, social reaffirmation, and active surveillance.

Jane Jacobs's book *Death and Life of Great American Cities* (1961) introduced the basis for crime prevention through environmental design and began the systematic search for how both physical and social urban factors affected people and their interactions. The book advanced a call for a comprehensive approach between micro and macro level environments as a way for healthy cities to function and be safe and the belief that all social interactions are affected by the physical layout (see Figure 2.2). For example, the impact of a sidewalk on contextual social interactions is discerned as the sidewalk is perceived on the street of a block, placed within a neighborhood, or located within the larger city. The notion of the sidewalk is translated in interior design into circulation paths and boundary demarcation, around which spaces and settings are organized and carried out. The social interactions and sense of protection and control occurring in public settings such as that of a coffee shop or a marketplace are clearly influenced by physical layout, circulation path, and the means of demarcation of space. Such interactions within the built environment exemplify an active "eyes on the street" behavior that is a cornerstone in studies of safety and security.

Based on the social control theory, which stipulates that the physical environment is perceived as a mediator for risk of crime, Jacobs developed a hypotheses she referred to as **eyes on the street**. Jacobs's "eyes on the street" theory is the belief that urban residential crime could be prevented by reducing conditions of anonymity and isolation in problem areas and increasing natural guardianship (Murray, 1994). This is a key principle in much of the security research that progressed following its introduction in 1961, and which holds great promise and adaptability for interior design applications. In *Death and Life of Great American Cities,* Jacobs listed three attributes needed to make a city street safe: a clear demarcation of private and public space; a diversity of use; and a high level of pedestrian use of the sidewalks. These three attributes can be translated into "eyes on the street," thereby affording the social framework needed for effective self-policing. Overall, Jacobs' contributions marked the introduction of safety and security conscious environmental planning for public spaces.

Shlomo Angel, a pioneer of crime prevention through environmental design, studied under the renowned architect and planner Christopher Alexander. Alexander is known for his renowned works, *A Pattern Language: Towns, Buildings, Construction* (1977) and *The Timeless Way of Building* (1979). Angel is one of the authors of *Pattern Language,* in which behavioral *patterns* are described in relation to a *problem* occurring over time within the built environment. The Pattern Language Theory also places behaviors in terms of "context and forces" and describes core solutions, referred to as a generative "solution"—a reemerging critical perspective in crime prevention research and design.

One particular problem Angel was interested in is how offenders choose their specific targets through a decision-making process in which they weigh the effort and risk against potential payoffs. With more opportunity and a higher potential payoff, it is more likely that at least one successful target offering little risk will be found. Angel stated in his dissertation, which he later developed and published, and which was widely distributed by the United States Department of Justice, that the "physical environment can exert a direct influence on crime settings by delineating territories, reducing or increasing accessibility by the creation or elimination of boundaries and circulation networks, and by facilitating surveillance by citizenry and the police" (1968). Similar to Jacobs, he asserted that crime was inversely related to the level of activity on the street (Luedtke, 1970). Angel's ideas regarding changing the physical design of environments revolved around channeling pedestrian traffic and zoning businesses into areas where mass transit and parking

2.3 Robberies in retail environments occur more often when an unfrequented or unobserved escape route is readily available for the perpetrator.

facilities are near. Robberies in retail establishments for example, occur more often when an unfrequented or unobserved escape route is readily available for the perpetrator (see Figure 2.3).

FYI: The "eyes on the street" concept that Jane Jacobs advocated remains a strong and central component of all security work in our present time.

—Jane Jacobs, *Death and Life of Great American Cities*

The Intermediate Years

Parallels between a focus on criminal behavior as well as on the environment became apparent during the "middle years" (1970s through 1990s). Oscar Newman, an architect and urban planner, defined **defensible space** as something that people can adequately defend from criminal attack. Newman's book *Defensible Space; Crime Prevention Through Urban Design* (1973) focused more on the architectural aspect than criminology. Criminologist Ray Jeffery first coined the term, defensible space, in his 1971 book, *Crime Prevention Through Environmental Design.* Jeffery's early work focused on crime prevention that would change the behavior of offenders by changing their environment.

Oscar Newman is credited with operationalizing previous work done by Jacobs and others. His early research projects in 1969, along with the National

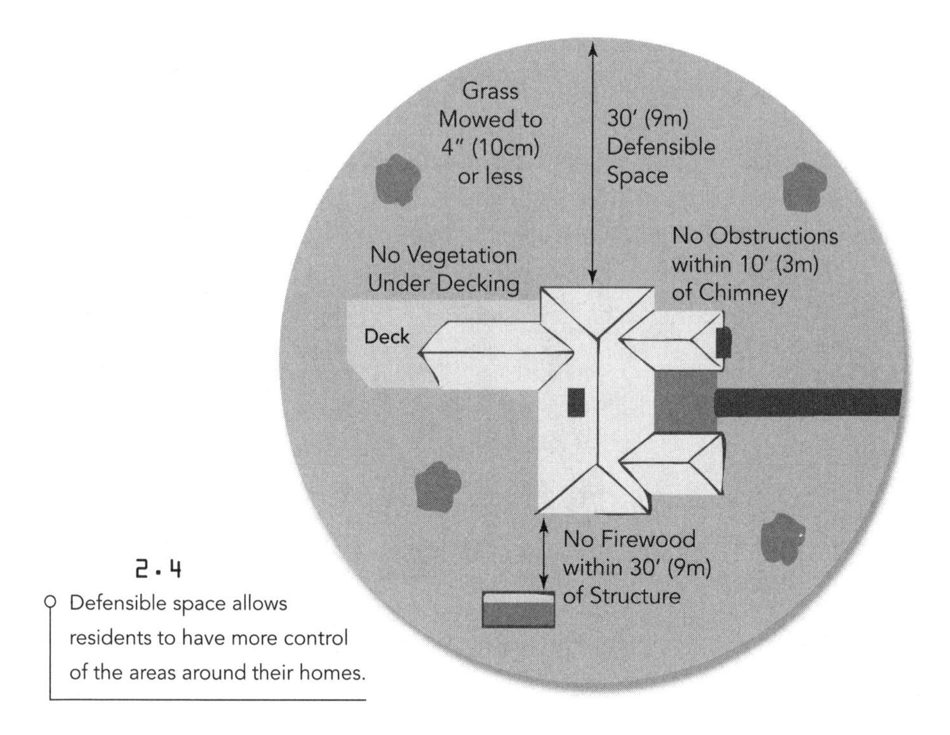

2.4

Defensible space allows residents to have more control of the areas around their homes.

Institute of Law Enforcement and Criminal Justice (NILECJ), now referred to as the National Institute of Justice (NIJ), appraised the relationship between the physical environment and its risk for criminal victimization. This study resulted in Newman's 1972 book *Architectural Guidelines for Crime Prevention,* which evolved into Defensible Space theory and its multifaceted applications (see Figure 2.4).

Following the introduction of Newman's Defensible Space theory, several research projects to study crime in various types of environments were initiated, and then translated into the design of public housing. The term "defensible space" is used most often to describe residential environments designed to enhance aspects of territoriality and surveillance of the environment by its residents. According to Newman's approach, areas low in defensible space are theoretically more vulnerable to crime. The goal of the defensible space approach is "to release the latent sense of territoriality and community among inhabitants so as to allow these traits to be translated into inhabitants' assumption of responsibility for preserving a safe and well-maintained living environment" (Newman, 1976, p. 4). Newman's work attempted to reduce both crime and fear of crime in a specific type of environment by means of reducing opportunity for crime and fostering positive social interaction among legitimate users (Taylor and Harrell, 1996, pp. 3–4).

FYI: "All 'Defensible Space' programs have a common purpose: they restructure the physical layout of communities to allow residents to control the areas around their homes. This includes the streets and grounds outside their buildings and the lobbies and corridors within them. The programs help people preserve those areas in which they can realize their commonly held values and life styles."

—Newman, *Creating Defensible Space,* p. 9, 1996

Concurrent to Newman's work, C. Ray Jeffery addressed crime prevention in his 1971 work *Crime Prevention Through Environmental Design,* which had a great impact on the field of criminology. Jeffery's work was based on modern learning theory, using a behaviorist model aimed at a change of behavior through the use of stimuli in the external environment. Jeffery's research, involving behavioral change and desired effect, directed the field of criminology toward appreciating the impact of environmental factors on human behavior.

Based on Jeffery's **Stimulus-Response** model, the role of the designer, policy maker, or involved parties is to arrange environments that elicit desired responses regarding crime and security, producing learned behaviors by providing punishments and rewards. This perspective arose out of his experiences with a rehabilitative project in Washington, DC, that attempted to control the school environment of juveniles in the area, while emphasizing the role of the physical environment in the development of pleasurable and painful experiences that would have the capacity to alter the behavioral outcomes of the offender.

Jeffery "emphasized material rewards . . . and the use of the physical environment to control behavior" (Jeffery & Zahm, 1993, p. 330). His major idea was that by removing the reinforcements for crime, it would not occur, and that the way to prevent crime is to design the "total environment" in order to reduce opportunities for crime (Robinson, 1996). Regrettably, Jeffery's work was ignored throughout most of the 1970s, as Jeffery later explains, "At a time when the world wanted prescriptive design solutions [his] work presented an overly broad comprehensive theory used to identify a wide range of crime prevention functions that should drive design and management standards."

Jeffery's later work in the 1990s shifted from a Stimulus-Response model of human behavior to an integrated systems approach that includes both the external environment of the place and the internal environment of the offender. For example, at the time, Jeffery's work as a criminologist led him to believe that psychology and social factors go hand in hand, while the commonly accepted paradigm was that external factors in terms of rewards and punishments were the main cause or deterrent of criminal behavior. In an interior environment this could be similar to an **environmental/architectural determinism** perspective, where behaviors are seen as predetermined by the environment where they occur, not as the

2.5 The broken window theory is an example of how unkempt, run-down, or unfrequented environments may provide the stimulus for crimes.

more commonly accepted environmental psychology perspective of **affordances**—the possibilities for actions as perceived by users of an environment. Whether as a Stimulus-Response approach, an affordance perspective, or from an integrated systems approach, crime and security demand a closer look at the various factors which lead to threat and threat mitigation in the built environment (see Figure 2.5).

The Later Years: CPTED

The 1990s and beyond provided research and exploration into crime prevention, emphasizing two critical elements to crime prevention through environmental design: the place where the crime occurs and the person who commits it. This is the approach that was advocated in the later Jeffrey's model, and brought to law enforcement and community planners a fresh approach that focused on the physical circumstances as well as the internal environment surrounding criminal activity. The work came to fruition in what we now call the **crime triangle**—a victim, an offender, and a place or opportunity—which has been a basis for the principles found throughout Crime Prevention through Environmental Design (CPTED). The **crime triangle** (see Figure 2.6) was articulated best by Al Zelinka (2001) co-author of *Safescape* who stated, "Those who commit crimes or other undesirable activities with a rational mindset do so based on judging the available opportunity to take advantage of a victim without being caught and/or identified as the perpetrator of the act. A victim, an offender, and an opportunity must be present for a

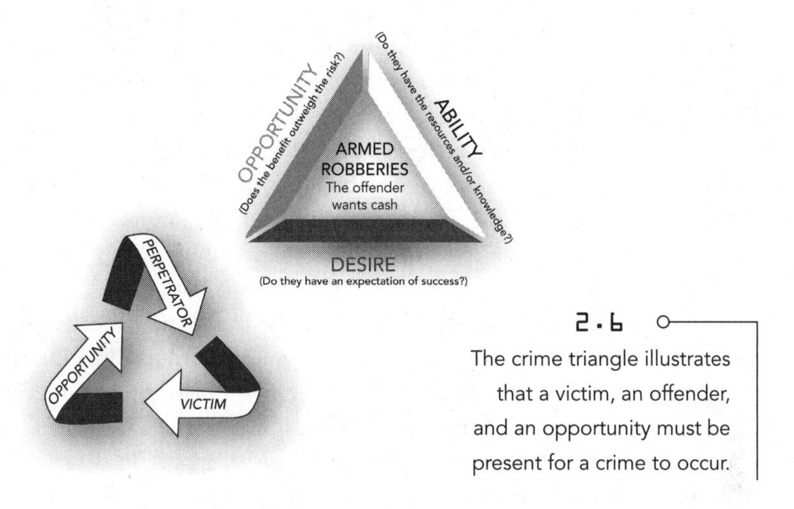

2.6
The crime triangle illustrates that a victim, an offender, and an opportunity must be present for a crime to occur.

crime to occur" (p. 6). If one part of the triangle is missing the crime will not occur. Conversely, opportunity to commit the offense can be addressed by increasing the risk of apprehension through increasing visibility, for example, ability to commit the offense may be minimized by increasing the effort required to commit the offense, and desire to commit the offense may be addressed by reducing the rewards available to the offender. All of these strategies can be seen through design and management of a place.

Globally, Crime Prevention through Environmental Design groups have articulated a framework for studying crime and eliciting means to combat it. Although the field is gradually expanding to encompass affective, psychological, and sociological environmental design—known as "second generation" CPTED—its traditional focus has emphasized physical design in the context of the normal and expected use of that space by the users, as well as the predictable behavior of people around the space. CPTED (see Figure 2.7) is built on four principles: natural

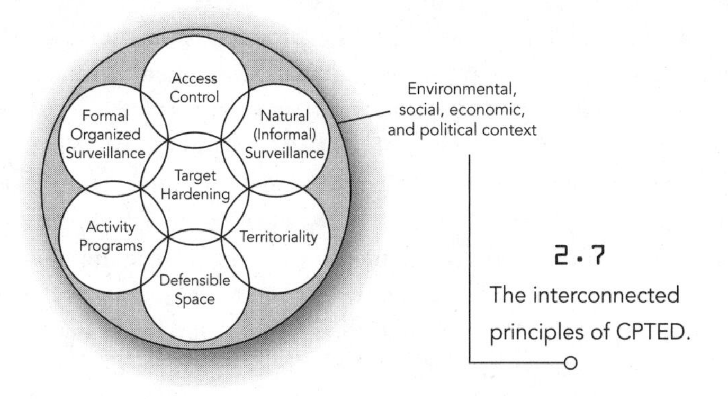

2.7
The interconnected principles of CPTED.

surveillance, natural access control, territorial reinforcement, and maintenance. Taken together, the four principles are used to delineate three levels of indicators of crime likelihood and intervention strategies. These levels are: First Order Determiners: pathways, activity nodes, and high-risk population; Second Order Determiners: areas of concealment, **access control**, engaged watching, and **target hardening**—increasing the resistance of a building; and Third Order Determiners: landscape, lighting, and climate. The interior designer's main scope of intervention is clearly seen in First Order Determiners (applied within an environment) and Second Order Determiners.

CPTED emphasizes the connection between the functional objectives of space utilization and behavior management. Conceptually, the four CPTED principles are applied through the **3-D approach**, or the three functions or dimensions of human space: **Designation**, **Definition**, and **Design**. The 3-D approach is a simple space assessment guide that helps the designer/user/manager in determining the appropriateness of how a space is designed and used.

Natural surveillance is the capacity to see what's occurring without having to take special measures to do so. Clear direct views, such as those provided by windows, provide natural surveillance. Unrestricted view ports from nurses' station and staffed information kiosks for example, afford natural surveillance of a premises.

Natural access control is the capacity to limit who can gain entry to a facility, and how. A school with dozens of unsecured exterior doors cannot hope to control comings and goings. Intruders have free rein, and schools must rely on other security measures. Without access control, a much greater emphasis must be placed on surveillance, territoriality, school climate, and security staffing in order to compensate.

Territoriality/Territorial Reinforcement is the capacity to establish authority over an environment, making a statement about who is in charge, who belongs, and who is an outsider. Graffiti is one way gangs establish territoriality; schools and semi-public facilities can take it back with vigilant maintenance. For example, signs directing visitors to the office or spelling out rules reinforce territoriality and influence behavior. School uniforms make it easy to identify intruders at a glance.

Maintenance as a CPTED principle follows the **Broken Window Theory**, which suggests that one "broken window" or nuisance, if allowed to exist, will lead to others and ultimately to the decline of an entire neighborhood. Neglected and poorly maintained properties are breeding grounds for criminal activity. Formalized, communicated, and carried out, CPTED-based maintenance plans not only assist in preserving safety and security, but also ensure a smooth functional operation of the facility. The nurse's station shown in Figure 2.8 demonstrates the 3-D approach reinforced by the four CPTED principles for optimal patient, staff, and visitor security and functionality of the health-care unit.

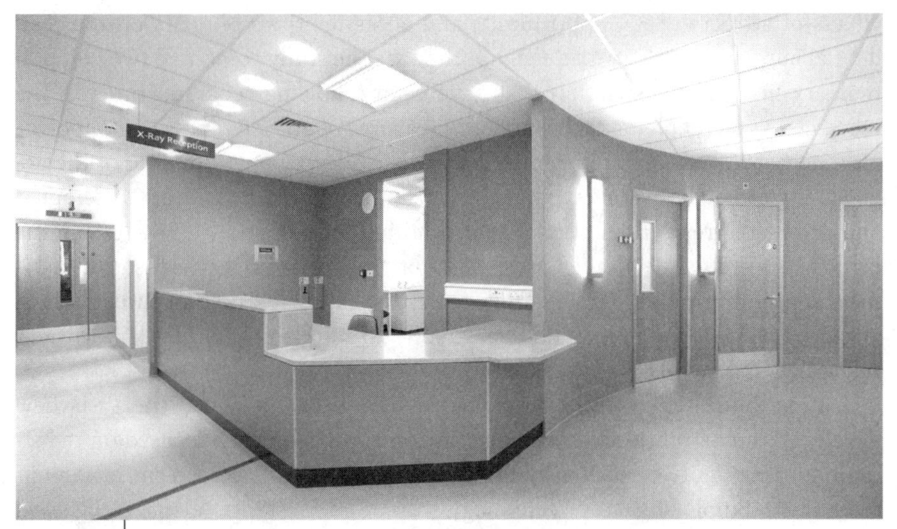

2.8 This 3-D approach for a nurse's station applies the CPTED's principles.

LEVELS OF SECURITY IN THE BUILT ENVIRONMENT

In the 1980s, much of the impact and application of security work in the built environment was limited to a focus on residential settings, varying from a focus on public housing to aspects of territoriality and its relationship to security. Less effective was the application in relation to non-residential settings; however, the research progressed in various directions.

Brower, Dockett, and Taylor's 1983 study, for example, measured responses to varying images of defensible space features and territorial signs utilizing line drawings with variations made in key features, such as entry features, spatial boundaries, and activity areas. They found that the presence of real barriers and plantings are interpreted as a deterrent to intrusion and an indication of stronger occupant territorial attitudes. However, it was found that in locations with higher incidents of crime, territorial displays, such as low hedges or spatially proximate furniture, were less effective in deterring crime or intrusion, a finding that is consistent with research on fear of crime and incidents of crime.

Along the same lines, Brown and Altman's 1983 study focused on use of environmental cues and burglary prevention. This study was instrumental in developing territoriality theories to great detail, specifically as the study applies to territorial behavior of private and public spaces. Their research findings were supported in a study done by Wim Bernasco and Floor Luykx from the Netherlands Institute for the Study of Crime and Law Enforcement (NSCR) (2003). In this recent study, Altman and Brown's former findings were utilized to assess the effects of attractiveness, opportunity, and accessibility to burglars on the residential burglary rates of urban neighborhoods. The study combined two complementary lines of investigation that have been following separate tracks in the research. As a complement to standard measures of attractiveness and opportunity, Bernasco and Luykx introduced and specified a spatial measure of the accessibility of neighborhoods to burglars. Using data on about 25,000 attempted and completed residential burglaries committed in the period 1996–2001 in the city of The Hague, the Netherlands, variation in burglary rates across its 89 residential neighborhoods were examined. Results suggested that all three factors, attractiveness, opportunity, and accessibility to burglars, pull burglars to their target neighborhoods (Bernasco & Luykx, 2003).

During the 1980s, British criminologists Ronald Clarke and Patricia Mayhew developed their **situational crime prevention** approach which focused on reducing the opportunity to offend by improving design and management of the environment. Employing lock technology, surveillance, siting, adequate lighting, enhanced visibility, avoidance of concealment areas, and mitigating escape routes are all examples of this situational crime prevention. This approach returned to the forefront in the later part of the 1990s during research into the relationship between crime and the physical environment discussed next.

A more interdisciplinary integrative perspective advocated in the 1990s, per the Jeffery model discussed earlier, evolved to one which assumes that, "The environment never influences behavior directly, but only through the brain. Any model of crime prevention must include both the brain and the physical environment" (Robinson, 1996). Nasar and Fisher's 1993 study takes a different slant on examining the geography of crime from a **Prospect-Refuge** approach. Prospect (i.e., victim—open or closed), offender's concealment (i.e., refuge), and boundedness (i.e., mental map and connection to the place) were the immediate or proximate cues studied, with female college students and campus police serving as subjects. Nasar and Fisher's study differentiates between macro- and micro-level site characteristics, examining how the latter may contribute to concentrated areas of fear of crime, crime, or "hot spots." Offenders desire environments exhibiting a high degree of refuge so that they can "wait, attack, and if need be, take the victim out of sight" (Fisher & Nasar, 1992, p. 38). Fear of crime was also examined on the same macro and micro levels. "Hot spots of fear and crime converged at the micro level. Both fear and crime increased in areas characterized by low prospect, high concealment, and high boundedness [cognitive knowledge of escape routes]" (Nasar and Fisher, 1993). Design measures are discussed regarding micro-level deterrence, such as employing appropriate lighting, minimizing unauthorized access, improving visibility, vegetation, maintenance, and security cameras.

NEW "RULES" FOR THE TWENTY-FIRST CENTURY

Consistent with the implementation patterns of defensible space founded in the 1970s, the current recommendations used in CPTED are based solely upon the theory that the proper design and effective use of the built environment can reduce crime, reduce the fear of crime, and improve the overall quality of life. This perspective has been embraced—either as is, or with modifications—by the majority of environmental design professionals, regardless of the theoretical approach they may use.

CPTED addresses the four most common built environment strategies of natural surveillance, natural access control, natural territorial reinforcement, and maintenance. CPTED believes that natural surveillance and access control strategies limit the opportunity for crime, whereas territorial reinforcement can promote social control of the built environment and maintenance can contribute to controlling operational functioning of designed environments. One problem that is encountered in public spaces such as restaurants, malls, and airports—usually referred to as **soft targets**—is that of anonymity. People expect to see strangers in public spaces, and currently outlined CPTED security strategies do not differentiate between individuals harboring criminal intentions from innocent citizens.

In 1997, an article entitled "Second Generation CPTED," by Greg Saville and Gerry Cleveland, criminologists and CPTED trainers articulated reasons why CPTED has recently resurfaced as an important base group in the overall security discussion. CPTED has emerged as an organization that has begun to focus on architecture, as well as other social and demographic factors that place security issues in the broader context of sense of place. It is argued that only focusing on architecture and ignoring social and demographic factors, traffic, and surrounding area patterns translates into ignoring the broad context of a place. Situational crime prevention mentioned earlier, as well as contextual risk assessment measures, attempts to correct this aspect. It is logical and meaningful to use a combination of approaches in addressing security in the built environment based on the context at hand, integrating both physical means of reducing crime, and ways of improving the quality of life in an area to achieve a greater effect.

Saville and Cleveland believe that CPTED advancements in training, increased involvement in project planning from the onset of design and construction, and increased dialogue among all parties involved have improved the organization's overall effectiveness. Increased cross-disciplinary dialogues and interdisciplinary collaboration, involving designers, builders, facility managers, and building owners all addressing issues of security, has improved the implementation and integration of crime prevention throughout the design process.

The third factor affecting adaptability and emergence of new generations of crime prevention is that of displacement. **Displacement** is described as the movement of crime as a result of some preventive action. Displacement can occur in the following five areas:

1. Place displacement: A problem is moved from one place to another.
2. Time displacement: A problem is moved from one time to another.
3. Method displacement: The problem, or the offender, changes methods, but the problem itself remains.
4. Target displacement: The problem, or the offender, changes targets. (The place, timing, and tactics are the same but target is different).
5. Offense displacement: The problem, or offense, changes to another type of problem or offense.

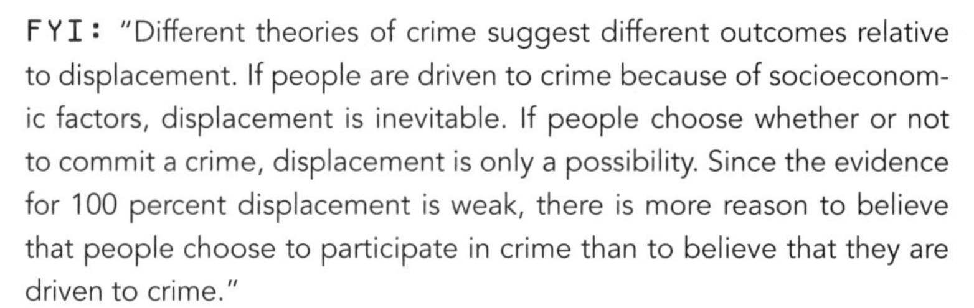

FYI: "Different theories of crime suggest different outcomes relative to displacement. If people are driven to crime because of socioeconomic factors, displacement is inevitable. If people choose whether or not to commit a crime, displacement is only a possibility. Since the evidence for 100 percent displacement is weak, there is more reason to believe that people choose to participate in crime than to believe that they are driven to crime."

—*Problem Solving Quarterly,* 1993.

Although the most common form of displacement is place or time displacement, many of these variations of displacement can occur concurrently. For example, Closed-Circuit Television (CCTV) placed in hallways and elevators, or directed to the cash/wrap location, may shift unauthorized behavior to blind spots for fear of detection. Displacement of crime or threat is either positive or negative, depending on the method by which it is utilized and managed. This factor brings to full circle the need for an inclusive integrated dialogue on security at both the macro and micro levels.

Often we either disregard the psychological aspects of security, the element of fear of crime, or attempt to address these issues in a roundabout way as Rachel Briggs (2005) articulates in her work on **invisible security**. "Ellin [Nan Ellin, urban designer and author of *Architecture of Fear,* 1997] has argued, 'form follows fear' on the urban landscape. In the wake of the anthrax attacks in the United States in Autumn 2001, for example, companies in London reported installing beefed-up security measures in their offices not because they believed there was a heightened threat, but to calm the fears of their employees" (Briggs, 2005). Briggs went on to critique current counterterrorism measures; "there are three main ways in which counterterrorism impacts in a physical way on the built environment: the militarization of space through the use of physical security barriers; the demise of **iconography** in the urban landscape—in other words what we choose not to build; and a process of decentralization as companies and ordinary people decide the risks of terrorism outweigh the benefits of city life."

For example, in a 2005 poll of businesses in London, while 40 percent of respondents said terrorism was the most important risk facing the capital city, only 3 percent said it was a factor that would influence whether or not they would relocate. The most important factors in their responses were business success and insurance rates (Briggs, 2005). Risk assessment in this instance for the business owners was not measured on the same axis as that for security personnel, thus the need for another set of determinants becomes obvious. The same is true when it comes to exploring means of addressing security in the interior environment, where security and civic life meet, thus necessitating the need for sensitive, unobtrusive, and integrated solutions.

Risk, threat assessment, and analysis, as well as mitigating the impact of risk have all been given more discussion and exploration in recent years. Risk as a concept has been studied and researched in the fields of economics, sociology, political science, and anthropology, culminating in asset analysis, threat analysis, vulnerability analysis, and risk analysis. In risk analysis for critical environments, such as highly sensitive laboratories and hospitals, the likelihood of a particular type of threat to breach the security of an environment is calculated and mitigating solutions are put in place. These methods of risk assessment and subsequent safety and security solutions take an economics approach focusing primarily on the likelihood a structure may be targeted, and the monetary value of the assets that may be affected. Such frameworks are widely used by various government and public agencies; however, the economic-only focus of assessment can negatively impact the human experience of place, and most certainly affect the core of what an interior designer does. Designers primarily focus on the meaning and user perception of the environment, and the creation of spaces and places for people's activities, aspirations, and growth, so an additional component that addresses human factors, human capital, and value-rich experiences must be included in risk assessment frameworks.

Transparent Security

One major development in the security dialogue for the twenty-first century is that technological developments and design imperatives are turning counterterrorism, community policing, and crime prevention from a largely physical and visible activity into one that is nearly invisible to the human eye, which brings both positive and negative ramifications to the social discourse. Planners, designers, and managers no longer have to depend on bulky security systems that restrict access, cause disruption, or alter architectural integrity, but rather can begin to appropriately and sensitively adopt measures of transparent or invisible security. This innovative and interdisciplinary approach to design can be manifested in NBBJ, one of the more dynamic, globally oriented architectural and design firms, originally housed in Seattle, Washington, and now with offices across the globe.

FYI: Risk analysis in the built environment demands both qualitative and quantitative assessments that take into account psychological, cultural, and economic perspectives. Any approach that addresses one of these perspectives alone is incomplete and may provide venues for inappropriate security solutions.

NBBJ's US Federal Courthouse design stands as a testament to the innovation and integration of transparent security in a highly visible and significant structure. As a federal building, the building met the newest General Services Administration guidelines for design excellence. The design aimed to "give contemporary form and meaning to the nation's democratic values: and as such, security needs have been met with creative strategies that emphasized an image of open access." According to NBBJ, "Site perimeter security has been achieved with the use of landscape buffers, courthouse steps, reinforced tree guards and low-height bollards designed as seating elements. Upon entry, an expansive public lobby conveys the importance of the courthouse to the public without perceived physical barriers. The security barriers include a reflecting pool, public artwork and an invisible infrared security curtain. Steel cables run parallel to the building's superstructure to prohibit progressive collapse in the event of a blast" (NBBJ, 2004).

Following the attacks of 9/11, perimeter security for public spaces gained popularity as requests increased from both the public and governmental sectors for solutions to building access (see Figure 2.9). Phifer (2003) found that due to the urgency—actual and perceived—mediocre or temporary solutions were often installed with the idea that something nicer could be installed later.

The means of conceptualizing and achieving this resistance is truly the core issue at hand. Several examples of perimeter security strategic modifications, including *jersey barriers* transformed into landscape planters and used as exterior architectural features accomplish the same security result but do not negatively affect the urban landscape. Intricate walkway systems that increase public participation and monitoring of public space; collapsible concrete sidewalks that appear similar to the typical sidewalk, but collapse into a concealed trench beyond a normal weight limit; and barriers that are utilized both as benches and as lighting features provide examples of transparent security solutions that offer increased resistance. All these strategies and products attempt to maintain the civic fabric of the surrounding environment while enhancing the security solution.

2.9

The courthouse's office wing flanks the courtroom tower. This structure includes column-free, clear-span floors that let in natural light—a feature that contributes to the building's sustainability goals. Physical security measures at major outsourcing service providers include guarded entrances, visible layered security throughout, and extensive indoor video monitoring.

FYI: Transparent security means unobtrusive, unrestrictive, and not readily visible technologies, systems, and approaches which address security in the built environment effectively but in ways that are not readily apparent to the public eye. The primary goal of transparent security remains the protection of assets as defined by the building owner, stakeholders, and codes; however, whether to use transparent security measures or visible security measures ought to be determined by context, stakeholders, and critical dialogue among design team members. Maxwell Stevens, director of security design in the security systems design group at RTKL in Baltimore, Maryland notes, "Prior to such events [terrorism incidents] and disasters, most people wanted to *see* security. But, as the public became more involved and there were more requirements to implementing higher levels of security, it became apparent that security could become visibly overbearing. As a result, developers, designers, and manufacturers began developing 'transparent' technology and systems."

As Rachel Briggs, former manager of the Risk and Security Research Programme at The Foreign Policy Centre, an independent European think tank, and current head of International Programmes for Demos—another globally oriented think tank—affirms, "'Transparent security' will certainly change the relationship between crime prevention and counterterrorism and the built environment, in both positive and negative ways. The urban landscape will no longer be marred by hasty obstructions and semimilitarization of the environment, but it also will raise many questions and debates about the delineation of public and private space as it relates to use of such 'invisible security'" (2005). Among these concerns is that, as designers, we must be informed about how the use of these technologies might differ between public and private spaces, who will define what is appropriate or suspicious behavior, how such interpretations vary depending on the local and regional context, and what impact would such strategies have on civil liberties as expressed in the built environment. These and other concerns will definitely give birth to new roles for the built environment professional.

Many citizens have already encountered **Closed-Circuit Television (CCTV)** used in tracking movement, however with the advent of smaller and more "invisible" means of security, the relationship between people and their environment will be radically altered. Since the September 11 attacks, people have reexamined their commitment to democratic norms and personal freedoms and now accept certain restrictions—more surveillance of their personal belongings, papers, and communications, as well as physical searches. As United States Supreme Court Justice Sandra Day O'Connor states, "We're likely to experience more restrictions on our personal freedom than has ever been the case in our country . . . it will cause us to reexamine some of our laws pertaining to criminal surveillance, immigration and so on" (2001). If safety and security are truly more basic needs than self-actualization and freedom (Maslow 1954), then individuals, in particular American citizens accustomed to freedom, broad civil liberties, and a safe and secure society, may be asked to sacrifice a great deal to maintain this comfortable aspect of the American way of life, even at the expense of greater limitations on their personal freedom. The design professional needs to be sensitive to the complex issues surrounding the discussion of personal freedoms as it relates to the built environment and how it is addressed in the design solution. Security analyst Paul Viollis in his article "A Wake-up Call for Not Only Terrorist Threats" maintains that, "Negative behavior—from theft to terrorism—migrates to the path of least resistance" (2002, p. 25). Reducing the likelihood of violence, crime, or any threat, therefore could be construed as a matter of increasing "resistance" (Bartholomew et al, 2004). The means of conceptualizing and achieving this resistance is truly the core issue at hand for the design professional.

Innovation and Integration

Another very critical security issue that has recently become more evident is the degree of reliance and connection to technology in our everyday life and the lack of a systematic approach to risk assessment. In an address on security in the twenty-first century, former United States Ambassador to Australia J. Thomas Schieffer stated "The recent blackout in the eastern part of the United States and Canada reminded us all of how vulnerable we are to attacks upon our infrastructure. Though not the work of terrorists, the blackout demonstrated that a world connected by technology and communication is a world that can be brought to its knees by terrorists or even mischief-makers. We must realize that we are threatened by some whose cause may only be the joy they derive from bringing the world to a halt. Cyber security will be an issue for us for many years" (2003).

A wider and more inclusive security assessment must become integrated into the design and management of our environment if we are to be proactive in this regard. To be prepared for the twenty-first century we need to utilize a fully integrated, seamless approach to design and security in the built environment. The many emerging security and safety standards and regulations, based on new standards of care, should be drawn upon and used as reference points, similar to the National Fire Protection Association (NFPA) Life Safety Code or the Americans with Disabilities Act (ADA) Accessibility Guidelines for Buildings and Facilities, as the interior design profession fulfills its professional obligation to the health, safety, and welfare of the public.

Global and Cultural Dimensions and Implications

Globally, we are becoming increasingly more aware of the threat of terrorism and need for security in the built environment. Following the tragic events of September 11, 2001, significant changes in the "security mindset" occurred. Currently there is widespread appreciation of the urgent need to tackle the terrorist threat head-on, and how the natures of these threats have shifted in targets from diplomatic staffs and specialist circles to targets within the business community and the general public. As a result, counterterrorism policymakers have gained the support needed to construct new and effective policies for improving security in the United States and abroad.

The 9/11 Commission Report (2005) provides an example of how governments are strategizing to improve, as stated in the language of the document, "failures of imagination, policy, capabilities, and management." One aspect of the commission report important to design professionals is the recommendation to encourage widespread adoption of newly developed standards for private-sector emergency preparedness—since the private sector controls 85 percent of the nation's critical infrastructure. But the threat to companies is not limited to terrorism. In fact, it is often the lower-impact but higher-frequency threats, such as petty street crime and medical problems, whose cumulative effects have more serious long-term consequences for business. "The policy-making community must now make the most of the heightened general interest in security issues, whilst avoiding the pressure to focus on terrorism to the exclusion of all other security threats" (Briggs, 2002). It is an exciting time for interior design and its allied professions, as the role of the designer to serve as an active participant in incorporating security solutions into the designed environment is great.

For example, The United States **Interagency Security Committee (ISC)** has issued new security standards for government leased spaces, and the General Services Administration (GSA) has incorporated the ISC security standards into its solicitation for bids. The aim of the new ISC standards is to provide a consistent level of security to federal tenants in leased spaces and buildings that fits with each agency's mission-specific risks, vulnerability, and market conditions (ISC, 2007–2008 and GSA, 2006).

In addition to CPTED chapters and UN security commissions and chapters, the Organization for Security and Co-operation in Europe (OSCE) represents the major international institution where competitive powers work together under a single security umbrella. Its normative core provides the foundation for the creation of a "pluralistic security community" based on the norms of democratic governance and the peaceful settlement of intrastate and interstate disputes within a framework of comprehensive, cooperative security. The work of this organization also needs to take a more integrated look at various aspects of threat and security though. Effective and grounded security is delivered through small acts rather than grand gestures; as seen through the research of Jacobs, Newman, Jeffery, Saville, Briggs, Nasar, Cleveland, Brown, and many others.

Our built environment—both far and near—is an important canvas for our hopes, dreams, fears, and everyday lives. There is an intimate relationship between the physicality and the perception of the environment; between our experience with the environment and the memories we carry with us about those environments. The personal and universal iconography of our spaces and places can be affected with the solutions we create as we face new security threats, the sense of place and place attachment can greatly become victims of such solutions. One can only contemplate the experience of national parks and monuments pre- and post-9/11. As Craig Obey, the Vice President for the National Parks Conservation Association (NPCA), stated, "Homeland security requirements have also changed the way visitors experience some national parks. Visitors to the Statue of Liberty for instance, go through a screening process more elaborate than most airports. At the St. Louis Arch, the first ranger a visitor might encounter isn't there to tell them the inspiring story of Lewis and Clark, but is instead standing guard, solemnly carrying a large weapon" (Obey, 2007).

Nadel (2006), for example, investigated the unique security challenges present in protecting security of places for worship for Muslims, Christians, and Jews in Israel. She states "Religious and lay persons must collaborate with security and design professionals to develop appropriate visible and transparent security measures that can be rapidly increased as needed based on event and community concerns. Above all, maintaining the powerful experience of worshiping in sacred spaces should remain paramount to all involved in protecting these facilities and those who use them" (2006). Nadel's statement highlights the complexity, need for flexibility, sustainability of security efforts, and protection of the essence of experience in the built environment.

The recent outcry for fear of huge queues and time demands associated with airport-style security solutions at London's Mainline Rail Stations (Murray, 2005), provides another example of protecting the essence of "experiencing a space." The British Transportation Secretary proposed that rail passengers should pass through body scanners and x-ray machines at all rail stations. Although the possible risks were not disputed, the public perceived the solution as not only "not practical," but also disrespectful of the quality of the interactions and experiences at those stations.

A similar situation occurred in Amman, Jordan, in 2005 when three simultaneous explosions shocked the structures of three hotels in the downtown causing much loss of life, property, horror, and an attack on the community's sense of security and safety. The significance of these attacks lies in the characterization of the targets as "soft targets," which essentially describes most of our everyday built environments. Although this was not the first soft target ever to be hit, comments made by reporters indicated that security measures were nonexistent, as there were no metal detectors, or physical searches, as one entered these hotels (BBC, 2005 and CNN, 2005). These two examples indicate a level of public acceptance or rejection for hastily imposed security solutions; as seen in a statement by the spokeswoman for Southeastern Trains, the busiest commuter operator in Britain. He characterized the reaction for the Mainline Rail Station scenario stating, "Security is a high priority but it has got to be practical. Any measures introduced would need to be practical" (Murray, 2005).

Issues of practicality were addressed in the British 2004 Buildingfutures, a joint initiative between the Commission for Architecture and the Built Environment (CABE)—which is the UK government's advisor on architecture, urban design, and public space and The Royal Institute of British Architects (RIBA). This venture put forward strategic issues that must be addressed as we move into the twenty-first century, a new era of flexibility and change.

Two primary initiatives dealt with by these organizations included schools and public libraries. Within each, the integration of security within design guidelines was evident. "If the provision for safe, accessible public space for children and young people—which libraries seem to be uniquely placed to provide—is a new priority, what forms of monitoring and security need to be developed which do not at the same time appear overly prescriptive or heavy-handed? How is the historic universalism of the public library to be squared with managerial requirements to separate out different user groups and their needs, particularly in a more culturally segmented and multimedia society?" (see Table 2.1) (Buildingfutures, 2004).

As a public space, the concept of a library in its own right provides an excellent example of the importance of the designers' increased sensitivity to the integration of security design solutions used within a much-respected and cherished public icon (see Figure 2.10). As we become more technologically connected, as the functions of the library are expanded, and service to a wider range of population is

TABLE 2.1

SCENARIOS RESULTS: FROM FORM TO FUNCTION		
Access and movement	Places with well-defined routes, spaces, and entrances that provide for convenient movement without compromising security.	This makes it easier to spot unusual behavior within these spaces.
Structure	Places that are structured so that different users do not cause conflict.	This enhances zoning and demarcation of space.
Surveillance	Places where all publicly accessible spaces are overlooked.	This is a human alternative to CCTV coverage and puts people rather than machines at the center of surveillance efforts.
Ownership	Places that promote a sense of ownership, respect, territorial responsibility, and community.	These attributes encourage people to be proactive rather than passive in the security of their spaces.
Physical protection	Places that include necessary, well-designed security features.	This enhances a sense of safety while allowing normal life to continue.
Activity	Places where the level of human activity is appropriate to the location.	This creates a reduced risk of crime and provides a sense of safety at all times.
Management and maintenance	Places that are designed with management and maintenance in mind.	This discourages crime in the present and the future.

Source: Adapted from the 2004 Buildingfutures: A joint initiative between CABE and RIBA twenty-first century. Retrieved January 2, 2006 from http://www.buildingfutures.org.uk/pdfs/pdffile_31.pdf

2.10 As a public space, a library needs security to protect its patrons and contents while remaining open and inviting.

increasing, security becomes an important issue to be handled sensitively so as not to create the wrong effect. "With this shift comes the need for sensitive management of key potential conflicts of design, function, and ethos. Getting the right balance between the safety and security of users, while at the same time providing a welcoming and more open plan layout" (Buildingfutures, 2004).

Another exciting development is the idea of **Sustainable Communities** which emerged as an alternative vision for governmental policies in countering crime and terrorism in the UK and are inspired by CPTED principles. They are described in a recent paper for the Office of the Deputy Prime Minister as "communities which succeed now, economically, socially, and environmentally, and respect the needs of future generations. They are well-designed places where people feel safe and secure; where crime and disorder, or the fear of crime, doesn't undermine quality of life or community cohesion" (2004). This vision has been reinforced by a new Planning Policy Statement, which has put crime prevention at the heart of the planning process: "Designing out crime and designing in community safety should be central to the planning and delivery of new development." Sustainable communities are organized around seven attributes, some of which are relevant to counterterrorism. These attributes are as follows (Briggs, 2005):

- Access and movement: Places with well-defined routes, spaces, and entrances that provide for convenient movement without compromising security.

- Structure: Places that are structured so that different uses do not cause conflict.
- Surveillance: Places where all publicly accessible spaces are overlooked.
- Ownership: Places that promote a sense of ownership, respect, territorial responsibility, and community.
- Physical protection: Places that include necessary, well-designed security features.
- Activity: Places where the level of human activity is appropriate to the location and creates a reduced risk of crime and a sense of safety at all times.
- Management and maintenance: Places that are designed with management and maintenance in mind, to discourage crime in the present and the future.

Briggs states that the concept of sustainable communities is currently focused on the potential for built-form and design features to tackle crime, and the results seem to be encouraging. However, lessons from such experiences have not yet been applied to larger-scale settings and across-the-board consideration.

CONCLUSION

"According to the latest Bureau of Justice Statistics' annual crime survey, nearly one million individuals become victims of violent crime in US workplaces each year. An estimated 8 percent of rapes, 7 percent of robberies, and 16 percent of all assaults occurred while victims were working or on duty" (National Center for Victims of Crime, 2004). The universal need for security and safety is not the issue in question, rather, it is how one can define and conceptualize parameters of the concept, and go about addressing it in the built environment. Theorists and researchers have addressed both the physical and psychological dimensions of security, and attempted to define the conditions necessary to increase safety and minimize crime and violence. Some of the methods advocated raise serious questions regarding issues of inclusiveness, displacement, psychological and social impact, design fit, and intrusion, as well as the sustainability of solutions.

A radically transformative approach to security considerations in the built environment has been in the making for over six decades. It is a prime window of opportunity for designers to become actively involved in the formation and emergence of a new era of security consciousness. Robert Peck, former Commissioner of Public Buildings Service, General Services Administration stated, "Our cities and towns need leaders who understand that vital, active places are critical to their health and long term sustainability" (Peck 2000).

The design community must be cognizant of the role they can play in facilitating and advancing a security plan that is seamless and integrated in their design, construction, and management of the environment. The concern for proactive and responsible security considerations that add to, not take away from, the civic vision of a place; that highlight, not hinder the identity of an environment; and empower, not stifle community participation and its inhabitants.

Jon Coaffee, author and specialist on urban regeneration for the Global Urban Research Unit at the School of Architecture, Planning, and Landscape at the University of Newcastle, England, for example, describes the use of *fortress architecture* and defensible space in the city, "notably around the central shopping area in Belfast where access to the centre was barred, first by concrete blockers and barbed wire, and then later by a series of high metal gates which became known as the 'ring of steel'—a term which was to gain new meaning in the 1990s in central London" (2003). In his research, Coaffee studied a series of place-specific security initiatives and risk management policies, and found that they led to increased fortification, a substantial rise in terrorism insurance premiums, and changing institutional relations at a variety of spatial scales. He describes how these design principles had a profound impact on the look of the city, the way residents and visitors used the space, and how they felt about being there.

Achieving a positive relationship and integrated solutions for security concerns will greatly depend on our ability to find ways of bringing together those who design spaces, those who secure them, and those who use them. Lessons from past experiences, from various disciplines, and contextual parameters, will help us all in defining, articulating, and creating appropriate solutions. Effective engagement in security dialogue, in educating others about the value of the built environment, and in maintaining an active appreciation and involvement in the impact security measures have on the built environment will further define the importance of the interior design profession and its significant role in the health, safety, and welfare of the public.

KEY CONCEPTS

- Lessons from security research over time and across disciplines provide an excellent foundation for application in the built environment.
- Perimeter security, structural security, and interior space security together can afford a more inclusive and integrated system that supports opportunities for active community policing, sustainable security solutions, and seamless integration in the built environment.
- Anonymity in public spaces, problems with security implementation, and displacement (the movement of crime) are some of the issues that must be addressed.
- Technological advancement and ethical implications of security solutions within the built environment need to be a central point of the security dialogue.
- Global and cultural dimensions of security in the built environment point to an increased awareness of threats and vulnerability, as well as the need to understand the context in which solutions are being offered.

- A radical, transformative approach to security is needed. **Sustainable security** solutions—i.e., solutions that grow and change with needs—encourage community engagement and provide design solutions within context.
- The design community must be cognizant of the role they can play in facilitating and advancing security plans that are seamless and integrated in the design, construction, and management of the environment.
- Achieving a positive relationship and integrated solutions for security concerns will greatly depend on our ability to find ways of bringing together those who design spaces, those who secure them, and those who use them.

ASSIGNMENTS

1. Discuss and further develop an understanding of the human need for safety and security.
2. Conceptually determine how to integrate security solutions into the built environment.
3. Provide examples of the security concerns and mitigation strategies in the twenty-first century and discuss how they impact the built environment.

ACTIVITIES

1. Journaling activity: Respond in written and graphic format. Questions may include remembering an experience or a space that heightened your sense of vulnerability, fear, or a space that did the opposite. Share your experiences while generating a list, look for patterns and lead discussion on issues in the built environment that could have been manipulated.
2. Read security theories and graphically illustrate concepts.
3. Create a project that requires as a component of the programming and design process the integration of security needs and theories in identifying and articulating design problems.
4. Visit a site that has implemented obvious security control measures with a required exercise in behavioral mapping.
5. Collect current information related to events and policies and analyze it based on theoretical perspectives in literature.
6. Windshield videography: Videotape a transition from areas that are perceived as vulnerable or less secure to areas that appear as more secure, determine characteristics that may have lead to such perception, and attempt to find if there is a "transition zone" or a balance point between the two. Follow up with systematic discussion.

CHARACTERISTICS OF PHYSICAL ENVIRONMENTS THAT PROMOTE SECURITY

Security-design strategies can most effectively minimize the loss of life and property through integrated use of technology, operational policies, and facility planning. Understanding the exact nature of what may threaten a building is important, especially in the early project development phases. From site selection and materials specification to structural systems, every design decision may someday be crucial to saving lives and preventing damage because of an attack, accidental explosion, or natural disaster.

—Barbara Nadel, AIA, 1998

OBJECTIVES

- Provide an overview of the basic psychological aspects of security as it relates to the built environment.
- Develop an awareness of the impact of the designer's role in regard to security design, perception, and use and management of the built environment.
- Increase awareness of how the built environment has changed as societies deal with acts of terrorism, workplace violence, and acts of aggression within schools.
- Increase awareness of basic security design programming issues, a variety of security related materials and products, including best practices principles of architecture, landscape architecture, and interior design principles as they relate to the design of safe and secure environments.

3.1 The aftermath of the Hurricane Katrina disaster in 2005.

"The devastating impact of Hurricane Katrina on the ability of school facilities to function, serves as a frightening reminder that the best disaster recovery (DR) plan may fail if steps are not taken to prevent or limit the impact of disasters before they occur. Disaster recovery plans are more likely to succeed if a *pre-disaster program of physical security* is in place prior to the advent of hurricanes, earthquakes, accidental and intentional explosions, and other potentially life-threatening events" (Watts, 2007). (See Figure 3.1.)

Events of the past ten years have shaped a wider appreciation of what "court security" entails and what must be involved in its provision. The earlier focus on law-enforcement functions, hardware-screening mechanisms, and some facility design considerations has been significantly expanded to include a much broader concept of protecting the health and safety of both the users and occupants of the courthouse (see Figure 3.2). There has also been an increase in safeguarding the full range of resources and judicial system activities necessary to sustain the functioning of the court system and the integrity of the judicial process (Cooper, 2007).

Considerations for architecture and design security are not only important for major civic and iconic buildings and structures but also for everyday places for people, with their dreams and aspirations. The design and construction professions are entrusted to design, build, and operate these environments in a way that assures public health and safety, preserves the environment, and promotes security. This role is perhaps one of the most significant as it directly affects physical, mental, psychological, social, and economic aspects of life.

Dennis, the gay owner of a bar in Lancaster, England, which is described as a "mixed" bar, offers an example of environmental boundary making and marking. "The relationship between the aesthetics of the place and safety from drunken violence is also a feature of boundary making and marking in Lancaster." He explains that while the bar is remotely situated across from a car park, it is close to several other pubs and bars where violence is common. He does not employ door staff, rather he uses an alternate technique to regulate access. This means, in his words, when, "lager louts" came to the bar, "they [would] just stand out and feel uncomfortable and that in itself makes them leave . . . it's a bit too pretty for them." He describes the aesthetics of the bar as "relaxed," which he explains in the following terms: "no juke box, no loud music, no pool table, no darts, no big screen, just a bar, a meeting place, with this big conservatory and a macaw [named Oscar]."

The built environment is a concept that is experienced, perceived, and communicated in parts and as a whole. Security and safety—both physical and psychological—are components of this concept that can be powerful tools and indicators of quality of life in an environment. According to Beverly Skeggs, "Americans are increasingly concerned about public safety and fears of crime are diminishing the quality of life in many communities. Public safety is the top priority in many communities, but while prison building is one of the fastest-growing industries in the United States, funding for crime prevention pales in comparison. People effectively read the environment as a barometer of risk and protective factors. To make these readings, people draw on the discourses to which they have access to, make sense of their own and others' occupation of space. This always involves visual evaluation of the built environment as well as visual evaluation of others" (2004).

Our environment is both a concern and a potent source of stress for many of us. While individuals experience stress due to personal events in their lives, communities experience environmental stressors linked to features of their neighborhoods

3.2

Hardware-screening mechanisms are used in courthouses to protect the health and safety of its occupants.

and general context such as traffic, crime, and abandonment of properties near their homes. The John D. and Catherine T. MacArthur Research Network on Socioeconomic Status and Health identified four main constructs conveyed in its research. These constructs include the following:

- Crime: crime victimization, perception, and observation
- Life stressors: individual experiences of community-level stressors
- Neighborhood conditions: conditions including graffiti, abandoned buildings, and untended lots
- Traffic: traffic volume, speed, and noise

This network on socioeconomic status (SES) and health also indicates that there are multiple pathways by which SES may affect health. These include the following:

- Access and quality of health care
- Health behaviors (e.g., smoking, lack of physical activity, nutrition)
- Psychosocial processes (e.g., stress, lack of personal control, hostility, depression)
- Physical environment (e.g., pollution, exposure to toxins, and crowding)
- Social environments (e.g., neighborhood, work and school environments, social capital, discrimination) (May 2005).

Safety and security constitute not only a construct for how SES and health are investigated but also act as a mechanism for affecting health and well-being in the built environment.

PSYCHOLOGICAL ASPECTS OF SECURITY

Violent actions that are random, unprovoked, and intentional, and often targeted at defenseless citizens, can set off a chain of psychological events culminating in feelings of fear, helplessness, vulnerability, and grief. Acts of violence, rampage shootings, and terrorism are incidents that threaten a society by instilling fear and helplessness in its citizens and communities.

Terrorism and Violence

In 2004, following the 9/11 attacks, a four-volume study *The Psychology of Terrorism,* edited by Chris E. Stout, (previously an advisor to the White House, and representative to the United Nations), was published. In this publication, respected scholars, academics, and clinicians from around the world applied their knowledge and experience in psychiatry and human behavior to issues of terrorism. This reference text provides information, approaches, methods, and understanding for those working to develop effective ways to respond to terrorism specifically and violence in general.

Tandem to the exploration of terrorism and crime, the psychological and health professions once again focused on the role of emotional processes in the face of such acts. Emotional responses are critical for human survival. Among other things, they help us learn from our negative experiences so that we can avoid harmful situations in the future, and may indicate an attempt to deal with a painful past similar to **Post-Traumatic Stress Disorder (PTSD)**, or can be seen as a part of reconciliation process. Undoubtedly, this is one of the main areas where interior designers can contribute through the design of a built environment that offer the perception of safety and security to its inhabitants.

FYI: "The goal of terrorism," according to Dr. Steven E. Hyman, the director of NIH's National Institute of Mental Health (NIMH), "is really to undercut coping and leave us with feelings of disorganization and panic. To combat this effect, we need to try to be rational about the real dangers we face and to do everything we can to cope with our very natural anxiety" (2002).

Workplace Violence

Across the globe, in times of economic upheavals, downsizing, layoffs, mergers, and bankruptcies, hundreds of thousands of workers have lost their jobs. Millions more have been shifted to unfamiliar tasks within their companies, and wonder how much longer they will be employed. Adding to the pressures that workers face are smaller personal spaces and overcrowded open offices, new bosses, computer surveillance of production, fewer health and retirement benefits, and the feeling they have to work longer and harder just to maintain their current economic status.

According to the United State's National Institute for Occupational Safety and Health (NIOSH), "an average of 1.7 million people were victims of violent crime while working or on duty in the United States, according to a report published by the Bureau of Justice Statistics (BJS), each year from 1993 through 1999. An estimated 1.3 million (75 percent) of these incidents were simple assaults, while an additional 19 percent were aggravated assaults" (2007).

"Of the occupations examined, police officers, corrections officers, and taxi drivers were victimized at the highest rates. For the same time period, more than 800 workplace homicides per year were recorded by the Bureau of Labor Statistics's Census of Fatal Occupational Injuries" (NIOSH, 2007). The rates range from 15 to 20 workplace related murders each week in the United States. The majority of these murders are robbery-related crimes. Most of these assaults occur in service settings such as hospitals, nursing homes, and social service agencies. Factors that place workers at risk for violence in the workplace include interacting with the public, exchanging money, delivering services or goods, working late at night or during early morning hours, working alone, guarding valuables or property, and dealing with violent people or volatile situations. Environmental factors ranged from unauthorized access to isolated situations.

FYI: The American Psychiatric Association offers the following statistics from a 2004 survey: 45 percent of workers say job insecurity has a significant impact on work stress levels; 61 percent of workers list heavy workloads as a significant impact on work stress levels; a majority of workers (52 percent) are more stressed because of work than home; and 73 percent of Americans name money as the number one factor that affects their stress level.

Youth Violence

Violence, the act of purposefully hurting someone, is a major issue facing today's young adults. One in twelve high school students is threatened or injured with a weapon each year. Young people between the ages of 12 and 24, face the highest risk of being the victim of violence. Statistics show that by the early 1990s, the incidence of violence caused by young people reached unparalleled levels in American society (APA, 2004).

There is no single explanation for the overall rise in youth violence. Many different factors may influence violent behavior: youth disengagement from school, hostility between social groupings, and violence used as a form of expression, manipulation, or retaliation. In Canada, a 1993 Environics poll revealed that Canadians believe school-based youth violence is the single most important issue facing public education (cited in Saskatchewan Schools Trustees Association, 1994). Canadian teachers themselves have reported dramatic increases in the type, frequency, and severity of antisocial, aggressive, and violent behavior in classrooms (Carney, 1999).

FYI: According to a 2005 American Psychiatric Association report on youth violence, one in twelve high-school students is threatened or injured with a weapon each year and 40 percent of youth have been concerned about a potentially violent classmate (See Figure 3.3).

Terrorism, workplace violence, youth violence, and other crimes as acts of violence, all exploit two very natural aspects of our brain, Dr. Steven Hyman, Director, National Institute of Mental Health (NIMH), explains, "The first is that novel

3.3

Schools are trying to combat youth violence with increased security and drug and gun awareness.

and uncontrolled situations are extremely stressful." From animal studies, he states, "we know that these situations can cause severe physical effects. Secondly, we normally empathize with others. When we face danger, we do not turn to the rational part of our brain and begin to do a statistically based risk analysis. Instead, we see these pictures . . . or hear stories in the media . . . and we begin to identify with the victims" (2002).

Fear can help us consolidate memories, Dr. Hyman further emphasizes, "Most citizens of the world can remember where we were on September 11th when we found out about the World Trade Center and the Pentagon. In the case of terrorist attacks, or other acts of violence at school or work, the mechanisms in the brain that are designed to ensure our survival can cause mental disorders that get in the way of normal life. And conditions like Post-Traumatic Stress Disorder (PTSD), depression, and anxiety disorders can plague not only the people who were directly in the line of an attack but also those watching events unfold in the media" (2002).

THE DESIGNER'S ROLE

The interior design profession can fulfill its specialized role in protecting the health, safety, and welfare of users of public spaces by partnering with clients, end users, and allied professionals to provide design solutions that increase the safety and security within the places where we live, work, and play. Proactive security design solutions will offer psychological comfort to inhabitants knowing that these spaces have been "secured" the best they can be through thoughtful risk assessment with measures added that may decrease the likelihood of harm, damage, and physical and/or psychological injury to improve quality of life and emotional well-being.

Designing for security ought to consider both physical and psychological aspects related to security and safety for the context at hand. As with all design solutions, cultural, environmental, economic, and other implications for the solution must be investigated for maximum benefit and a seamless fit. Security issues can be investigated and addressed by analyzing function, location, and personnel-related requirements (and vice versa, meaning designating security solutions based on function, location, and personnel).

Reactions

On September 11, 2001, Laurie Balbo, an architect in the engineering department of the Port Authority of New York and New Jersey, was at her desk on the eighty-second floor of the World Trade Center's north tower. Balbo's heartrending account of her escape from the building, written on the recommendation of a trauma counselor and published in *Metropolis* magazine (October 2002), provided a forum to share with friends and relatives an explanation of that horrific day—and save herself the anguish of telling the story again and again.

Still with the Port Authority, Balbo now works in downtown Newark, New Jersey. She is on the fifteenth floor of her new building. "It's a nice place," Balbo says, "but I keep asking myself, 'How do I get out of here?'" She compares her heightened safety awareness to suddenly being confined to a wheelchair and realizing how hard it is to get around. "After being in the WTC on 9/11," Balbo says, "you realize that the most important thing about a building is how to get out of it." In Balbo's reflections, the most basic of codes, egress, takes on a unique and central presence of experiencing an environment on a daily basis.

"It was not the buildings that killed people, it was the terrorists," she emphasizes in a follow-up interview with *Metropolis* magazine. (October 2004). "People died, yes. But an astounding number of us walked out." Designers and engineers cannot prevent another attack, Balbo says, but they can better equip the occupants to escape. She feels strongly that architects [and designers] need to think beyond meeting safety codes. "It's teaching people how to survive," Balbo says. "How do you break out of a stopped elevator? How do you kick through the drywall and get out of a sealed conference room? We have to give the people inside as much information as we can. It's a role we never thought of architects [or designers] as having." In addition, it's a change, she says, that has to happen: "How do you lure people back into those tall buildings? You can't unless you can make them feel safe" (October 2004).

One survivor's account of the attacks of September 11, 2001, illustrates the profound impact the attacks had on the standards of care in design. Since 9/11, within the United States, there has been a broad-based legislative response, including the Homeland Security Act, Terrorism Risk Insurance Act, and the Maritime Transportation Security Act. In addition to these legislative responses, governmental "embedded economic incentives" are being provided to encourage businesses and organizations within the private sector to adequately secure the nation's critical infrastructure.

Although none of the legislative incentives directly target the mainstream architecture, design, or construction communities, the homeland security environment increases potential liability for injuries sustained in terrorist attacks, places additional regulations on owners of critical infrastructure components, and creates the need to revise contracts to allocate risks arising from new security perspectives. This increased security awareness will undoubtedly create business opportunities for contractors, architects, and designers, while fulfilling our professional mission of protecting the health, safety, and welfare of the public.

CHANGING STANDARDS OF DESIGN AND CONSTRUCTION CARE

Most fundamentally, owners, designers, and contractors are held to a higher standard of care in performing their work. The professional standard of care applies most frequently in cases alleging the negligence of physicians, architects, engineers, and attorneys, but it may be used to hold any professional to apply the acceptable degree of knowledge, training, and skill ordinarily possessed by others in the profession, which includes interior designers. *Negligence,* in relation to planning for safety and security within the built environment, has become evidence for not meeting the **reasonable standard** of care for the architectural and design community.

Generally, reasonableness is determined by foreseeability—such as what a reasonably prudent person could be expected to foresee as a possible consequence of his or her acts or omissions. For example, traditional premises liability rules in Florida apply to hotels, motels, and restaurants, imposing a standard of reasonable care to guests, and those who gratuitously visit guests, but retaining a no-duty rule to trespassers. The rule is one requiring reasonable care for the safety of patrons in their ordinary use of the facility, consistent with the facility's design and operation.

Until September 11, 2001, no reasonable person would have foreseen an event involving the coordinated highjacking of four airliners for the sole purpose of flying them into landmark buildings such as the World Trade Center and the Pentagon, or that two young male high school students would walk through corridors in a rampage based on violence and revenge. The occurrences of these types of events require designers of the built environment to contemplate such attacks. Because such acts are now foreseeable, developers, designers, and contractors arguably have a duty to take the possibility of these, and like scenarios, into consideration when designing future projects.

Similarly, owners of existing facilities may have a duty to evaluate those environments in terms of security threats and respond appropriately to counter those threats—a **duty to care**. Such measures such as building access, visitor screening,

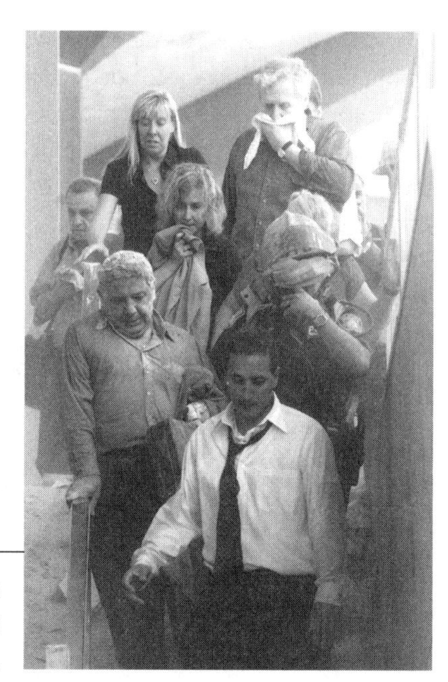

3.4

People make their way down a crowded stairwell inside one of the World Trade Center towers on September 11, 2001.

installation of additional escape routes, wayfinding methods for building evacuation, and protection of HVAC systems, are just a few examples of how increased reasonable standards will affect facility design, planning, and construction (see Figure 3.4).

Enhanced Security Expectations

The enhanced expectation regarding security in the built environment has been in place in relation to federal buildings for many years. According to the General Service Administration (GSA) of the United States government, which manages and supports the functioning of its federal agencies, designers should include some evaluation of the potential threats to that project as part of the programming and review process for each specific new project. Selected GSA initial evaluative questions include:

- Whether the project has any landmark significance (i.e., does the project have sufficient symbolic significance to merit terrorist attention?) (See Chapter 5.)
- Would the project have a government tenant? (See Chapter 7.)
- Would an attack on the project have a significant ripple effect on the economy or a region? For example, a pipeline could pose a more attractive target than a warehouse because an attack on a pipeline could affect millions of people and the entire economy, while an attack on a warehouse might affect only a few people.

- Would an attack on the facility have a secondary physical impact? For example, an attack on chemical plant could release a toxic plume, killing or injuring thousands of people.
- Is the project in close proximity to an attractive terrorist target? Recall that many neighboring buildings were damaged in the World Trade Center attack.

Although these questions appear to assess risks associated with governmental structures, the same premise applies to the private sector. Once potential threats are identified, designers should take into consideration design features necessary to eliminate or mitigate the losses from acts of violence, crimes, attacks, or threats. For example, while it may not be possible to design a building to withstand the impact of a plane loaded with jet fuel, safe from suicide bombers, or secured from sniper shootings, it may be possible to mitigate the impact by adding more segregated stairwells than required by code, or bridging twin towers. Allowing tenants to move to another structure if their escape route is cut off, as seen in the Petronas Towers (see Figure 3.5), or designing educational facilities with an "eyes on the street" approach to increase student safety and security are also ways to mitigate the impacts of attacks.

3.5 The Petronas Towers have a bridge that joins the two structures, which allows for an additional escape route in the case of an emergency.

It is important for designers to note in design contracts that **force majeure clauses**, clauses which excuse parties from contract obligations if certain events outside their control occur, have changed in the design of built environments of the twenty-first century. "Acts of war" typically are events of *force majeure.* Terrorism has been held to *not* constitute an "act of war" under insurance policy exclusion. Accordingly, contracts should be revised to specifically allocate the risks of terrorism. The risks include not only the direct impact from a terrorist attack but also impacts caused by responses to such attacks. For example, projects located in Manhattan were impacted not only by the loss of work time attributable to the attacks themselves, but also by resulting government restrictions preventing trucks from freely crossing onto the island following the attacks.

The concept of reasonable standards of care necessitates that designers keep abreast of innovations in materials, technology, and practices. Architects and engineers have developed blast-resistant glass for windows, modified decontamination showers outside hospitals, and designed landscaping to absorb the force from a blast. These innovations can be quite expensive and cost prohibitive, however lessons from them can be the pathways for more readily available, affordable solutions. Any determination of what a reasonably prudent person should do to guard against a terrorist attack must be made on a case-by-case basis, factoring in the use of the facility, the surrounding circumstances, the cost, and regulations particularly applicable to the project.

Regulations Arising from Homeland Security

A number of legislative mandates in the United States and Canada now require security reviews and upgrades for existing facilities, and certainly for new ones. The mandates provide significant opportunities for contractors and design professionals in the following areas:

- Public utilities: water, power, and pipelines
- Transportation: airport, maritime, rail, and mass transit
- Science and industry: biohazard and chemical hazards

All of these legislative mandates will have some impact on the design and construction industry and require project research on the part of the design professional.

For example, in the United States, the Bioterrorism Preparedness and Response Act (P.L. 107–188) signed into law in June 2002, authorizes monetary incentives to assist states in preparing for a **bioterrorism** attack—the intentional release of biological agents such as bacteria, toxins, or viruses—by developing preparedness plans and enhancing preparedness of hospitals and other clinics. The implications for design and architecture in terms of **scenario planning**, programming, space planning, zoning, materials selection, and other design considerations is considerable. (See Chapter 6 for case study analysis within the health-care environment).

Social Justice and Security

Although architects have to design buildings that are fire resistant and accessible to people with disabilities, they don't have to make buildings resistant to crime. Designing for fire resistance and accessibility means complying with building codes and industry standards. The purpose of building codes is the protection of the health, safety, and welfare of the building occupants. Thus, architects and designers need to design for the safety and security of the users of the environment. Architects and designers of the future must design against threats of criminal behavior, workplace violence, and acts of terrorism as part of their commitment to designing a building that protects its users.

The first contact a person has with a particular architectural project is accessing the site to gain entry to a property or building. With the increasing threats to people and property from acts of terrorism, workplace violence, and street crime, as discussed earlier in Chapter 2, the first and most important line of defense is securing the site perimeter and the careful placement of buildings on the given site. Care should be taken to ensure that the boundary between the outside, or the public, and the inside, or the private domain, is clearly demarcated. Entry points are extremely important in terms of their location; they are seen as the mediator between outside and inside, and become important points of vulnerability to the interior design.

According to the RAND Corporation, a nonprofit institution that helps improve policy and decision making through research and analysis focusing on issues of national security, acts of terrorism are dynamic and ever-changing. Terrorists may change their methods, adapt to changes in security or perceived value of the target, or adapt techniques that were used successfully against other targets when planning attacks. As terrorism is dynamic, and terrorists adapt their methods to suit changes in weaponry and defense tactics, terrorism prevention and security measures therefore also needs to be dynamic. Buildings are essentially static, so this makes it extremely difficult, and expensive, to design built environments that will be as secure against attacks 20 years from now as they may be today (RAND, IP-251).

In response to changes in airport security and growth in airport traffic, a new look is needed at the circulation and security of passengers, cargo, and personnel throughout airports and into surrounding communities. New and innovative approaches that are "User-Centered Designed" and create open environments with minimal disruption along with a strong level of security is needed. As previously discussed, security and safety are contextual and call for the implementation of a **User-Centered Design (UCD)** approach, as discussed in the next section.

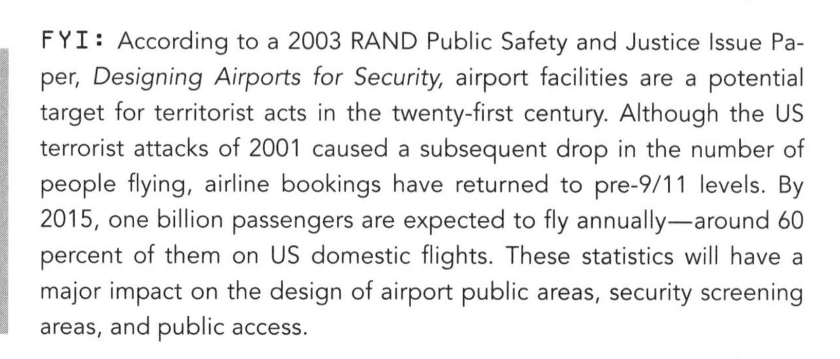

FYI: According to a 2003 RAND Public Safety and Justice Issue Paper, *Designing Airports for Security,* airport facilities are a potential target for territorist acts in the twenty-first century. Although the US terrorist attacks of 2001 caused a subsequent drop in the number of people flying, airline bookings have returned to pre-9/11 levels. By 2015, one billion passengers are expected to fly annually—around 60 percent of them on US domestic flights. These statistics will have a major impact on the design of airport public areas, security screening areas, and public access.

DEFINING USER-CENTERED DESIGN

What is User-Centered Design (UCD)? UCD is both a philosophy and a process. As a philosophy, it places the person (as opposed to the "thing") at the center; as a process, it focuses on cognitive factors (such as perception, memory, learning, problem-solving, etc.) as they come into play during people's interactions with people, places, and things.

UCD seeks to answer questions about users and their tasks and goals, and then uses the findings to drive development and design. UCD seeks to answer questions such as the following:

- Who are the users of this space/product/service?
- What are the users' tasks and goals?
- What are the users' experience levels with this space/product/service, and spaces/products/services like it?
- What functions do the users need from this space/product/service?
- What information might the users need, and in what form do they need it?
- How do users think this space/product/service should work?
- How can the design of this space/product/service facilitate users' cognitive processes?

UCD can improve the usability and usefulness of everything from "everyday things" (D. Norman) to software to information systems to processes . . . anything with which people interact. As such, User-Centered Design concerns itself with both *usefulness* and *usability.*

Thomas Mellins, a prominent architectural author, writes, "airports, like the grand nineteenth- and early twentieth-century railroad stations they have in large part replaced, are symbolically rich gateways that reveal our need to create lasting expressions of civic pride" (2005). In many cases, especially in smaller cities, the airport can be an important public building, serving as the city's gateway for visitors and reflecting its heritage, people, and values.

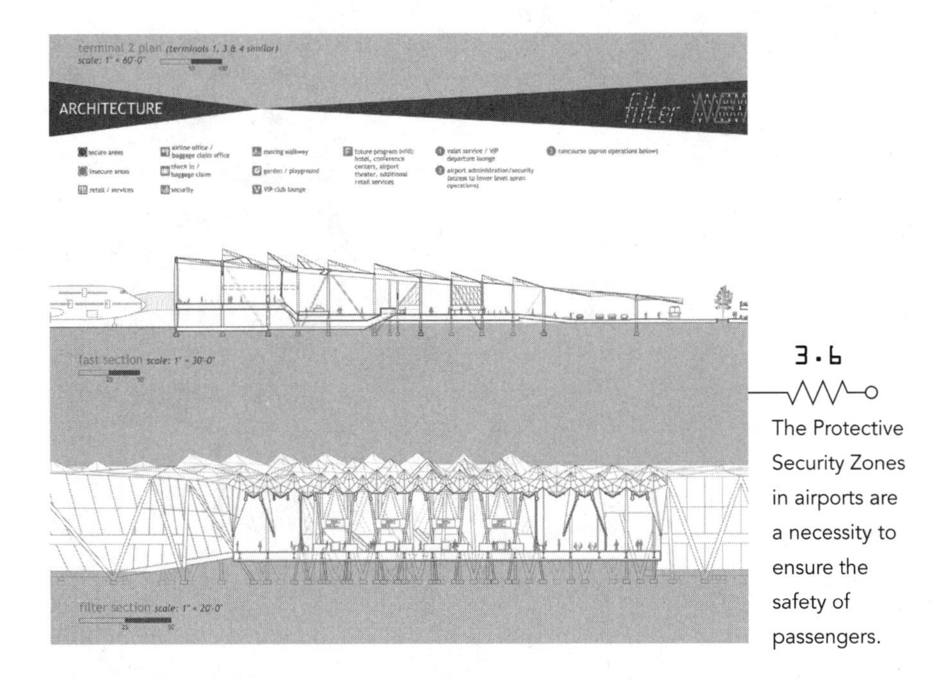

3.6

The Protective Security Zones in airports are a necessity to ensure the safety of passengers.

One of the most visible recent trends in airport design is the increase of retail and entertainment components; these facilities expand the overall size of the airport, making efficient pedestrian movement a challenge. One challenge for the designer is to seek airport security design solutions that merge the airport's functional aspects with innovative solutions through architectural design. In exploring potential solutions to security threats, attention must focus not only on operational innovations and practices, but also on better approaches to facility planning, material exploration and use, and other design solutions.

One such area, referred to as the **Protective Security Zone** (see Figure 3.6), includes access points for loading and unloading passengers or cargo, ticketing areas, and passenger screening areas. The Protective Security Zone is a complex and integrated system that must successfully integrate high levels of security, respond to circulation of passengers, cargo, and personnel throughout the airport, as well as respond to central architectural concepts such as human activity needs, climate considerations, and structural integrity.

The Lessons of 9/11

The tragedy of 9/11 was a shocking moment for the world, and since then, much has been done to try to make New York City, and other large urban communities, safer places. Based upon the 2003 recommendations of the *World Trade Center Building Code Task Force* (WTCBCTF, 2003), 13 proposals have been presented that are intended to prevent the kind of structural failures that contributed to

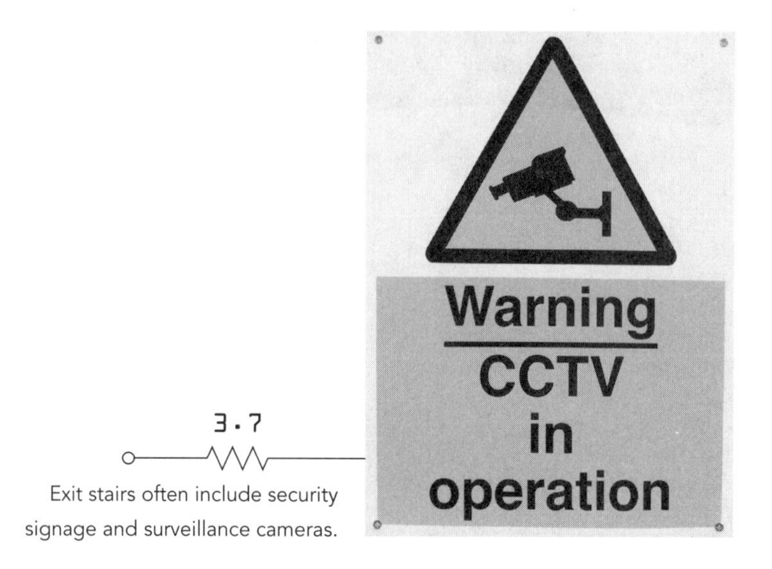

3.7

Exit stairs often include security signage and surveillance cameras.

the World Trade Center's (WTC) collapse, and to make it easier for people to evacuate tall buildings in case of emergency. Selected recommendations that are applicable for interior design and architectural consideration include the following:

- *Full sprinkler protection for office buildings.* Owners of all existing office buildings 100 feet or greater in height which are not already fully equipped with sprinklers will be required to do so on or before January 1, 2019.
- *Improved markings, exit signage, and back-up power to exit signs.* Exit stairs and doors in new or existing high-rise office buildings will be required to have glow-in-the-dark markings (see Figure 3.7).
- *Impact-resistant stair and elevator enclosures.* In many accounts of the WTC tragedy, the drywall encasing the stairwells in the impact area disintegrated, blocking egress for some. The use of more impact-resistant stair and elevator enclosures will be required in high-rise office buildings constructed or altered after January 1, 2006.
- *Restricted use of scissor stairs.* As discussed in Chapter 1, "scissor" stairs are two intertwining sets of staircases that are separated by a common wall and floors. Scissor stair assemblies will be prohibited in new high-rise office buildings with relatively large floor plates (see Figure 3.8).
- *Smoke-stop elevator vestibules.* A smoke-stop elevator lobby reduces the possibility of smoke spreading to other floors through the elevator shaft. (See Figure 3.9.)

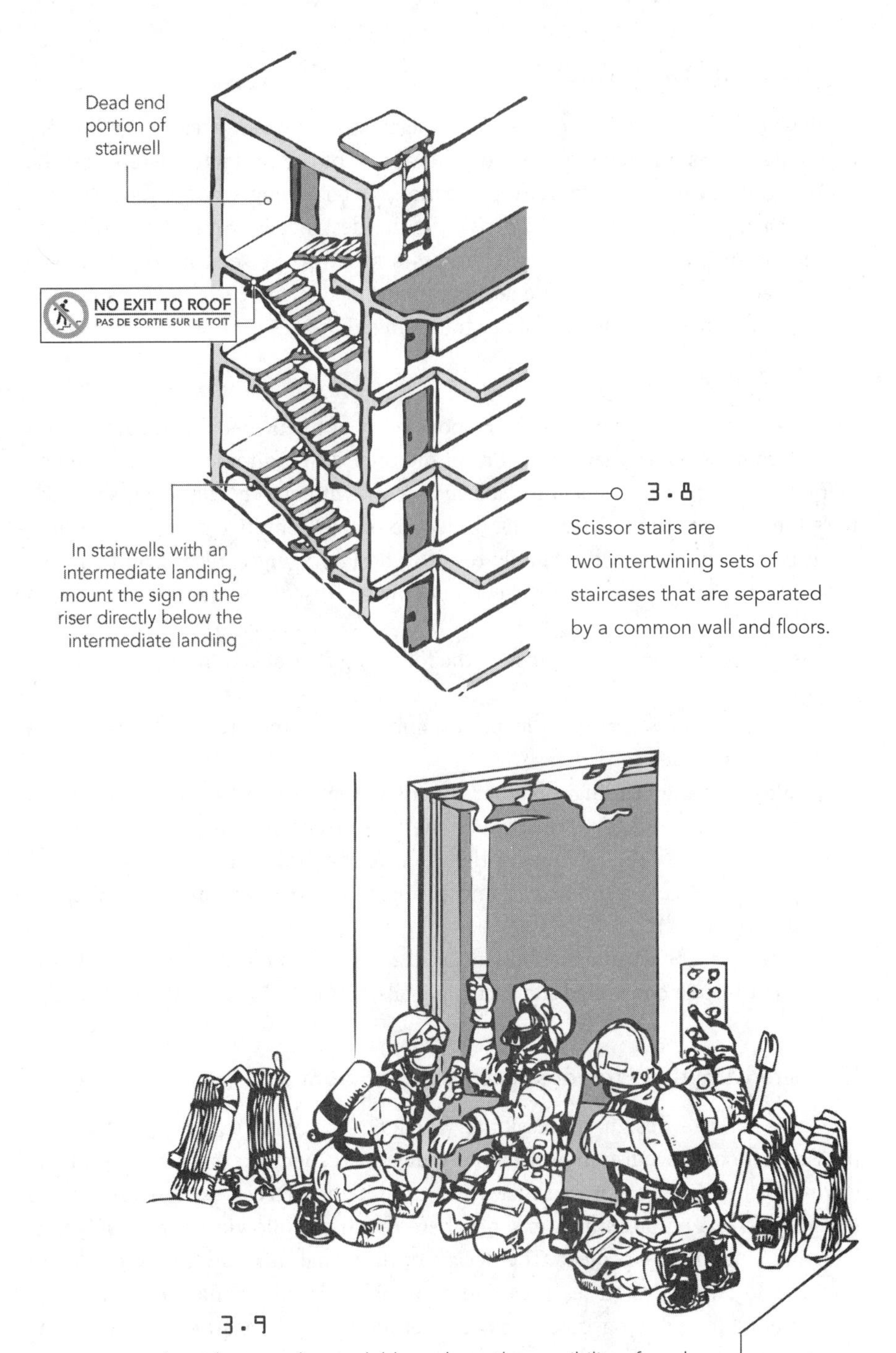

3.8

Scissor stairs are two intertwining sets of staircases that are separated by a common wall and floors.

3.9

A smoke-stop elevator lobby reduces the possibility of smoke spreading to other floors through the elevator shaft.

PROGRAMMING ISSUES

Achieving the correct level of protection against site-based threats may be very expensive and is highly dependent on the nature of the protected assets and the threat against which they require protection. Determining what is required is a matter of managing the perceived risks. If the designer is to assist in providing protection in the design of the site, an assessment of the security requirements must be accomplished before the design process begins, but certainly no later than the beginning of the architectural programming phase.

Site Assessment

Although the site assessment is the responsibility of the owner, it is incumbent on the designer to assure that the nature of the security requirements is determined before the design process begins. Failure to work with closely with clients throughout the programming phase of the project to obtain definitive answers regarding security-related issues will certainly result in design changes, delays, and cost increases to the owner and the architect if the owner "discovers" their security needs later in the design process.

The site assessment should answer the following four questions:

1. What are the assets (people, places, information, and property) that require security protection?
2. What are the criminal or other threats (street crimes, workplace violence, terrorism, sabotage) against which the assets must be protected?
3. What are the vulnerabilities of the assets to the threats (for example, if workplace violence is a threat, can uncontrolled people enter a private workspace unchallenged)?
4. What are the countermeasures (for example, does the design channel visitors through controlled site access portals) required to mitigate the threat?

Characteristics that Promote Security: Function/Spatial Issues

The goal for the design professional when dealing with security issues is to provide safe and secure environments that also respect the civic nature of the environment. The goal in a sense is to minimize **fortress design** (prisonlike design) and target hardening, except where required, following a thorough analysis and study of the project. The design professional must address the issue of how architectural design features and approaches can be enhanced with security without introducing objectionable measures on the aesthetics, functionality, and experience of the building. How can electronic and automated physical security systems be integrated with the increasingly complex management and monitoring systems for fire protection, building environmental control, communications, and accessibility?

The CPTED principles and guidelines provide us with a framework that can be integrated into the design process and simultaneously afford us opportunities to draw upon the interior design body of knowledge. The CPTED 3-D approach, (see Chapter 2), can be the overarching umbrella for security consideration within any context. The 3 "D's" are as follows:

- *Designation.* What is the purpose or intention for the space?
- *Definition.* How is the space defined? What are the social, cultural, legal, and psychological ways the space is defined?
- *Design.* Is the space defined to support prescribed or intended behaviors?

Security Layering: The Onion Philosophy

The first layer of the **Onion Philosophy** is the outside skin of the onion, which translates to the site perimeter of the property. The building skin of the architecture is the next layer. Sensitive areas within a building are deeper layers requiring protection, and finally special people, information, or property may require point protection—the center of the onion. The site perimeter is the first, not last, line of defense. For example, the US State Department seeks setbacks of at least 100 feet for new buildings, and even that distance is difficult to obtain in most urban settings. Although most perimeter fences and walls are designed to discourage intruders, they are of little use against a determined person or bomb vehicle.

The building skin is the next layer of protection. It is possible, but never simple or inexpensive, to minimize openings, orient them away from the perimeter, raise them above the ground, and provide windows, doors, grills, and other devices that resist ballistic weapons, explosives, and forced entry, all the while trying to retain a sense of openness, unobstructed views, and adequate natural lighting.

The next layer is the interior space planning and security. The most sensitive areas should be located high and away from exterior zones. Thought must be given to the use of spaces behind or near windows. Inside the building, zones or layers of security may be established with various types of access-control devices reinforcing physical separations. Protected workstations are critical in many occupations, as well as safe rooms for staff protection.

The process of risk assessment and security design is especially relevant in the design and architecture of schools, hospitals, airports, office buildings, multifamily apartment buildings, and so on. During the risk assessment process, the design team must be aware that recently buildings have been targeted for bombing by terrorists, or sieged by violent teenagers, due to their "architectural vulnerability," and assess all design security solutions accordingly.

DESIGN CRITERIA AND RISK ASSESSMENT

During the initial client interviews and programming phase of any security-minded project, four elements are necessary for exploration. These should be viewed as design challenges, and not separate from other functional, aesthetic, or environmental considerations. The programming stage of any project should ask the following four basic security questions:

- What are the possible threats?
- What are the assets?
- What are the needed levels of protection?
- What are the constraints?

The result of the preliminary security assessment should be integrated as a seamless countermeasure within the overall design solution. In the case of required government standards, such as any federal building, the assessment results are assigned a defined Level of Protection (LOP) with specified countermeasures and design solutions. When the LOP is defined, the required countermeasures are priced and the owner may select appropriate measures depending on a prudent level of protection and the cost effectiveness of the measure.

The GSA Security Standards: Applicability to the Public Domain

The 1995 bombing of the Murrah Federal Building in Oklahoma City, Oklahoma, gave birth to a federal effort to develop security standards that would apply to all federal facilities. The Interagency Security Committee, created in 2002, has recommended their adoption as a US Government–wide standard. The Government Security Association (GSA), formed in the United States in 2003, has developed Security Standards that address the functional requirements and the desired application of; security glazing, bomb-resistant design and construction, landscaping and planting designs, site lighting, and natural and mechanical surveillance opportunities, such as; sight lines, blind spots, window placement, and proper applications of CCTV.

These standards reinforce and encourage a defensible space/Crime Prevention through Environmental Design (CPTED) (see Chapter 2) approach to clearly defining and screening the flow of people and vehicles through layering from public to private spaces. It is further recommended that edges and boundaries of properties should clearly define the desired circulation patterns and movements. The screening techniques and funneling of people through public spaces is an effort to screen legitimate users of a building from illegitimate users, who might look for opportunities to commit crime, workplace violence, or acts of terrorism.

The GSA has produced a set of Security Design Criteria covering four levels of protection. These recommendations are further subdivided according to various levels of security (e.g. a level one facility might not require an entry control system while a level four facility would require electronic controls with CCTV assessment).

The requirements of the Security Design Criteria that affect facility design and engineering are summarized here in four general categories of "corrective action" as used by the GSA. The designer and/or architect and engineering team for renovations or new construction projects on any federal building must address these criteria. Overall, the GSA Security Design Criteria information provides a basic overview of the issues that are important design considerations for the overall assessment of design and security issues in the built environment regardless of building type.

Perimeter and Exterior Security

- Parking area and parking controls
- CCTV monitoring
- Lighting to include emergency backup
- Physical barriers

Entry Security

- Intrusion detection system
- Upgrade to current life-safety standards
- Screen mail, people, packages
- Entry control with CCTV and electric door strikes
- High security locks

Interior Security

- Employee ID, visitor control
- Control access to utilities
- Provide emergency power to critical systems
- Evaluate location of day-care centers

Security Planning

- Evaluate locations of tenant agencies as concerns security needs and risk
- Install Mylar film on exterior windows
- Review/establish blast standards for current projects and new construction
- Develop a design standard for blast resistance and street set-back for new construction

The GSA Security Design Criteria is an excellent example to use as a resource for designers seeking to take a balanced approach to security design solutions

3.10 Union Station in Washington, DC, maintains tight security, yet still offers an open and attractive design.

while considering cost effectiveness, acknowledging acceptance of some risk, and recognizing that buildings should be not bunker or fortress-like, but open, accessible, attractive, and representative of the spirit of a community. (See Figure 3.10.)

Application of GSA Security Standards to All Building Types

Whatever the building or its use, security and crime prevention should be a design criteria that is similar to fire safety, accessibility, and structural integrity. Every piece of public architecture should establish a hierarchy of space that transcends from open access by the public, to semipublic, to semiprivate, to private spaces. Any areas or spaces that are unassigned to a specific purpose or capable guardian should be avoided, as they become "no man's land" and not claimed, protected, or defended by any individual or group. Traffic patterns of pedestrians and vehicles into sites and buildings should be carefully thought out, controlled, and should maximize the potential for natural observation by legitimate building users.

Key defensive architectural and landscape design site considerations selected from the GSA Security Standards include:

- Establish a secured perimeter around the building that is as far from the building as is feasible. Setbacks of 100 feet are desired.

- Design artistically pleasing concrete barriers as flower planters or works of art and position them near curbing at a distance from the building with less than four feet of spacing between them to block vehicular passage.
- Build new buildings in a simple geometric rectangular layout to minimize the "defraction effect" when blast waves bounce off U-shaped or L-shaped buildings causing additional damage.
- Drastically reduce or eliminate ornamentation on buildings that can easily break away causing further damage to building occupants or pedestrians at street level. All external cladding should be made of lightweight materials that will minimize damage when they become flying objects following an explosion (or hurricane).
- Eliminate potential hiding places near the facility.
- Provide unobstructed view around the facility.
- Site or place the facility within view of other occupied facilities.
- Locate assets stored on site, but outside of the facility, within view of occupied rooms of the facility.
- Minimize the signage or indication of assets on the property.
- Eliminate lines of approach perpendicular to the building.
- Minimize the number of vehicle access points.
- Eliminate or strictly control parking beneath facilities.
- Locate parking as far from the building as practical (yet address ADA spaces and proximity) and place parking within view of occupied rooms or facilities.

Key defensive interior design considerations selected from the GSA Security Standards include:

- Provide employee and visitor identification systems.
- Secure the utility closets and vulnerable utilities.
- Develop emergency plans, policies, and procedures.
- Have day care located and protected from unauthorized access.
- Establish screening points where applicable for weapons, pilferage, or identification.
- Secure and control shipping and receiving areas with integrated access
- Control CCTV, intercoms, data logging, and report capabilities.
- Employ the concept of security layering, i.e., the Onion Philosophy.
- Locate assets in spaces occupied 24 hours a day where possible.
- Locate activities with large visitor populations away from protected assets where possible.
- Locate protected assets in common areas where they are visible to more than one person.
- Place high-risk areas, such as the mailroom, on the perimeter of the facility.

Security and Design: Crime Prevention through Environmental Design (CPTED)

As previously introduced in Chapter 2, CPTED strategies (See Figure 2.7) use natural access control, natural surveillance, territoriality and boundary definition, maintenance and management enforcement, and legitimate activity support. Any crime prevention strategy must accomplish the following:

- Increase the effort needed to commit a crime
- Increase the risks associated with committing a crime
- Reduce the rewards of committing crime
- Remove the excuses to commit crime

These goals are accomplished with organized methods of employing people at **security posts**, such as security guards, police, or capable guardians, or mechanical solutions such as technology systems and barriers, together with natural methods involving design decisions based on behavioral psychology that determines how people (and vehicles) use buildings.

Crimes are committed because they are easy to commit. A person sees an easy opportunity and commits a crime regardless of the legality or consequences. Oftentimes, casual criminals are eliminated by increasing the effort needed to commit an offense. *Target hardening* is one method of increasing the effort to combat crime by using techniques such as: improving locks to be dead bolts, upgrading window screens, using break-resistant glazing, increasing the use of fencing, and using magnetic locking doors. If not done thoughtfully, these security solutions may lead to what can be termed "architecture of fear" or fortress architecture.

Additional CPTED recommendations are in the area of access control that include; installing barriers and designing paths, walkways, and roads so that unwanted and unauthorized users are prevented from entering vulnerable areas. Barriers may include limiting entrance to specific individuals, places, or times; security vestibules; parking lot barriers; entry phones; visitor check-in booths; guard stations; vehicle control systems; and biometric screening for access control.

The following list provides valuable CPTED principles that are significant interior and architectural design considerations. It is important to note that these recommendations are similar to those required by the GSA Design Security Standards:

- Control access to the facility by pedestrian and vehicular traffic.
- Divide interior and exterior spaces into small easily identified areas that are associated within a specific group of individuals or users.

- Have detection devices easily visible to increase the perceived risk to the offender and by posting signs advertising the use of such devices.
- Minimize the number of entrances to the interior of a building with the function of the remaining entrances clearly identified. Entrances should be secured when not in use.
- Provide keyed access to vulnerable areas such as laundry rooms, storage areas, elevators, and bathrooms.
- Restrict emergency stairs and exits to their intended use by equipping them with alarm panic bars with time egress delays and no exterior door handles.
- Install barriers on vulnerable openings such as ground floor windows, exterior fire stairs, roof openings, and skylights. Fence off problem areas to prevent unauthorized access and funnel movement along desired paths.
- Provide lockable security areas for items that are stored in low-surveillance areas or items that are easily portable.
- Control access for servicing and deliveries.

Increasing the risks associated with crime contributes to crime prevention by improving the probability that the criminal will be observed, identified, and arrested. Criminals commit crimes because they believe they will not be caught. Ways to increase the risk of being detected include; entry and exit screening, formal surveillance, increasing surveillance capabilities by employees, and improving natural surveillance. All are CPTED recommendations for deterring crime.

Additional CPTED recommendations that should be considered by the interior design professional include:

- Screening devices used when appropriate to allow legitimate building users and guests. Employee screening should be separate with the use of badges or IDs.
- Formal surveillance uses security personnel and hardware such as CCTV and intrusion detection systems.
- Informal surveillance by use of the facility employees uses the existing resources of door attendants, concierge, maintenance workers, and secretaries to increase site surveillance and crime reporting.
- Improving natural surveillance by careful architectural placement of windows, doors, lighting, and controlled landscaping and plantings.
- Interior lighting enhances opportunities for casual or formal surveillance in spaces visible through doors and windows. Lighting should be even without deep shadows and fixtures should be vandal-proof.
- Interior blind spots such as alcoves and dead-end corridors create vulnerable entrapment areas and should be eliminated when possible.
- Clearly defined regulations and signage prevent offenders from excusing their crime with claims of ignorance or misunderstanding.

3.11

The federal government installs security systems and equipment to help prevent terrorism.

The overall goal for designers, architects, and allied design professionals is to minimize fortress design and target hardening, except where required, after a thorough analysis and study of a project. The design professional must address issues of how architectural design features, approaches, and interior spaces can be enhanced with security without intruding objectionably on the aesthetics and functionality of a building. Designers must ask, how can electronic and automated physical security systems be integrated into the increasingly complex management and monitoring systems for fire protection, building environmental control, transportation and communications, and accessibility?

Key Security Systems and Equipment

In recent years, the security of public places and federal sites has become an increasingly urgent concern. The federal government has moved swiftly to install a full range of security responses to thwart terrorism. Physical barriers, surveillance, metal-detection devices, and protocols have either been strengthened or established. By their nature, these measures channel and restrict personal movement. The challenge has become to protect citizens without erecting barriers that have a detrimental impact on how people interact with the government and with each other. (See Figure 3.11.)

Consider space for placement of hardware (see Figure 3.12) and its use by planning for use of the following:

- Generous wiring
- Backup power
- Intrusion-detection devices
- Site intrusion detection

3.12 It is important to consider the placement of security hardware within a design.

- Boundary penetration sensors
- Motion-detection systems
- Access-control systems
- Contraband and weapons detection
- Explosive detectors
- Credential readers and positive personnel identification systems
- Security control and information display systems

There are currently thousands of new security products available for integration into the design solution that assist in providing safer and more secure built environments. It is essential that designers research and understand the use and integration of these products in overall design solutions, as well as their applications, costs, and overall function to educate clients on their use.

BEST PRACTICES—ALLIED PROFESSIONS

The architectural and landscape architecture design communities both play a valuable role in the overall site design solution of any project, from site planning, building shape and form, selection of architectural materials and finishes, and access to buildings. It is important for the interior design professional to understand these considerations while serving as a member of the design team.

Architectural Design Considerations

Best safety and security practices implemented by the architectural team may include:

- Establish a secured perimeter around the building that is as far from the building as is feasible. Setbacks of 100 feet are most desirable.
- Use poured-in-place reinforced concrete for all framing including slabs, walls, columns, and roofs. Roof and base slabs should be at least 8 inches thick, exterior walls 12 inches thick, and columns spaced no more than 30 feet apart.
- Use "seismic detailing" at connection points (i.e., interconnect rebar in slabs with rebar in columns and beams so framing within a building becomes an integrated whole). Reinforce floor slabs and roofs using a two-way reinforcing scheme (i.e., place rebar in a crisscross pattern in concrete).
- Design windows that comprise no more than 15 percent of the wall area between supporting columns.
- Reduce flying-glass hazard by using a plastic Mylar coating placed on the inside face of the windows (see Figure 3.13).
- Install specially designed blast curtains inside windows that can catch pieces of glass while permitting air blast pressure to pass through the curtain.
- Design artistically pleasing concrete barriers as flower planters or works of art and position them near curbing at a distance from the building with less than four feet of spacing between them to block vehicular passage.
- Build new buildings in a simple geometric rectangular layout to minimize the "defraction effect" when blast waves bounce off U-shaped or L-shaped buildings causing additional damage.
- Drastically reduce or eliminate ornamentation on buildings that can easily break away causing further damage to building occupants or pedestrians at street level. All external cladding should be made of lightweight materials that will minimize damage when they become flying objects following an explosion (or hurricane).

Landscape Architectural Design Considerations

Landscape architects are uniquely qualified to develop and highlight design principles that achieve an appropriate balance between security measures, freedom of movement, and accessible public spaces. According to the American Society of Landscape Architects (ASLA), the principles for combining security and good landscape design include:

- Provide an adequate balance between threats and the beauty of the public realm.
- Recognize that good design and good security are compatible.
- Expand the palette of elements that can gracefully provide perimeter security, producing a coherent security and urban design strategy that embraces whole streets and districts without dampening pedestrian activity and the vitality of the environment. (See Figure 3.14.)

3.13

These windows have a plastic Mylar coating on the inside to reduce the hazard of flying glass.

3.14

Planters provide both perimeter security and beauty.

- Address security issues dealing with; bollards/planters, curbs, vehicle barriers, security lighting, exterior signage, and ground rules and gates.

CONCLUSION

Architecture and design are not only about major civic and iconic buildings and structures; they are also truly about the everyday places and spaces in which people live, work, and play. The design and construction professionals of the twenty-first century are trusted to design, build, and operate these environments in a way that assures public health and safety, preserves the environment, and promotes security. This role is perhaps one of the most significant as it directly affects the physical, mental, psychological, social, and economic aspects of daily life.

The interior design profession can fulfill its specialized role in protecting the health, safety, and welfare of users of public spaces by collaborating with clients, end-users, and allied professionals to provide design solutions that increase the safety and security within the built environment. Proactive security design solutions will offer psychological comfort to inhabitants knowing that these spaces have been "secured" the best they can be through thoughtful risk assessment. The designers' use of added security measures might decrease the likelihood of harm, damage, and physical and/or psychological injury, with the professional goal of improving the quality of life and emotional well-being of users of the built environment.

KEY CONCEPTS

- The built environment is experienced, perceived, and communicated in parts and as a whole. Security and safety—both physical and psychological—are components of this experience that are powerful tools and indicators of quality of life.
- The interior design profession can fulfill its specialized role in protecting the health, safety, and welfare of users of public spaces by partnering with clients, end-users, and allied professionals to provide design solutions that increase the safety and security within the places where we live, work, and play.
- Risk assessment in reviewing security considerations assists in adding measures that may decrease the likelihood of harm, damage, and physical and/or psychological injury to improve quality of life and emotional well-being.
- Within the design professions, negligence, in relation to planning for safety and security within the built environment, has become evidence for not meeting the reasonable standard of care for the architectural and design community.
- Enhanced expectations regarding security in the built environment have been in place in relation to federal buildings by the General Service Administration (GSA) of the United States government.
- User-Centered Design (UCD) is both a philosophy and a process. As a philosophy, it places the person (as opposed to the "thing") at the center; as a process, it focuses on cognitive factors (such as perception, memory, learning, and problem-solving), as they come into play during peoples' interactions with people, places, and things.
- Programming for security considerations assists in providing protection in the design of the site, and must be accomplished at the beginning of the design process. Security assessments should be viewed as design challenges, and not separate from other functional, aesthetic, or environmental considerations.
- The security of public places and federal sites has become an increasingly urgent concern. The challenge has become to protect citizens without erecting physical barriers that have a detrimental impact to how people interact with buildings and with each other.
- The interior design, architectural, and landscape architecture design communities all play a valuable role in the overall design solution of safe and secure environments.

ASSIGNMENTS

1. Discuss the psychological role that security plays in humans' needs for safety and security.
2. Develop an understanding of the changing standards of care in design and construction as integrated security solutions into the built environment.
3. Discuss the issues of programming, design criteria, risk, and security concerns of the twenty-first century and their impact on the built environment.

ACTIVITIES

1. Journaling activity: Respond in written and graphic format. Probes may include visiting sites that have obvious and obtrusive security measures versus sites that provide more transparent security design solutions. Share your experiences while generating a list about the psychological differences between the varied spaces. Look for patterns in the built environment that could be manipulated to improve the psychological well-being of end-users.
2. Research some security equipment–related Web sites and compile a list of five products. How might these products be integrated into the built environment?
3. Using the information you learned in this chapter, create a project that requires as a component of the programming and design process the integration of security needs and theories in identifying and articulating design problems.
4. Interview members of the allied professions, i.e., architects, landscape architects, facility managers, engineers, etc., for an overview of how professional practices have changed with the added security measures of the twenty–first century. Follow up with a systematic discussion.

3 4 1 0 7 2 9 6 5

4 WORKPLACE VIOLENCE AND SECURITY-RELATED NEEDS

Violence in the workplace is a serious safety and health issue. In its most extreme form, homicide, it is the fourth-leading cause of fatal occupational injury in the United States. According to the Bureau of Labor Statistics's Census of Fatal Occupational Injuries (CFOI), there were 564 workplace homicides in 2005 in the United States, out of 5,702 fatal work injuries.

OBJECTIVES

- Provide an awareness of the epidemic of workplace violence and the designer's role in providing safe and secure workplaces.
- Develop an awareness of conducting security assessments that identify existing and potential hazards within the workplace.
- Increase awareness of the variety of prevention strategies that are important security design considerations within the workplace.
- Increase awareness of a range of risk factors associated with various types of workplace violence.
- Review the principals of Crime Prevention through Environmental Design (CPTED) and their relationship to workplace safety and security.
- Increase awareness of the roles of the interior designer, architect, landscape architect, facility manager, and building owner as they relate to the design of safe and secure workplace environments.

Thanks to new security precautions, Bob's surprise party held no surprises.

4.1

It is important to consider security design within the workplace.

On February 5, 2001, William D. Baker, a former employer of Navistar International, brought a cache of guns to the Rose Park, Illinois, diesel engine plant, killed four people, and wounded four others before killing himself. Baker was one day away from starting a federal prison term for a felony conviction for stealing from Navistar.

Another incident, involving Connor Peripheral, a Security Company in San Jose, California, stemmed from the firing of an employee. The company notified the contract guards that the employee was not allowed back on the premises. The following day, the former employee returned through a normally secured entrance to the parking lot and shot a company executive in the back, permanently disabling him. According to testimony, guards had been advised of the ex-employee's presence on two occasions, but failed to remove him. This case shows the danger of the appearance of a failure to take action and the extreme importance of responding to warning signs and reports of threats from current or former employees.

On July 29, 1999, Mark Barton, 44, walked into a day trading firm in Atlanta, Georgia, at about 3 P.M. and began shooting, and then walked across the street to another brokerage firm and continued shooting; nine people were killed, and a dozen others seriously wounded (see Figure 4.2).

CONTEXT AND EXPERIENCE

Physical attack or assault resulting in death or physical injury of an employee in a place of business is the standard definition of workplace violence (WPV), but *victimologists* have argued strongly that psychological and verbal abuse ought to be included in this definition. The National Institute for Occupational Safety and

Health (NIOSH) therefore defined workplace violence in 1991 as any physical assault, threatening behavior, or verbal abuse occurring in the work setting. These violent acts include homicide, forcible sex offenses, kidnapping, assault, robbery, menacing, reckless endangerment, harassment, disorderly conduct, berating language, physical or verbal threats, or vandalism of personal property. About the only thing that is not included (though it sometimes is) in the definition of workplace violence is terrorism (NIOSH, 1993).

Violence in the workplace has become an epidemic. Not only is workplace violence increasingly common in those workplaces where violence is expected—for example, corrections, law enforcement, and mental health—but in almost every occupation that deals with the public.

According to the study, "Violence at Work," conducted by Vittorio Di Martino, an international expert on stress and workplace violence, and Duncan Chappell, past president of the New South Wales Mental Health Review Tribunal, Australia, and the Commonwealth Arbitral Tribunal, United Kingdom, workplace violence is increasing worldwide and, reaching epidemic levels in some countries. According to a 2007 publication by the International Labour Organization (ILO), the global cost of workplace violence is enormous and costing untold millions of dollars in losses in other countries due to causes including absenteeism and sick leave. The study also notes that professions once regarded as sheltered from workplace violence such as

4.2 A tragic workplace violence incident took place at Navistar International, in Atlanta, Georgia, in 1999.

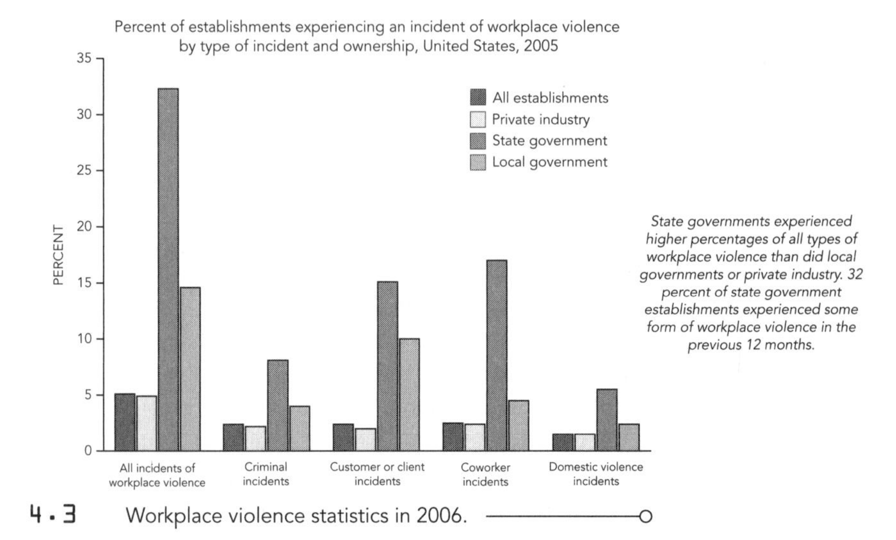

State governments experienced higher percentages of all types of workplace violence than did local governments or private industry. 32 percent of state government establishments experienced some form of workplace violence in the previous 12 months.

4.3 Workplace violence statistics in 2006.

teaching, social services, library services, and health care are being exposed to increasing acts of violence, in both developed and developing countries.

"Bullying, harassment, mobbing, and allied behaviors can be just as damaging as outright physical violence," the authors state. "Today, the instability of many types of jobs places huge pressures on workplaces, and we're seeing more of these forms of violence." In addition, the authors also address growing concerns about terrorism, calling it "one of the new faces of workplace violence—contributing to the already-volatile mix of aggressive acts taking place on the job (Di Martino and Chappell, 1998)."

Growing awareness of the need to tackle workplace violence has spawned the development of new and effective prevention strategies, the ILO states (2007). The study highlights a number of "best practice" examples from local and national governments, enterprises, and trade unions from around the world that have successfully implemented "zero tolerance" polices and violence-prevention training programs.

According to the US Bureau of Labor Statistics (BLS), homicides were the second leading cause of death in the workplace in 1992, accounting for 17 percent of all workplace deaths (see Figure 4.3). Although the press focuses on "postal worker-type violence," where a berserk worker kills his supervisor or coworkers, such "worker-on-worker" violence makes up only 4 percent of all workplace homicides. The rest are the result of robberies, or assaults by residents, patients, or customers against workers (BLS, 1993).

According to a Bureau of Labor and Statistics survey, homicide was the leading manner of traumatic workplace death among women in the United States from 1992 to 2001. Forty-one percent of women's workplace deaths were the result of homicide, compared with 10 percent among men. Although women account for only 7 percent of all worker fatalities, they were the victims in 17 percent of reported workplace homicides (Richardson and Windau, 2003).

Each year, at least 1,000,000 people are victims of workplace violence, and about 1,000 of these cases are homicides. Accurate numbers are hard to come by since at least 50 percent of the more minor incidents go unreported and there are other reporting problems. In some states, more people die from being murdered at work than in traffic accidents. Homicide is the second leading cause of death for most retail, industrial, and office jobs, accounting for 17 percent of all injuries, and females are three times as likely to be murdered as males. Homicide is the first leading cause of death for people who work in mobile occupations such as taxicab drivers, health-care workers, social service, or schools, or in criminal justice settings that encounter unstable or volatile people. The majority of this violence involves the unexpected presence of someone who is not supposed to be at a certain place, as they do not work there and do not have approved access to the workplace. It is important to note that most WPV incidents involve people known to each other, and that no place or occupation is immune from violence in the workplace.

FYI: According to a 1995 US Bureau of Justice Statistics report, violence-related fatalities are only the tip of the iceberg. According to the Department of Justice, one million individuals become victims of violent crime each year while working or on duty. A half million employees miss 1.8 million days of work each year, resulting in more than $55 million in lost wages, not including days covered by sick and annual leave. Workplace violence accounts for 16 percent of the more than 6.5 million acts of violence experienced by individuals age 12 and over.

—US Dept. of Justice, 2005

In addition to the human cost, businesses suffer economic losses when they are the victims of workplace violence. According to a 2005 US Department of Justice survey, assaults at work cost 500,000 employees 1,751,100 lost days of work each year, which averages out to 3.5 days per crime. In terms of just lost wages, the estimated annual total was more than $55 million. When lost productivity, legal expenses, property damage, diminished public image, increased security, and other factors are included, total losses from workplace violence probably can be measured in billions of dollars.

Another cost borne by employers is liability for the injuries suffered by victims of workplace violence and/or liability claims in negligent or wrongful deaths occurring on the job. Third parties assaulted and/or seriously injured in the workplace have won significant awards in suits against businesses or others with responsibility in the workplace that were found to be negligent in this area. In addition, while

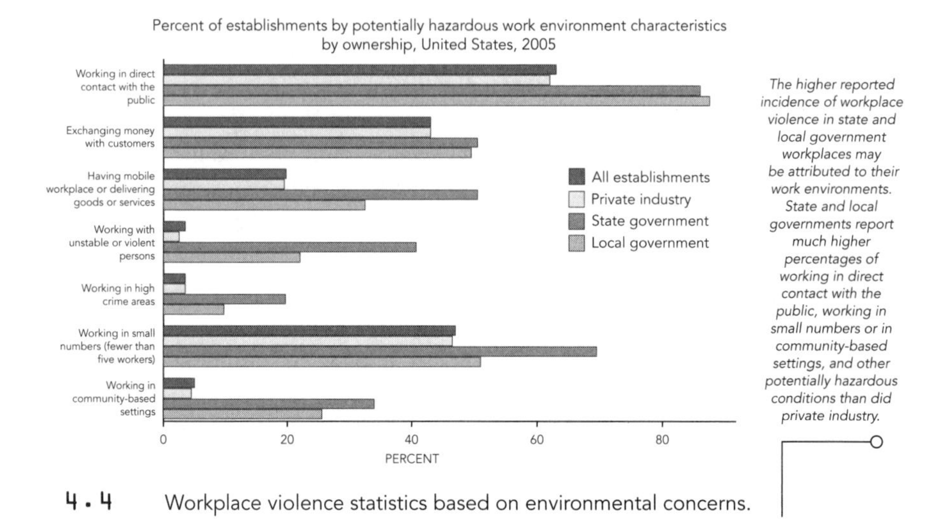

4.4 Workplace violence statistics based on environmental concerns.

The higher reported incidence of workplace violence in state and local government workplaces may be attributed to their work environments. State and local governments report much higher percentages of working in direct contact with the public, working in small numbers or in community-based settings, and other potentially hazardous conditions than did private industry.

workers' compensation insurance is generally the employee's only remedy for on-the-job injuries from assaults, in certain states, employees have successfully sued their employers in civil court for incidences of workplace violence.

According to the Bureau of Labor Statistics (BLS), workplace violence (WPV) incidents are divided into four categories depending on the relationship between the assailant and the worker or workplace (see Figure 4.4). These categories are:

1. *Violence by strangers.* In this type of incident, a stranger commits the violence. This stranger has no legitimate relationship to the worker or workplace and enters the workplace, usually on the pretense of being a customer, to commit a robbery or other violent act.
2. *Violence by customers/clients.* In these incidents, someone who receives a service provided by a business, such as a current or former customer, client or patient, a passenger, a criminal suspect, or a prisoner commits the violence.
3. *Violence by coworkers.* In coworker incidents, the perpetrator has an employment relationship with the workplace. The perpetrator can be a current or former employee, a prospective employee, or a current or former supervisor or manager.
4. *Violence by personal relations.* In personal relations incidents, someone who has a personal relationship with the worker, such as a current or former spouse or partner, a relative, or a friend commits the violence. Included in this category is the perpetrator, who has a personal dispute with the worker and enters the workplace to harass, threaten, injure, or kill.

Employers have both a legal duty and a moral obligation to provide a safe workplace. Under the General Duty Clause, Section 5(a) (1) of the Occupational Safety and Health Act (OSHA) of 1970, employers are required to provide their employees with a place of employment that "is free from recognizable hazards that are causing or likely to cause death or serious harm to employees." The OSHA General Duty Clause has been interpreted to mean that an employer has a legal obligation to provide a safe workplace. This duty includes inspecting the workplace to discover and correct a dangerous condition or hazard, which for the interior design professional equates to providing natural surveillance, **safe havens** for employees, and the integration of security technology to mitigate the loss of life in a workplace violence scenario.

CONDUCTING A SECURITY ASSESSMENT

To be successful, workplace violence prevention efforts must have commitment from top management and involve supervisors, employees, and employee representatives. Many organizations have implemented a WPV Prevention Program that identifies existing and potential hazards. The design professional should become familiar with the organization's WPV Prevention Program in the initial phases of the design process, as it will become a valuable tool in understanding and implementing the organization's safety and security concerns. Typical elements of a WPV Prevention Program include the following:

- A clearly written company Workplace Violence Policy statement
- Establishment of a Threat Assessment Team
- Hazard assessment
- Workplace hazard control and prevention
- Training and education
- Incident reporting, investigation, follow-up, and evaluation
- Recordkeeping

The role of the internal Threat Assessment Team within an organization is to inspect the workplace to determine the presence of hazards, conditions, operations, and situations that might place workers at risk of occupational assault incidents. In addition, the Threat Assessment Team often identifies and institutes a combination of control methods designed to eliminate or minimize risks. These may include, but are not limited to the following:

- General building, work station, and area design, security measures
- Security equipment
- Work practice controls and procedures
- Workplace Violence Prevention Policy statement

4.5 A workplace design that incorporates open communication and minimizes the potential for assault incidents, using the CPTED 3-D approach.

Additional components of the WPV Prevention Program in the areas of general building design, workstation layout, and overall space planning that are most applicable to the interior design professional include:

- The review of the design of all new or renovated facilities to ensure safe and secure conditions for employees. A well-developed WPV Prevention Program will make certain that the facilities are designed to ensure the privacy, safety, and security of patients, clients, and customers, yet permit employees to communicate with other staff in emergencies. (Such communication could be via clear partitions, video cameras, speakers, alarms, and so on as appropriate to the workplace situation.)
- Designed work areas and furniture arrangements that prevent entrapment of the employees and/or minimize potential for assault incidents. Figure 4.5 shows an example of an open and accessible workplace that provides open communication between employees.
- Controlled access to employee work areas. (Use of locked doors, buzzers, card access, etc.)
- Appropriate lighting systems for all indoor building areas, as well as for the grounds around the facility and in parking areas. Lighting meets the requirements of nationally recognized standards such as the American National Standards Institute (ANSI), as well as local building codes.
- Security does not conflict with Life Safety Code requirements. Although it may be tempting to keep doors locked to prevent intrusion, egress from inside the building must not be impeded.

The following work practice controls and procedures are additional WPV Prevention Program considerations as interior designers work closely with administrators and staff in the creation of safe and secure workplaces:

- If appropriate, provide identification cards for all employees, establish sign-in and sign-out books, and escort policy for non-employees.
- Develop internal communication systems to respond to emergencies.
- Develop policy on how to deal in emergency or hostage situations.
- Modify existing work practices that are identified by the workplace hazard assessment where employees face increased risk of violence.
- Arrange office space so unescorted visitors can be easily noticed, as shown in Figure 4.6.

In reducing threats in the workplace, the interior design professional should consider the following preventative measures as solutions that assist employees at risk within the workplace:

- Make sure that employees who have client contact within the facility have work areas designed to ensure that they are protected from threats by clients.
- Arrange desks and chairs to prevent entrapment of employees.
- Install Plexiglas payment window for employees who handle money and/or take payments from clients.
- Install locks on restroom doors with keys provided to each department.

4.6 An open reception area creates a safe and secure workplace.

- Install panic buttons in employees work areas.
- Control and monitor access to the building.
- Require all clients to enter through the main entrance to gain access to facility.
- Require visitors to sign in at the front desk; providing appropriate informational and directional signage.
- Avoid the use of unobstructed office exits.
- Post floor plans that show exits, entrances, location of security equipment, and so on.

A single explanation for the increase in workplace violence is not readily available. Some episodes of workplace violence, like robberies of small retail establishments, seem related to the larger societal problems of crime and substance abuse. Other episodes seem to arise more specifically from employment-related problems.

What can be done to prevent workplace violence? How can the interior design professional improve the health, safety and welfare of the public in the workplace? Most importantly, the interior design professional must begin to understand the threats, the level of risk, and the preventive measures associated with the various types of workplace violence. Even though our understanding of the factors that lead to workplace violence is not perfect, sufficient information is available which, if utilized effectively, can reduce the risk of workplace violence through environmental design.

FYI: According to the NIOSH (2007), when one examines the circumstances associated with workplace violence–related events, they can be divided into three major types. However, it is important to keep in mind that a particular occupation or workplace may be subject to more than one type. In all three types of workplace violence events, a human being, or "hazardous agent," commits the assault.

Types of Workplace Violence

Workplace violence is considered to be any threatening type of behavior that happens in a work environment. This includes shaking fists, throwing objects, or other overt physical acts, as well as any verbal or written threats to cause harm to anyone or anything. There are three main types of workplace violence committed by people within and outside of the workplace:

1. *Type I:* The person has no legitimate business relationship to the workplace and usually enters the affected workplace to commit a robbery or other criminal act.

2. *Type II:* The person is either the recipient, or the object, of a service provided by the affected workplace or the victim, for example, the assailant is a current or former client, patient, customer, passenger, criminal suspect, inmate, or prisoner.
3. *Type III:* The person has some employment-related involvement with the affected workplace. Usually this involves an assault by a current or former employee, supervisor or manager; by a current/former spouse or lover; a relative or friend; or some other person who has a dispute with an employee of the affected workplace.

The Type II workplace violence event involves fatal or nonfatal injuries to individuals who provide services to the public. These events involve assaults on public safety and correctional personnel, municipal bus or railway drivers, health-care and social service providers, teachers, sales personnel, and other public or private service sector employees who provide professional, public safety, administrative, or business services to the public.

Of increasing concern, though, are the rising numbers of Type II events involving assaults to the following types of service providers:

- Medical care providers in acute care hospitals, long-term care facilities, outpatient clinics, and home health agencies
- Mental health and psychiatric care providers in inpatient facilities, outpatient clinics, residential sites, and home health agencies
- Alcohol and drug treatment providers
- Social welfare service providers in unemployment offices, welfare eligibility offices, homeless shelters, probation offices, and child welfare agencies
- Teaching, administrative, and support staff in schools where students have a history of violent behavior
- Other types of service providers, e.g., justice system personnel, customer service representatives, and delivery personnel

Increasingly, some occupations and workplaces are at risk of more than one type of workplace violence event. Hospital emergency rooms, in addition to being at risk for Type II events involving assaults by patients, are also at risk for Type I events (see Figure 4.7). For example, gang members can enter a hospital emergency room to disrupt the medical care of a rival gang member who survived an initial attack. In the process, emergency room personnel can be physically harmed. Similarly, retail establishments at risk for Type I events, for example, convenience stores, can also be at risk for Type III events. For instance, a convenience store employee can be fatally injured in the course of a robbery by an unknown assailant (Type I), or because of a dispute with a spouse or co-employee or acquaintance (Type III).

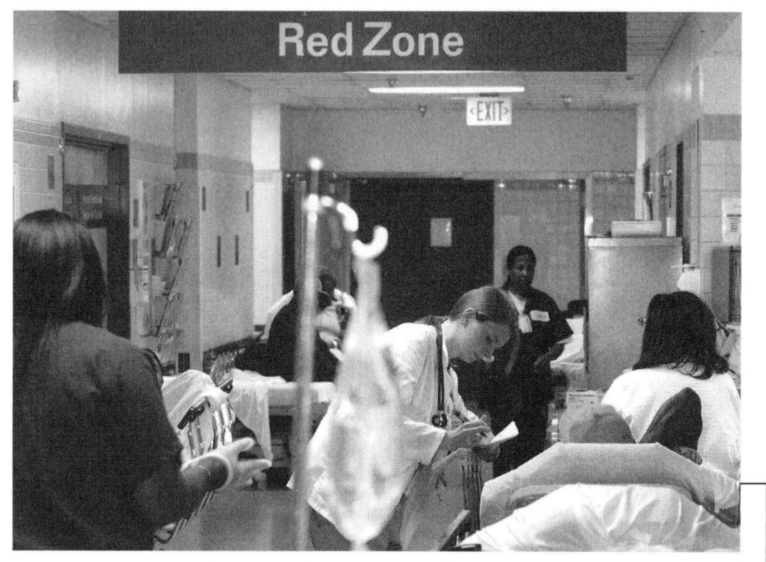

4.7 Emergency rooms are at risk for Type II events within the workplace.

RISK ASSESSMENT CONSIDERATIONS

Although risk assessment is ultimately the responsibility of a building's owner, it is incumbent upon the design professional to make certain that the overall nature of security requirements are determined prior to beginning the design process. The designer's failure to work closely with clients to obtain definitive answers regarding security-related issues throughout the programming phase of the project may result in design changes, delays, and cost increases to the owner.

Site Assessment

Interior designers should help clients concerned with workplace safety and security understand that the control of physical access through workplace design is an important preventive measure. This can include controlling access into and out of the workplace, freedom of movement within the workplace, and placing barriers between clients and service providers. Escape routes for an organization's employees is a critical component of a security-minded workplace design, and in certain situations, so is the installation of alarm systems or "panic buttons" as a security back-up measure.

FYI: Averages of 1.7 million people were victims of violent crime while working or on duty in the United States, according to a report published by the Bureau of Justice Statistics (BJS), each year from 1993 through 1999. An estimated 1.3 million (75 percent) of these incidents were simple assaults while an additional 19 percent were aggravated assaults. Of the occupations examined, police officers, corrections officers, and taxi drivers were victimized at the highest rates. For the same period, more than 800 workplace homicides were recorded by the Bureau of Labor Statistics's (BLS) Census of Fatal Occupational Injuries.

ENVIRONMENTAL DESIGNS—PREVENTION STRATEGIES

When involved in the design of built environments of the twenty-first century, the interior design professional will be addressing clients' workplace safety and security concerns on a multitude of levels. Each project is unique in client type, site, location, number of employees, and so on. Therefore, the designer must be aware of the prevention strategies that contribute to workplace safety such as:

- Physical separation of workers from customers, clients, and the public through the use of bullet-resistant barriers or enclosures has been proposed for retail settings such as gas stations and convenience stores, hospital emergency departments, and social service agency claims areas. The height and depth of counters (with or without bullet-resistant barriers) are also important considerations in protecting workers, since they introduce physical distance between workers and potential attackers.
- Visibility and lighting are also important environmental design considerations. Making high-risk areas visible to more people and installing good external lighting should decrease the risk of workplace assaults.
- Security devices may reduce the risk for assaults against workers and facilitate the identification and apprehension of perpetrators. These include closed-circuit cameras, alarms, two-way mirrors, card-key access systems, panic-bar doors locked from the outside only, and trouble lights or geographic locating devices in taxicabs and other mobile workplaces.
- Access to and egresses from the workplace are important areas to assess. The number of entrances and exits, the ease with which non-employees can gain access to work areas because doors are unlocked, and the number of areas where potential attackers can hide are issues that should be addressed. These issues have implications for the design of buildings and parking areas, landscaping, and the placement of garbage areas, outdoor refrigeration areas, and other storage facilities that workers must use during a work shift.

Personnel Control

For most building owners, security is primarily related to personnel. Therefore, personnel access control is fundamental to a sound security program and is greatly influenced by facility design. The electronic access-control industry has provided a broad array of tools that control personnel flow based on a combination of memorized personal identification numbers (PINs), electronic credentials (access cards), or some physiological feature, such as a palm print of the individual requesting access (**biometrics**). These types of systems have become as essential as HVAC and lighting in a building, because they are less expensive to install and manage than lock systems and are effective in controlling unauthorized access. Efficient application of the available technological tools, however, is dependent on the facility layout.

Nowhere is this more evident than in the facility lobby. In this location, the population consists of individuals authorized access to the facility, visitors who will be allowed into the facility either escorted or unescorted, and, potentially, individuals who, for a variety of reasons, will not be granted access. In addition, the lobby becomes that first point where the reception person/security officer first greets all people entering the building. Especially for visitors, that person becomes the company's ambassador, chief representative, and security overseer.

Effectiveness

Balance must be achieved between the aesthetics of the lobby and its ability to provide a natural flow of personnel past the security/reception desk. Personnel traffic must ultimately flow past a minimum number of security/reception desks from a purely economic standpoint. Close cooperation between all design parties is necessary to achieve the desired function within the defined architectural context.

Efficiencies

The security/reception desk must be designed to provide the utmost efficiency in performing a wide range of required tasks. This will involve everything from assisting lost visitors to helping longtime employees with malfunctioning access credentials. The desk should have sufficient space for Closed-Circuit Television (CCTV) monitors, a PC tied to the facility's local area network (LAN), and a PC monitoring the facility's access-control system, badge printers, and various communication devices.

Convergence

The lobby, as shown in Figure 4.8, is also the common traffic-flow point between the above-grade and below-grade floors. Under these circumstances, all stairwells should empty into the lobby to prevent an individual from gaining access to the facility without first passing through the security/reception screening point.

4.8

Stairwells and escalators that empty into the lobby prevent individuals from gaining unauthorized access to a facility.

FYI: **Understanding Liability.** Building owners and managers are not expected to guarantee the safety of their tenants, visitors, and guests, but they are required to exercise reasonable care to protect them from foreseeable events. "Courts are imposing increasingly higher duties on building owners and managers to protect tenants," notes Stephen G. Bushnell, product director, real estate, for Fireman's Fund Insurance Company's Commercial Business Division in Novato, California. Bushnell adds that municipalities and states are imposing more statutory requirements for building owners and managers, and that the growing numbers of industry association standards also influence the level of duty and liability incurred at the ownership/management level. Often, the focus of duty extends beyond the safety measures inside a building.

It is important to stress the importance of identifying foreseeable events based upon such things as the level of crime in the neighborhood and what it means to the building in question (and its tenants). Building owners need to ask themselves if their building's environment is a target and if crime or terrorism [are] foreseeable—not just in their building, but in the neighborhood. It is incumbent for building owners to understand the liabilities in the areas where properties are located. For example, a building might be crime-free, but assaults might have occurred in the parking lot across the street. Alternatively, perhaps a block away, someone is hiding in shrubbery outside an office building, confronting and harming tenants. "If building owners do not do something about the safety of their tenants walking to that parking lot, or take into consideration the assaults occurring on the next block, they will not have a defense against liability claims, as it is their duty as building owner or manager to have some measure of security to keep employees and tenants safe," Bushnell further states.

The design professional must be aware that although it is the violent attacks that capture the media headlines, and the public interest, it is the everyday security breaches that make a comprehensive, effective security plan a must for every facility. While terrorism still makes prominent headlines and remains a possible threat to buildings and their occupants, businesses are more likely to face such everyday crimes as theft, violence, and fraud. Because of the high concentration of people on-site—and in some building types, a transient population—commercial and institutional buildings are ripe targets for criminal activity. It is not just limited to high-rise, multitenant office buildings; mixed-use facilities, shopping centers, hotels and motels, office and college campuses, and busy hospitals are at risk, too.

"We have to be careful of the day-to-day threats," says Carlos X. Villarreal, vice president of national security and life safety for Chicago-based Trizec Properties Inc. For example, consider "creepers"—individuals who enter multitenant buildings or hotels and seek out empty offices to steal laptop computers, handbags, briefcases, and other items of value. Building access controls have helped curb this behavior to some extent, Villarreal notes, and although it is not as prevalent as it used to be, it is still relevant.

FYI: What about workplace violence? According to Geoff Craighead, vice president, high-rise and real estate services, at Securitas Security Services USA, Inc. in Los Angeles, in the last four out of five years, Corporate 1000 security directors listed workplace violence as the number one threat, ranking it higher than terrorism. "Terrorism went up, but workplace violence remains a primary concern," he explains. "If you start adding up all the incidents you hear about in the news, you realize it really is an issue.

"Look at your program and your building," Craighead states. "Assess potential threats in building and perimeter control, tenant and visitor access, package acceptance and mail delivery, security staffing and training, and tenant security awareness. The initial reaction [was] that we needed to rely on technology," he says. "A lot of technology application after 9/11 might have been misspent or misused. There is a moment to step back, take a deep breath, assess what you are trying to accomplish, and look at whether technology should be a supplement to a plan or if it should be a foundation for a plan. If you skip over the assessment process and go right to design, you might be misusing funds" (Craighead, 2003).

For the design professional that thorough analysis should include focusing on the security concepts as discussed in Chapter 2, provided by CPTED (Crime Prevention through Environmental Design). These concepts center on the idea that the proper design and effective use of the physical environment can lead to a reduction in the incidence and fear of crime. As discussed, the basic tenets of CPTED include lighting design, clear sightlines, landscaping for visibility, and natural access control. CPTED creates opportunities for tenants or occupants to maintain vigilance of their space and to make it uncomfortable for trespassers to move into the space. A space created with CPTED principles, as shown in Figure 4.9, makes a facility and its surroundings more open, visible, and occupied.

4.9 This commercial lobby follows the CPTED principles, by enabling designation, definition, and design.

DETERMINING SECURITY PREPAREDNESS

Determining preparedness requires the designer to ask probing questions about security policies and procedures, potential threats, the quality of technology, and the knowledge and capabilities of the property's security staff. When working on an existing facility, the designer can assess potential threats and examine the effectiveness of current security measures in the following eight areas:

1. Building and perimeter controls, including entry to under-building parking garages
2. Access control of tenants and visitors to the building, including access to loading docks by delivery people, contractors, and vendors
3. Package acceptance, mail delivery, and removal-control measures
4. State of existing physical security measures such as; architectural features, lighting systems, locking and key-control systems, access control, intrusion detection and alarm systems, Closed-Circuit Television systems (CCTV), and communication systems
5. Security staffing and training
6. Building policies and procedures
7. Building emergency plan and building emergency procedures manual
8. Building emergency staff preparedness and evacuation drills

A Checklist for Security and Fire and Life Safety

As previously stated, building owners and managers have a legal duty to protect tenants and guests. Regularly inspecting a facility for security breaches and trouble zones is a necessity. Some "musts" for any routine inspection program that will assist the designer in understanding the design security scenario include:

- Secure and inventory all keys
- Control access to the roof and all mechanical spaces
- Trim landscaping to maximize visibility and eliminate hiding spaces
- Maximize nighttime illumination as necessary
- Inspect that all emergency exits are visible, operable, and accessible
- Inspect that all access control systems are operable
- Train personnel to constantly monitor CCTV systems
- Conduct an annual security risk analysis, including review of area crime statistics and upgrade/update security policies as needed (Fireman's Fund Insurance Co., 2004)

Security Management

The tragic events of 9/11 spurred increased vigilance and security measures in commercial facilities nationwide. Some measures boosted building security for the better; others wound up being excessive and impossible to sustain over any period of time, both practically and financially.

The United States building industry has become much more aware of what it takes to create a good security management program, but the question of what is necessary versus what is too much, still remains. "There is no cookie-cutter approach to security," says Russell W. Riddell, director of school security, planning, and design services of The Thomas Group, a TetraTech Company, based in New York State. "Each [building] has unique circumstances. The principles of security management are the same. How they are applied and instituted vary depending on the needs of the facility," he notes. "There might be site-specific issues that you have to deal with, but the overall conceptual philosophy in security management and how to protect a facility are generally the same."

> **FYI:** Barbara Nadel, FAIA, noted security expert, states, "I think there is a tremendous amount we can learn from each other, and there needs to be a dialogue that brings us together to consider and address mutual issues of concern. Admittedly, my knowledge is rather limited when it comes to specific issues of architecture, design, and construction, but we could probably share a great deal of collateral expertise with those in the architecture, design, and construction communities. I could not, for example, begin to comment credibly on the technical aspects of how to design and construct emergency exits and stairwells, but I could probably offer some insights into the behavior of crowds under crisis situations—insights that might figure prominently in that design and planning."
>
> —Barbara Nadel, FAIA

ASSESSING THE RISKS

Designing secure workplace environments begins with the development of an overall security assessment. This assessment addresses multiple issues, providing information to be analyzed, and if appropriate, integrated into the design solution. In general, risk assessment analysis should include a review of an organizations assets, threats, vulnerabilities, and risks.

Asset analysis identifies and prioritizes the assets to be protected, including people, operations, information, trade secrets, and property. This analysis should prioritize the assets in order of importance by the ability of an organization to survive should an asset be destroyed or stolen.

Threat analysis assesses the types of threats that can occur against the organization. These threats can cause harm or death to employees, destruction to property, disclosure of sensitive material, interruption of operations, or denial of services. Types of threats can include forced entry, bomb, or ballistic (e.g., gun/rifle, mortar, vehicular, or flying craft). This analysis also identifies the potential individuals or groups who represent a threat and the level of motivation they might have, as well as factors such as:

- Have past threats or actions been carried out against the organization?
- What types of political events may bring on new threats?
- Does the location of the facility increase the level of threat by exposure?
- Does the facility or organization have symbolic value?

Vulnerability analysis identifies weaknesses that can be exploited or taken advantage of to carry out a threat. This analysis—which includes site topography and facility location on-site, as well as facility security operations and facility hardening—is conducted on either existing-facility conditions or proposed projects in development.

Risk analysis examines the security measures that will be taken against identified threats, along with the extent of the costs of each measure (monetary and operational). Ultimately, a plan is developed that identifies which level of security will be provided against each threat.

Because of its complex nature, the development of a security assessment frequently involves the use of specialty consultants to assist in the analyses by offering special, detail-oriented, current knowledge of security tactics. The outcome of the security assessment is the development of functional criteria outlining security requirements and strategies. This criterion provides the project team, including the designer, architect, landscape architect, and engineer with the information needed to develop programmatic safety and security requirements.

CPTED PRINCIPLES IN THE WORKPLACE—FROM THEORY TO APPLICATION

When designing a workplace environment, once functional project criteria have been identified, security design concepts can then be applied. As previously reviewed in Chapter 2, safety and security in the built environment is based on several premises: detection, deterrence, and response. Using these premises, CPTED—Crime Prevention through Environmental Design—developed several concepts that reduce crime through proper facility and site design to create safer built environments such as the following:

- *Natural strategies* (natural surveillance). These incorporate the natural conditions of the site with facility placement and design to provide visual surveillance and territorial reinforcement of ownership. Natural strategies use the principles of line-of-sight visual control for facility occupants and security personnel, while incorporating features such as shrubs, gates, and fences to instill a feeling of ownership, sending the message that trespassers will be identified.
- *Mechanical strategies* (natural access). There are multitudes of electronic technologies that can provide facility security. Video cameras, Closed-Circuit Television, electronic locks using keycard or proximity devices, scanning devices, and interior and exterior sensor devices are just a few of the items from which to choose.
- *Organizational strategies* (territoriality). These strategies rely on the occupants of the facility to provide surveillance and access control. For these to be effective, occupants need to understand the overall security concept, including what is expected from them if an event occurs.

An important CPTED principle, known as layering (or defense-in-depth), creates various layers of security, also known as zones. Zones begin at the perimeter of the site, where methods to control pedestrian and vehicular traffic form the initial defense. Providing facility-hardening techniques at the perimeter forms the next defense. Layering then continues from the facility envelope to the interior areas. Once inside, the facility's interior walls can create zones of protection throughout until reaching the highest secured area within the center of the facility.

As learned in earlier chapters, CPTED principles include the 3 "D"s, which are designation, definition, and design. They reduce the fortress-like look that is often associated with highly secure facilities by using a site's natural security defenses to provide some (or all) of the facility-hardening design criteria. This approach considers these three aspects of space to gather functional security-design information, as follows:

1. *Designation:* Questioning the proposed use(s) of the facility. For example, who will use it and when will it be used?
2. *Definition:* Questioning how the space is to be defined. For example, is the space being used for social or cultural uses?
3. *Design:* Questioning whether the design supports concerns that were raised in the areas of "designation" and "definition."

Up-front Planning is Critical

During the predesign phase of a project, an organization must first determine the level of security features and considerations to be included in its facility—information that can also serve as baseline programming requirements and facilitate preliminary project design.

As discussed previously, risk assessment and the identification of any potential threats are two of the first action items in the development of a security design scenario. Threats can be external (a group or individual that is opposed to a method of operation, a product being produced, or an affiliated/parent company); internal (disgruntled or recently dismissed employees); or natural (tornadoes, floods, earthquakes, fires, etc.). Once potential threats are determined, the organization then needs to decide how and what it is willing to do to prevent and/or respond to an event.

During the predesign phase of a project, facility managers and design professionals must review a variety of access points to the facility that deal with security. Examples of access points to be covered include:

- *Site access.* Site access looks at how people approach the facility. This portion of the review determines whether the site requires a security fence around the perimeter, a guardhouse, or a secured gate entry with voice communication and/or Closed-Circuit Television (CCTV) at parking areas, docks, building entries, the site perimeter, and other areas.
- *Building/lobby access.* Once people enter the site, building/lobby-access security becomes important. This part of the review covers how the building is accessed both from outside and from within, and determines whether measures such as secured entry (requiring an electronic magnetic card or proximity reader), an attended reception desk, CCTV in the lobby, secured doors from the lobby to the remainder of the building, a walk-through metal detector, biohazard protection, exterior-door access throughout the facility, or building-hardening features are required.
- *Sensitive-area access.* Because of the often-critical nature of the information being stored and/or processed, certain areas within a facility (such as a data center, laboratory, senior-executive area, process/work area, and human-resources area) must typically contain a higher level of security. The designer, along with the building owner, manager, or facility manager must determine whether secured entry (requiring electronic magnetic card or proximity reader), entry restricted to specific employees, motion-detection devices within a room, lockable files, secured access from the parking lot, or other measures may be required.

A well-developed security design scenario and its related strategies take into account how people behave in an environment, how that environment lends itself to productive and safe use for those using the space, and how crime prevention principles may be applied. Issues such as the building orientation, entrances and exits, parking lot location, landscaping, lighting, fences, sidewalks, and signage are just a few examples of what is considered when a site plan is reviewed. Interior colors, lighting, ceiling heights, reception-area design, hallway size, and width of counters make environments feel safe, yet pleasing, to staff and clients, while deterring would-be criminals.

For example, rather than overt security devices, such as cameras, guards, and metal detectors, an organization, such as a nonprofit youth-serving organization, could be designed with a single point of entry into the building leading to a reception area, visible through glass, from the administrative offices. These offices and parent conference rooms would be accessible to visitors without entering the main service providing areas. The youth are then separated by age into pods that radiate off a central atrium located down a hallway from the reception area. In this scenario, should an incident occur in one pod, it can be isolated from the rest of the building by closing discreet steel doors. An additional layer of security would be to provide secondary exits that are accessible only in emergencies.

Cost-effective Solutions to Help Reduce Crime

As the cost of any design project is typically an important consideration, designers can apply the basic principles of CPTED easily, innovatively, and less expensively to improve the safety and security of the workplace environment, for example:

- Lowered ceilings, softer and lower-wattage lighting, and calming paint colors reduce anxiety that can lead to shouting, acting out, and other violence.
- Narrow hallways, as they leads from the main entry doors to the reception area, naturally slow people down and direct them.
- Customer-service counters constructed wider than the comfortable reach of a tall person's arm, protects employees and volunteers without caging them behind steel bars and bulletproof plastic.
- A neat, cared-for front makes a site less of a target.
- Provide reception areas at the entrance of offices, in which the receptionist has an unimpeded view of the door, parking lot and, if possible, the doors to the restrooms. If there is no receptionist, this job should be assigned to the person whose office is across from the entrance, with clear visibility provided.

Not only do these solutions tend to de-escalate situations for those with larceny on their minds, they make the site welcoming for the majority of people coming into a facility.

Physical Security Options

The designer should evaluate the following areas and security options that can reduce risk in the workplace:

- *Public and nonpublic areas.* A clear delineation between public and nonpublic areas of the premises and agencies should be considered. The approach to workplace design should be sensitive to the needs of clients while at the same time maximizing the physical security for employees. For example, security can be enhanced by the effective use of foyers, counters, and screens.
- *Reception areas and counters.* The risk assessment will help to determine what measures are necessary for a particular reception area. If the assessment indicates it is necessary, a counter should be designed to protect employees from physical attack by clients. The counter should be functional and in keeping with the design of the reception area.
- *Interview rooms.* Interview rooms should be designed to protect employees from assault and aid the conduct of interviews. For instance, furniture should be arranged so that employees can leave the room quickly if needed. The risk assessment might indicate that duress alarms should be fitted in some or all interview rooms where judged necessary. Organizations might also consider the use of Closed-Circuit Television in interview rooms.
- *Duress alarms.* Duress alarms enable employees to discreetly call for assistance from other employees, security staff, or police in response to threatening incidents. Duress alarms can enhance security in public contact areas, including reception areas, counters, and interview rooms.
- *Lighting.* Lighting, both internal and external, can make an important contribution to physical security. Security lighting can also provide deterrence and can help security guards detect intruders. Motion-detection devices can also be set up so that any detected movement will activate a CCTV or a floodlight or both.
- *Security guards.* In special circumstances, guards or security staff may be required. Guards can deter criminals or disgruntled members of the public who might harm people or property. If a guard presence is necessary, agencies should think about where the guard will be positioned.
- *Closed-Circuit Television.* CCTV systems can be used for the surveillance of entrances, passages or other areas such as interview rooms.

In summary, the CPTED principles, based on the belief that behavior, both normal and abnormal, is heavily influenced by the natural and built environment, is a valuable tool in making the appropriate changes to an organization's environment to ensure that staff members feel safe and secure, while providing a powerful deterrent to intruders. Often these changes can increase productivity, profitability, and employee morale.

CPTED principles that most relate to the interior environment and that address interior design and architectural design solutions, are identified in the next section. These sections illustrate the application of CPTED principles, security assessment processes, and educational considerations that are integral to the design of a safe and secure workplace environment.

Security Technology—Utilization in the Workplace Environment

Security technology, and related security equipment, has become yet another layer of the body of knowledge required of designers of the built environment. Here are some of the types of security technologies that have become an integral part of the design of safe and secure workplaces for the twenty-first century:

- *Video-surveillance system.* This system is available with sophisticated features, such as remote control pan/tilt/zoom, internal motion detection, and networking capabilities. They can identify the location of the room (or employee) by means of an alarm sound and/or a lighted indicator.
- *Biometric system.* This type of system is activated by fingerprint, iris of the eye, voice recognition, hand or palm geometry, and facial characteristics. Biometrics in the workplace are also being integrated into individual workstations, using a mouse with an embedded fingerprint scanner and computer-mounted security cameras using iris recognition technology.
- *Electronic alarm system.* This system is activated either visually or audibly. Systems identify the location of the room (or employee) by means of an alarm sound and/or a lighted indicator.
- *Closed-Circuit Television.* The use of this security permits security guards and other personnel to monitor high-risk areas, both inside and outside the building.
- *Metal-detection system.* This system identifies people with weapons.
- *Cellular telephones, beepers, CB radios, or handheld alarms.* These can be used as security alarm systems.

FYI: Security Technology. Business Controls, Inc. (BCI), a consulting firm offering background screening and other employee-related investigations, offers the *MySafeWorkplace* service, a third-party incident reporting system that offers employees an anonymous way to communicate with their employer and provide details on any issue of concern regarding safety and security.

The service offers employees several communication options. One is a secure Web site. The site is available around the clock and can be accessed in nearly 170 languages, according to Steven Foster, executive vice president and chief operating officer for BCI, headquartered in Colorado. Once a report is received, it is encrypted, forwarded electronically to appropriate individuals within the organization, and handled in accordance with the company's internal policies.

ALLIED PROFESSIONS

As a valuable member of the design team, the interior design professional must appreciate many of the basic safety and security solutions undertaken by allied design professions, such as architects and landscape architects, when involved in the planning of safe and secure workplace environments.

Numerous architectural and landscape architectural considerations are implemented within the design of workplace environments to mitigate the effects of a bombing, shooting, and/or an act of violence in a commercial facilities. Detailed information regarding safety and security solutions and considerations as defined by the architecture and landscape architecture professions respectively, can be found at www.aia.org and www.asla.org. Identified below are selected examples of considerations important to members of these professionals in the planning process:

- *Stand-off distance.* A concept used in the site placement and design of office facilities as a security solution to unwanted access to a building. The basic concept of stand-off distance is to allow as much room between a vehicle and a building as possible.
- *Passive barriers.* These include concrete planters, high curbs, berms, fences, and trees and are used to protect against stationary bombs, and can help deflect blast shockwaves away from a building.
- *Active barriers.* These include cable-beam barriers, retractable bollards, and sliding-gate barriers and are designed to stop a moving vehicle, such as those used in a suicide bombing attempt. When used correctly, active barriers can present formidable challenges to cars and trucks.

Best Practices in Architecture and Landscape Architecture

Here are some best practices to follow when making architecture and landscape decisions:

- Avoid eaves and overhangs, because they can be points of high local pressure and suction during blasts. When these elements are used, they should be designed to withstand blast effects.
- Set the facility back from the street or angle the facility to reduce blast impact. If the facility must be at the face of a street, using laminated glazing will reduce the fragmentation from glass.
- Facility façades can be strengthened using additional reinforcement or steel members. These methods are employed in multistory facilities to prevent progressive collapse.

- Shrubs, trees, and landscape features should not impede visual surveillance on the exterior site.
- Locate site entry points in high-visibility areas where they can be easily observed and monitored by office personnel.
- Perimeter protection using operable vehicular bollards, fixed bollards, fences, and concrete planters can also be used.
- Secure the building's perimeter with both passive and active barriers.

CONCLUSION

At one time, workplace security was little more than a passing thought, considered only after the facility had been constructed and was in normal operation, and only, perhaps, if some incident occurred that affected the workplace. There was a time when, as a facility owner, you could get by with simply placing locks on doors. Today, however, security has exploded into a high-tech, daily necessity. Threats to an organization's personnel or products can come from exterior sources or from inside the organization.

Due to their increased importance within contemporary society, security solutions must be built-in from the beginning of design and construction to be flexible and responsive to new threats as they develop. As with many components of any design projects, it is much more cost-effective to provide safety and security–designed solutions in the beginning than to retrofit after the fact. During the initial stages of any project, a security program should be developed and implemented, forming a specific basis for the site, facility, and operations layout. This program enables architects, designers, and engineers to design proper accommodations for current security measures, as well as provide practical alternatives, as security needs change.

Environmental design has a tremendous impact on human behavior. The behavioral aspects of disasters, workplace violence, and terrorism are examples of the dialogue that must take place when assessing risks to a commercial facility. Professionals in different areas of specialization and expertise, such as interior designers, architects, landscape architects, facility managers, and building owners, all play a valuable role in the risk-assessment process and the development of workplace environments that offer safety and security to employees, as well as the public.

KEY CONCEPTS

- The interior design profession can fulfill its specialized role in protecting the health, safety, and welfare of users of public spaces by partnering with clients, end-users, and allied professionals to provide design solutions that increase the safety and security within the places where we live, work, and play.
- Violence in the workplace is a serious safety and health issue and has risen to epidemic proportions.
- Physical attack or assault resulting in death or physical injury of an employee in a place of business is the standard definition of workplace violence (WPV).
- In addition to the human cost of WPV, businesses suffer economic losses, incur legal expenses, property damage, and diminished public image when they are the victims of workplace violence.
- According to the Bureau of Labor Statistics (BLS), workplace violence is divided into categories depending on the relationship between the assailant and the worker or workplace. These categories include violence by strangers, customers/clients, coworkers, or personal relations.
- Risk assessment in reviewing security considerations assists in adding measures that may decrease the likelihood of harm, damage, and physical and/or psychological injury to improve safety and security within the workplace.
- CPTED concepts and strategies take into account how people behave in an environment, how that environment lends itself to productive and safe use for its end-users, and how crime prevention strategies can be applied.
- Environmental design prevention strategies, such as physical separation, visibility and lighting, and access/egress from the workplace are important areas to address.

ASSIGNMENTS

1. Discuss the important role that security plays in the design of workplace environments.
2. Provide examples of the how design standards and construction change as security solutions are integrated into the workplace.
3. Discuss the types of programming, design criteria, and risk assessment issues that are involved in securing the workplace environment.

ACTIVITIES

1. Journaling activity: Respond in written and graphic format. Probes may include visiting workplace environments that have obvious and obtrusive security measures versus sites that provide more transparent security design solutions. Share your experiences while generating a list about the psychological differences between theses varied workplaces.
2. Conduct interviews with peers, friends, and family to identify a variety of workplace security scenarios. Research examples of the types of security measures and/or equipment stated in interviews. Discuss how these products might be integrated into the built environment.
3. Research security equipment–related Web sites and compile a list of five products. Note the dimensions, installation methods, maintenance requirements, finish selections, and so on, to become familiar with security technology products.
4. Create a project that requires as a component of the programming and design process the integration of security needs/theories in identifying and articulating design problems.
5. Visit a site that has implemented obvious security control measures with a required exercise in behavioral mapping.
6. Interview members of the allied professions, such as architects, landscape architects, facility managers, engineers, and so forth, for an overview of how professional practice has changed with the added security measures of the twenty-first century. Follow up with a systematic discussion.

1 6 5 8 3 4 1 0 7 2

5 SECURITY-RELATED NEEDS IN HISTORICAL INTERIORS

Preservation of our landmarks provides a sense of community between past and present, and an appreciation of the accomplishments that outlast the individual life. We are reminded that the values and aspirations these landmarks embody possess continuing relevance today and make us aware of the past's importance to the future state's renowned preservationist.

—Barbara Lee Diamonstein-Spielvogel, Hon. AIA

OBJECTIVES

- Create an awareness of the many challenges faced in providing security for historic facilities, whether they are public or private.
- Understand the design objective of creating a balance between openness and free access within historic settings, while satisfying security requirements.
- Learn the concept of transparent security design and its integration into historical interiors.
- Review the varied types of historical design considerations as defined by the National Trust for Historic Preservation, the General Services Administration, and the Standards Department of Interior Rehabilitation.
- Identity aspects of security risk assessments as related to historic interiors and settings.
- Review the principles of CPTED and their relationship to the security of historic interiors and national landmarks.
- Increase knowledge of the role of the interior designer, architect, landscape architect, facility manager, and building owner as they relate to the design of safe and secure historic settings.

5.1

Security rules for visiting the Statue of Liberty in New York Harbor changed after the terrorist attacks on September 11th.

Liberty Enlightening the World, now known as the Statue of Liberty, (see Figure 5.1) soars from a 150-foot-high stone base on Liberty Island in New York Harbor and is an icon among European immigrants. In the 1890s, the United States threw open its doors to newcomers, funneling almost all of them through Ellis Island, a near neighbor to the statue in the harbor. For the 22 million immigrants who passed through there between 1892 and 1924, catching sight of the Statue of Liberty became the poignant confirmation that they had arrived at the threshold to a new life.

After September 11, 2001, concerns over terrorists targeting this American icon lead to the indefinite closing down of the statue itself. Visitors were free to visit Liberty Island and tour the grounds, but could not go into or up the statue. The American government felt that the Statue of Liberty was a target because of its symbolic value as an artistic representation of America's values, and that all measures should be taken to protect the landmark. "Lady Liberty" reopened for full public viewing in 2004.

CONTEXT AND EXPERIENCE

Historic public places and buildings are preserved precisely because they inspire, educate, and uplift (see Figure 5.2). Historic landscapes, approaches and entrances, and significant interior spaces contribute greatly to the public's experience and appreciation of a society. They are prized examples of architecture, landscapes, and the fine art and decorative arts that form and define cultures and artistic heritages. One of the greatest security challenges is the dilemma of balancing public safety with protection of historic places and their art, sculpture, records, and landscape that often are the destination for thousands of visitors every day.

Historic properties are active and vital parts of every community. They provide many of the places where we work, live, attend schools, worship, enjoy leisure time, and conduct government business. These often-irreplaceable places and settings inspire and teach us about our past. They also provide an important source of present and future economic growth through heritage tourism. Providing security for operations and personnel located in or near historic sites presents unique, and sometimes difficult, challenges for the design professional. In some cases, security measures implemented at historic and archaeological sites are obtrusive, lack design sensitivity, discourage public access, and

5.2 It is a difficult challenge to maintain public safety in historic places that have visitors everyday, such as Grand Central Station, New York.

5.3 People pass through security checks as they enter the Smithsonian National Air and Space Museum.

threaten the design integrity of the resources they are designed to protect. (See Figure 5.3.)

Within the United States, from the Statue of Liberty in New York, to Independence Hall in Philadelphia, Pennsylvania, to the Lincoln Memorial in Washington, DC, and thousands of other federal, state, and local historic properties, our national heritage and the story of American democracy are reflected in historic resources. Just as they are for all civil societies, these varied historic properties are a living legacy of the rich and diverse assets that comprise the fabric of our lives. The stories and oral histories associated with their creation, occupancies, use, and preservation ultimately describe and define who we are as a people and what we value.

There are many challenges to face in providing security for historic facilities, whether they are public or private. The design objective though is largely the same: the challenge of creating a balance between openness and free access, while at the same time satisfying security considerations. How do we provide for both appropriately? For those of us entrusted with interior design, architecture, and historic treasures, there is an additional dimension—how do we preserve a structure's historic and architectural integrity, and its aesthetics, while improving its security? What are the security design challenges for historic places?

DESIGNER'S ROLE

A brief review of the varied types of historical design considerations as defined by the National Trust for Historic Preservation will assist design professionals in understanding the difference between **Historical Preservation** and **Historical Restoration.** Regardless of the building classification, the designers' role is one of sensitivity to a building's historical past when integrating the new safety and security requirements of the twenty-first century.

The National Trust for Historical Preservation, a division of the United States Government Services Administration (GSA) defines these differences as follows. Historical Preservation is the act of maintaining and repairing existing historical materials and the retention of a property's form as it has evolved over time. Specifically, the United States Department of the Interior's interpretation is; "Preservation calls for the existing form, materials, features, and detailing of a property to be retained and preserved. This may include preliminary measures to protect and stabilize it prior to undertaking other work—or protection and stabilization may be an end in itself." Basically, Historic Preservation is a tool to save older buildings; whereas, Historical Restoration is the process of the renewal and refurbishment of the interior and/or exterior fabric of a building. As buildings are structures, which have, from time to time, particular purposes, they require ongoing maintenance to prevent them from falling into disrepair as the result of the ravages of time and use. Historical Restoration is the set of activities that are greater than year-to-year maintenance, while maintaining the architectural integrity of the structure. The scope of restoration typically depends upon the need, the state of the building, and the affordability of the work required (Dickenson, NPS, 2007).

FIRST IMPRESSIONS AT HISTORIC BUILDINGS

Of importance to the design professional is the 1998 Government Services Administration's (GSA) First Impressions Program. This program is a federal initiative to improve the architectural integrity of visitor and tenant gateways into federal buildings. The program guidelines focus on a building's lobbies and landscapes, the portions of federal buildings that often shape a visitor's first impression of the federal government.

In 2000, the GSA published a Technical Preservation Guideline, *First Impressions of Historic Buildings,* specifically related to historic interiors. These guidelines, as outlined below, are a valuable resource for the interior design professional faced with the complex issues of preservation and restoration within historic places. These guidelines provide a valuable tool when integrating safety and security solutions within historic settings.

The GSA Technical Preservation Guidelines and recommendations are intended to be consistent with the general objectives of the First Impressions Program, which is to improve the architectural integrity of historic settings when accessing historical buildings. The overall purpose of the guidelines is to provide specific design direction to ensure that changes are consistent with the buildings original design, features, and materials, as listed in the following sections.

Design Principles

- *Direct visitors' focus to the original space.* Changes to an historic space should help visitors appreciate the original design including volume, spatial quality, and materials. Preserve original materials in place.
- *Use original documentation.* Where it exists, use historic documentation to draw design ideas. For example, new signage for the Department of Justice is replicated from existing sign frames. New work may be a simplified version of more elaborate historic work.
- *Design contextually.* Design should respond to materials, colors, textures, and detailing of an historic space. Design using comparable quality materials and construction.
- *Create opportunities to restore.* Use First Impressions as an opportunity to restore historic features. For example, if a lighting upgrade is necessary in an historic space, use the opportunity to replicate historic fixtures, if possible.

First Impression Improvements

- *Consider functions and furnishings in public space.* Limit furnishings to support only functions necessary to welcoming, informing, and securing both visitors and tenants. For example, vendors and commercial activities should be located elsewhere (e.g., near cafeterias). Temporary furnishings for receptions and other events should be promptly removed and stored.
- *Use of signage.* Use original signage typeface. For prewar buildings, signage usually uses a serif typeface. ADA generally recommends sans serif typeface but serif is permitted as long as letter contrast and size is sufficient to ensure visibility. Attach signage systems in a manner that does not damage original finishes.
- *Security design.* Design guard booth and guard desk architecturally (as built in architectural furniture), matching original detailing and materials in the space. Design desk to conceal computer monitors and equipment.
- *Temporary displays.* Design displays to work with the materials and colors original to the space. Install in a manner that does not harm historic materials. (For example: never bolt banners into masonry units; instead, use spring-loaded rods or mounting rings held by friction around columns.)

- *Permanent and semipermanent displays.* Use historic features as showcases. For example, abandoned directories can be effectively converted to house exhibits or interactive displays (describing nearby artwork).
- *Utilitarian items and equipment.* Locate utilitarian items and equipment such as ATMs and trash receptacles, outside of lobby areas and primary spaces whenever possible. When not possible, use the smallest apparatus in finishes sympathetic with space, consolidating the equipment to the greatest extent possible.
- *Lighting.* Maintain original fixtures whenever possible. Where necessary, to meet required light levels, install low-energy, high-output bulbs (where concealed by globes). Use torchères, freestanding lights, task lighting, and other discreet supplementary light rather than permanently mounting new contemporary fixtures on ornamental walls and ceilings.
- *Doors and other original features.* Retain original doors and trim. Where missing, replicate originals. Do not remove original doors.

Design professionals can be strong stewards of historic resources through a commitment to preserving the past as a way of inspiring future generations. Former Congressman and Ambassador Richard N. Swett, FAIA, author of *Leadership by Design,* observes: "In today's world of terrorism and heightened security requirements, there is a need for experts who not only understand how to create defensible space, but who can address security solutions that maintain the character and accessibility of our nation's most treasured historic resources." Architects and designers with this understanding and sensibility will contribute greatly to the built environment by assessing potential risks and recommending the needed design solutions, with the goal of enhancing public safety and the quality of our daily lives. "This approach allows societies to maintain openness and accessibility in public buildings that continue to reflect the similar, fundamental principles of their democracies," Swett adds.

Preserving and protecting historic resources is an important civic responsibility, and one in which the design professional plays a valuable role. Those involved in the creation of the built environment can—and must—play a vital leadership role by understanding the unique needs of historic resources within communities, and creating appropriate security design responses in keeping with the spirit and intent of such recommendations as given by the National Trust for Historic Preservation, and the GSA's, *First Impressions of Historic Buildings* programs.

NATIONAL HISTORIC PRESERVATION ACT OF 1966

Realizing the need to protect America's cultural resources, Congress established the National Historic Preservation Act (NHPA) in 1966, which mandates the active use of historic buildings for public benefit and preserving our national heritage. Cultural resources, as identified in the National Register of Historic Places, include buildings, archeological sites, structures, objects, and historic districts.

The NHPA encourages the identification and preservation of cultural and historic resources through partnerships with state, tribal, and local governments. It states, among many important principles, that national historic and cultural foundations should be preserved as a living part of community life and development in order to give a sense of orientation to the American people. The act goes on to say that federal government policy shall contribute to the preservation of non-federally owned historic resources and give maximum encouragement to organizations and individuals undertaking preservation by private means. It encourages the public and private preservation and utilization of all usable elements of the nation's historic built environment. (NHPA, 1966)

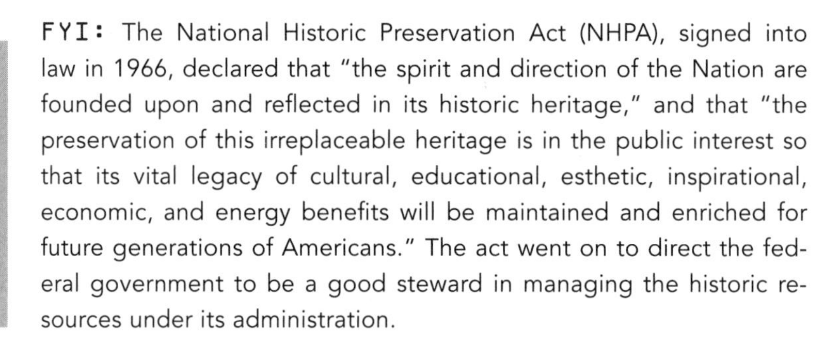

FYI: The National Historic Preservation Act (NHPA), signed into law in 1966, declared that "the spirit and direction of the Nation are founded upon and reflected in its historic heritage," and that "the preservation of this irreplaceable heritage is in the public interest so that its vital legacy of cultural, educational, esthetic, inspirational, economic, and energy benefits will be maintained and enriched for future generations of Americans." The act went on to direct the federal government to be a good steward in managing the historic resources under its administration.

Historic Preservation Terminology

Within the NHPA, the Secretary of the Interior's *Standards for the Treatment of Historic Properties* provides standards for four distinct approaches to the treatment of historic properties: preservation, restoration, rehabilitation, and reconstruction. As discussed previously, preservation focuses on the maintenance stabilization and repair of existing historic materials and retention of a property's form as it has evolved over time, while restoration depicts a property at a particular period in its history, removing evidence of other periods. The two additional approaches as defined by the Secretary of the Interior include rehabilitation and reconstruction. Rehabilitation acknowledges the need to alter or add to a historic property to meet continuing or changing uses while retaining the property's historic character while Reconstruction re-creates vanished or non-surviving portions of a property for interpretive purposes.

Although each treatment has its own definition, they are interrelated. For example, one could "restore" missing features in a building that is being "rehabilitated." This means that if there is sufficient historical documentation on what was there originally, a decorative lighting fixture may be replicated or an absent front porch rebuilt, but the overall approach to work on the building falls under one specific treatment.

FYI: "The new security constraints on Federal building are opportunities for enriching architecture. Once you understand the limitations, they should be cause for invention and analysis that allows you to push beyond your preconceptions. The security issues should allow you to invent a vocabulary that not only solves the problem, but also creates an appropriate architectural image."

—Charles Gwathmey, FAIA

One example of a project that successfully uses the principles of historic restoration can be found in the physical elements for improving security at the United States, Washington, DC, Visitor's Center (see Figure 5.4). The safety and security of design solutions for the project are based on principles applied from the National Capital Planning Commission report *Designing for Security in the Nation's Capital.* This case study provides designers with an excellent overview of design considerations appropriate to the integration of safety and security solutions within any historical building, such as:

- Improved evacuation procedures and protocols, and refined plans for evacuating the building.
- Improved security systems aesthetically appropriate for location.
- Improved egress and circulation of people, especially for visitors unfamiliar with evacuation routes and procedures.
- Reduced vehicular access to the exterior of the Capitol. (Remote vehicle screening and underground access to a loading dock to avoid cutting the landscape to the ground while enhancing security).
- Maintained having multiple sets of building and system plans readily accessible in multiple secure locations, as well as off-site locations for plans.
- Defined different needs for different types of situations. A chemical-biological attack requires a different response than other types of threat.
- Emergency plans are available for relocations and responses depending upon the situation being faced. Computer-Aided Design (CAD) data was used as an essential tool and useful for a great many purposes—such as providing mechanical drawings, creating emergency evacuation procedure plans, and for **hazmat** (hazardous material) planning. CAD is a powerful tool, but the world operates on 11 by 17-inch drawings during a crisis. The Capitol Visitor Center now has 11 by 17-inch bound and numbered sets available and regularly updated.

- Use of a relatively new technology, a laser scan, accurate within two millimeters as it scans the exterior façade of a structure, throughout the project. This provided a historic record that will be useful in years to come and provides important building documentation.

Addressing Security Expert Panel

In 2006, at The Preserve America Summit, a task-force was developed entitled, *The Addressing Security Expert Panel,* that consisted of a 14-member multidisciplinary team of design, security, and preservation professionals, assigned to collaborate on developing program and policy recommendations answering the principal question: How can we more effectively balance security concerns with the preservation and interpretation of historic properties?

The Addressing Security Expert Panel provided the following statement to those involved with providing security design solutions within historic settings, "For security interventions in a historic setting, project planners must balance the historical and architectural character and integrity of a property with the use of the property, the identification and analysis of risk, and possible design and engineering solutions. Multi-disciplinary project teams and reviewers are best able to create security interventions that preserve the public's use and enjoyment of a historic resource for its intended or designed purpose" (Preserve American Summit, 2006).

It is important for the design professional to provide sensitive security design measures that preserve the visual and physical access to publicly accessible landscapes and sites, and provides continued freedom of movement through a building's approaches and significant interior public spaces. The Addressing Security Expert Panel recommends the following in its Executive Summary on security:

5.4 The proposed Visitor's Center in Washington, DC, suggests good options for physical design elements to ensure a secure environment.

1. *Keep public historic properties open to the public.* Design and implement security measures for a property of historic significance that preserves its integrity and continues to provide public access in a manner consistent with the property's historic purpose and current use. Respect the character and visibility of a historic public property and the importance of its story.

   For all historic properties, preservation of integrity is of vital importance. The designation of historic public properties recognizes that these places are significant and should be an active and accessible part of culture and society. The consideration of new physical security designs and their implementation must recognize existing conditions, programs, building context, and presence, all of which contribute to a property's significance and all of which can be affected by the need for increased levels of security. Security measures must provide for, and enhance wherever possible, public access.
2. *Develop risk assessment methods appropriate for historic and archaeological properties.* Develop an All-Hazards risk assessment methodology that recognizes the special challenge of protecting historic and archeological properties from natural hazards and man-made threats. As historic and archeological properties are unique because they represent our cultural heritage, they are at the same time, living places fulfilling contemporary purposes. Property owners, designers, architects, security experts, and community groups should collaborate to reduce exposure to natural hazards and man-made threats while preserving historic integrity.

   Security planning should be coordinated with other community planning issues and begin with a comprehensive security risk analysis and threat assessment.

   An **All-Hazards approach** encompasses natural hazards and man-made threats (criminal, workplace violence, technological accident, terrorism) while dealing with hazards in a more comprehensive manner.

   All-Hazards risk assessment for historic and archaeological properties is not currently a defined process in codes or standards. Code and standard writers and administration organizations must collaborate to develop All-Hazards risk assessment methods for historic and archaeological properties. These assessments must recognize the need for the development of an educational and outreach program that teaches practicing professionals, students, the public, and standards officials how to apply risk assessment and management-based decisions to historic properties.
3. *Incorporate security-related provisions into national building codes.* The Council recommends a review of existing security principles and technical facilities standards for developing security-related provisions for new construction, existing buildings, and historic properties to be incorporated into

national building codes. This review should include provisions to address architectural, operational, structural, mechanical, electrical, plumbing, and landscape design requirements for historic properties.

Because there are currently no nationally recognized codes for new or existing buildings that specifically addresses security issues, the Council recommends that such national standards should be developed first, with special provisions applicable to historic buildings developed subsequently. Federal agencies should work cooperatively to evaluate existing building codes and standards and how they address historic properties, identify consistencies/inconsistencies, and develop a coordinated solution, while understanding that as historic properties, risk and building use vary, therefore the solutions must vary accordingly.

4. *Design matters—sensitive security solutions must be selected to protect the property's historic integrity.* Historic buildings and sites must meet a high standard to be determined significant and worthy of protection, including the qualities of their architecture and setting, their importance to historical events and people, and the information they embody about our past. The design and placement of necessary security interventions must be held to the same high standard. Multidisciplinary design teams, including; interior designers, architects, landscape architects, engineers, community planners, archaeologists, historians, and security experts should be selected for their experience and expertise, ability to collaborate, talent, and passion for creating lasting designs that meet the security requirements and yet are compatible with a historic setting.

Designers must strive to go beyond **prescriptive solutions** in order to find creative, historically, and aesthetically appropriate solutions suitable to the individual historic property that do not diminish or compromise its purpose or architectural character. Throughout the design process, the collaborative team, including property owners, interior designers, architects, landscape architects, engineers, archaeologists, historians, security experts, and community groups must realize that security concerns should not outweigh historic significance, but must be addressed collectively and sensibly.

General Services Administration's Design Excellence Program

In addition to the GSA First Impression Program and the recommendations provided by the Addressing Security Expert Panel, as previously discussed, interior designers will also find the GSA's Design Excellence Program a valuable resource when faced with the challenge of balancing security issues within historic properties. Selected recommendations from the Design Excellence Program include:

5.5

Ellis Island manages to preserve the aestheticism of the site, while keeping it safe for visitors.

- Preservation of the aesthetic sensibility and historic character of the resource (see Figure 5.5)
- Security measures that protect all aspects of the property's historic integrity, design, materials, workmanship, setting, feeling, association, and location
- Public access to significant interior spaces such as lobbies, main corridors, and principal and ceremonial rooms
- Sensitive security design measures that preserve visual and physical access to publicly accessible landscapes and sites, and provide freedom of movement through a building's approaches and significant interior public spaces
- Uninterrupted visual/physical access to publicly accessible landscapes and sites
- Continued freedom of movement through a building's setting and approaches
- Minimization of the effect of perimeter security for both pedestrians and motorists on freedom of movement in public areas

The GSA's program serves as an excellent model for both process and results when faced with the challenge of integrating safety and security design solutions within historic settings. Additional resources for the design professional include: the United States *Secretary of the Interior's Standards for Rehabilitation,* which serves as the current authoritative source for the review of security design proposals at historic properties; the Department of Defense's *Unified Facilities Criteria for Minimum Antiterrorism Standards for Buildings;* and the *National Capital Planning Commission's Security Plan,* all providing useful examples of how to balance security issues within historic properties.

FYI: An Architect's Perspective. "Change is inevitable. If we are to design changes to improve the physical security of historic buildings, we will have to accept the fact that the altered building will not be a true restoration back to a specific period or style. This is NOT a bad thing; nor should we be afraid of it. Change is inevitable, but with historic structures, changes should be very carefully managed."

—Bob Loversidge, Jr., FAIA

The Secretary of the Interior's Ten Standards for Historic Rehabilitation

An additional resource for the design professional involved in safety and security concerns within historic settings is the *Secretary of the Interior's Standards and Guidelines for Federal Agency Historic Preservation Programs* (36 CFR 67). Even though these standards do not address safety and security design issues specifically, they do provide an overall appreciation for the philosophy of design and construction when working with historical structures. These standards pertain to historic buildings of all materials, construction types, sizes, and occupancies, and encompass both the exterior and the interior, related landscape features, and the overall built environment such as attached, adjacent, or related construction. (See Figure 5.6).

The GSA's 10 Standards for Historic Rehabilitation are:

1. A property shall be used for its historic purpose or be placed in a new use that requires minimal change to the defining characteristics of the building and its site and environment.
2. The historic character of a property shall be retained and preserved. The removal of historic materials or alteration of features and spaces that characterize a property shall be avoided.
3. Each property shall be recognized as a physical record of its time, place, and use. Changes that create a false sense of historical development, such as adding conjectural features or architectural elements from other buildings, shall not be undertaken.
4. Most properties change over time; those changes that have acquired historic significance in their own right shall be retained and preserved.
5. Distinctive features, finishes, and construction techniques or examples of craftsmanship that characterize a property shall be preserved.
6. Deteriorated historic features shall be repaired rather than replaced. Where the severity of deterioration requires replacement of a distinctive feature, the new feature shall match the old in design, color, texture, and other visual qualities and, where possible, materials. Replacement of missing features shall be substantiated by documentary, physical, or pictorial evidence.

5.6 When restoring a historical site, it is important to respect the historical integrity of the built environment..

7. Chemical or physical treatments, such as sandblasting, which can cause damage to historic materials, shall not be used. The surface cleaning of structures, if appropriate, shall be undertaken using the gentlest means possible.
8. Significant archeological resources affected by a project shall be protected and preserved. If such resources must be disturbed, mitigation measures shall be undertaken.
9. New additions, exterior alterations, or related new construction shall not destroy historic materials that characterize the property. The new work shall be differentiated from the old and shall be compatible with the massing, size, scale, and architectural features to protect the historic integrity of the property and its environment.
10. New additions and adjacent or related new construction shall be undertaken in such a manner that if removed in the future, the essential form and integrity of the historic property and its environment would be unimpaired.

CONDUCTING A SECURITY ASSESSMENT WITHIN HISTORIC SETTINGS

For a number of reasons, the issues in balancing public safety and protection of property are different for historic places than for other properties. As historic buildings and landmarks are symbols of a unique way of life, such symbols are targets for anyone who wants to destroy the values they stand for. As designers, we must be concerned for the safety of visitors at historic places who at the moment of a disaster are caught in an unfamiliar environment and often far from home. Finding the balance of protecting those places identified with a society's heritage, while protecting visitors and workers, is one challenge faced by the design professional.

Is your historic property prepared for a disaster? "Probably not" was the conclusion by many who attended the 2002 national conferences on *Balancing Public Safety and Protection of Historic Places* by the Federal Preservation Institute, a program of the National Park Service in the United States. This conference examined the broad range of issues regarding protection at historic places and heard from people in the historic preservation fields, engineers, security experts, public officials, designers, architects, and community planners about the concerns of the public, administrators, and preservationists of historic places and related collections.

Information exchanged and points of view shared throughout this 2002 conference revealed that the impact of 9/11, assassinations in public buildings, and the occurrence of natural disasters illustrated that even places with an emergency plan often failed to practice it, failed to coordinate it with local disaster offices, and failed to have an off-site copy with information about the historic site and its contents. It became evident that securing people and property at historic places must be part of the preservation agenda for the twenty-first century.

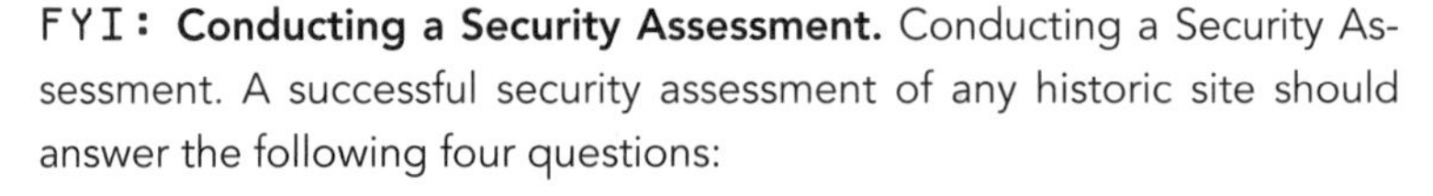

FYI: **Conducting a Security Assessment.** Conducting a Security Assessment. A successful security assessment of any historic site should answer the following four questions:

- What are the assets (people, places, information, and property) that require security protection?
- What are the criminal or other threats (street crimes, acts of violence, terrorism, or sabotage) against which the assets must be protected?
- What are the vulnerabilities of the assets to the threats (for example, if violence is a threat, can uncontrolled people enter the historical setting unchallenged)?
- What are the countermeasures required to diminish the threat?

When focusing on the historic preservation agenda in regards to issues of safety and security within historic structures, the Federal Preservation Institute and the Advisory Council on Historic Preservation, teamed in 2002 to create the five *Principles for Development of Security Measures for Historic Places.* These principles are a guide for planning and response to disasters as they affect historic settings. The five principles grew from the premise that though the protection of human life is paramount, is not enough when dealing with historic structures. The places that embody a society's history, values, and ideals must be protected. The overall spirit of the principles is that heritage protection is in the public interest and that safety and security should not be used as an excuse for insensitivity to those values or for failure to consider feasible ways to safeguard visitors at historic places. The five Principles for Development of Security Measures for Historic Places, as prepared by the Advisory Council on Historic Preservation and the Federal Preservation Institute, include:

1. *National Park Service Heritage Preservation is in the public interest.* While protection of human life is paramount, planners and public officials should respect, consider, and protect heritage values, which are fundamental to preserving the American way of life. "Safety" and "security" should not be used as an excuse or pretext for poor planning, insensitivity to heritage values, or failure to consider alternatives if they are feasible in safeguarding the public at historic places.
2. *Balancing public safety and heritage protection is an evolving field.* Security information, methods, and technologies, particularly for historic places, are changing and improving daily. Base security solutions upon the appropriate risk assessment. Design preparedness upon an understanding of effects of disasters on people and places. When making decisions, emphasize commonsense measures and consider changes in technology, professional practice, and other relevant factors.
3. *Accurate information about heritage resources is fundamental to effective preparedness plans.* Ensure complete survey information and resource documentation in order to improve preparedness and response for natural or man-made disasters. Place redundant key records and documentation in several on- and off-site locations. Develop a systematic means for factoring risk assessment into decisions on inventory and documentation priorities at the regional, state, or local levels. Remember that complete site mapping is important for post-disaster orientation and for identification of fragile archeological sites.
4. *Sensitive preservation of historic values is integrated into all actions.* Plan and execute disaster preparedness and security measures in or adjacent to historic areas in as sensitive and design-conscious a manner as possible. Make physical modifications—including fencing, bollards, and other landscape elements—compatible with significant historic features to the maximum extent feasible. Do not permit temporary or interim installations for security and related purposes to become permanent fixtures of the property or its

surroundings. Avoid compounding disaster damage by poorly designed response and clean-up efforts that may further damage historic and archeological sites and fragile landscapes.

5. *Consultation with others during planning and implementation is necessary and important.* Plan disaster preparedness and security measures in consultation with emergency organizations and other concerned parties, not in a vacuum. Determine how much insformation can be made public and how much can be shared with other public officials and review authorities. Err on the side of releasing information as long as that release would not jeopardize public safety or national security. Strike an appropriate balance among timeliness, security, and allowing for reasonable public processes.

These principles recognize that a best practice for both public safety and heritage protection is an evolving field. As risk assessments become more sophisticated and potential disaster impacts more clearly identified, common sense, along with the use of technology, will allow us to recognize the ineffectiveness of such practices as using moveable concrete barriers and placing guards inside, rather than outside, buildings.

It is essential for the design professional to note the importance of the documentation of heritage resources as highlighted in these five principles. Historic places must have complete information about their landscape, archaeological sites, buildings, structures, and collections, or have copies of that documentation at off-site locations. This is still a rare occurrence. Complete survey information and resource documentation needs to be identified to improve preparedness and response plans within historic settings. For example, fire and water, even in small amounts, can be a disaster from which recovery could be impossible without good documentation. At the same time, mitigation measures must take into consideration the historic values of places and not desecrate them through insensitively designed physical modifications. When temporary and interim installations for security, such as the many that were put in place following 9/11, are no longer effective against the intended risk, they should be removed and not become permanent fixtures of an historic property.

The principles also address the need for disaster preparedness. Lessons learned from past disasters emphasize the reliance on common sense, assessment of the values inherent in the property and collections, knowledge of technological advances, and coordination with neighbors and communities. As Christie McAvoy, an expert in developing disaster plans for historic places in Los Angeles, states, "Learn from the Boy Scouts, be prepared!" She recommends the following: (1) identify and assess the risks to your historic property and identify your security objectives and priorities; (2) document your collections, archives, libraries, interior decorations, and architectural and structural elements; and (3) investigate and implement technologies and experiences that save lives and protect historic properties from different types of threats (Historic Resources Group, 2005).

John H. Stubbs, Vice President of the World Monuments Fund, puts the security discussion into historic and international perspective by noting, "Through time, history is replete with examples of threats to historic structures as well as attempts to preserve or document endangered sites. Human beings have always found intrinsic value in places, shelters, and objects defined as cultural heritage. We have made efforts to protect those valued places from man-made disasters, such as wars and physical attacks, and from natural disasters, such as floods. Throughout history, surviving cultures have risen after disasters to rebuild those places that symbolize themselves. Heritage destruction is an integral part of war, and today heritage protection should be an integral part of homeland security." Stubbs concludes that heritage preservation faces new challenges undreamed of a few years ago. "Could it be," he asks, "that the next cycle in American preservation has been defined by the challenges posed to the United Sates after September 11th?" (World Monuments Fund, 2006).

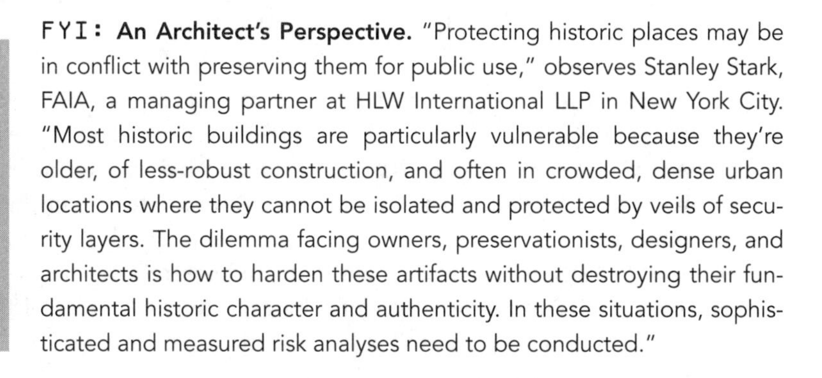

FYI: An Architect's Perspective. "Protecting historic places may be in conflict with preserving them for public use," observes Stanley Stark, FAIA, a managing partner at HLW International LLP in New York City. "Most historic buildings are particularly vulnerable because they're older, of less-robust construction, and often in crowded, dense urban locations where they cannot be isolated and protected by veils of security layers. The dilemma facing owners, preservationists, designers, and architects is how to harden these artifacts without destroying their fundamental historic character and authenticity. In these situations, sophisticated and measured risk analyses need to be conducted."

Designers must be aware that within historic settings there is no single, one-size-fits-all, security solution that applies to every facility of significance and that security planning is a multidisciplinary, team effort that requires collaboration. Historic property owners who are responsible for capital construction, annual operations, and insurance costs should work in partnership with architects, designers, engineers, landscape architects, preservationists, security personnel, and others to develop transparent security solutions, along with required visible security elements, as needed, depending on potential threats and vulnerabilities as identified in the risk assessment process.

These threats can include acts of terrorism (such as blasts and biohazards), natural disasters (from hurricanes and tornadoes to floods and wildfires), and regional crime. Each facility has a unique set of circumstances that should be addressed in the threat assessment and risk analysis, even for similar building types in different locations. The factors to be considered in the risk assessment of historic settings typically include: location, owner, occupancies, tenants, adjacent uses, regional assets that may be at risk, and various other site-specific factors. Age of the facility, replacement value, cultural importance, construction materials, and code compliance are additional criteria to be considered.

CPTED PRINCIPLES AND HISTORIC STRUCTURES

How can the key elements of Crime Prevention through Environmental Design (CPTED) be applied to historical settings? As previously discussed, the three key elements of CPTED include:

1. *Natural surveillance.* Keep an eye on the whole environment without taking extraordinary measures to do so. Within historical settings, typical obstacles to natural surveillance include solid walls and lack of windows that provide visibility to other areas of the building. Pruning shrubbery is one step that can be taken to improve the natural surveillance of historic grounds.
2. *Natural access control.* Determine who can or cannot enter a facility. Within historical settings, the addition of information desks, ticketing areas, or guests services serve as control areas that determine who is entering or exiting a facility, while maintaining the architectural integrity of the built environment.
3. *Territoriality.* Establish recognized authority and control over the environment, along with cultivating a sense of belonging. As cited earlier, historical considerations provide a controlled entry with visible authority, while remaining welcoming to employees and visitors.

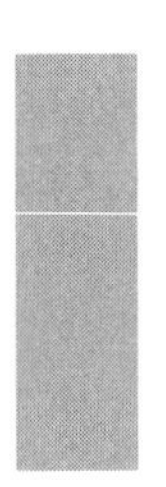

FYI: **An Architect's Perspective.** "The new security constraints on Federal building are opportunities for enriching architecture. Once you understand the limitations, they should be cause for invention and analysis that allows you to push beyond your preconceptions. The security issues should allow you to invent a vocabulary that not only solves the problem, but also creates an appropriate architectural image."

—Charles Gwathmey, FAIA

5.7 Street barriers can sometimes be unattractive, impede pedestrian traffic, and pollute the urban landscape.

A Historical Case Study

The threat of terrorism, underscored by the events of 9/11, made security a necessary feature of life in the nation's capital. Understandably, the federal government's initial response to threats adversely affected Washington's historic urban design and streetscape (see Figure 5.7). Street closures increased traffic congestion; disrupted local business activities; and marred the beauty and historic design of the nation's capital with hastily erected jersey barriers, concrete planters, and guard huts that surrounded buildings and lined the streets.

In 2001, to address the challenge of increased security, while maintaining the historical and architectural significance of the city, the National Capital Planning Commission (NCPC) formed an Interagency Security Task Force to identify permanent, comprehensive solutions to the problem. The result was the release of the *Designing for Security in the Nation's Capital,* a report that makes recommendations for improving security and urban design in the monumental core of Washington, DC. In addition, a more comprehensive security plan was introduced in 2002, the *National Capital Urban Design and Security Plan,* that has led the nation in exploring innovative urban design solutions to meet heightened security requirements. (See Figure 5.8.)

In 2004, the NCPC released an addendum to the 2002 plan providing an update on the status of several major projects, including the redesign of Pennsylvania Avenue in front of the White House and a new security scheme for the Washington Monument. Recently, the NCPC developed a complementary brochure, *Designing and Testing Perimeter Security Elements,* which provides guidance to designers, architects, security professionals, and building managers on applying the latest creative perimeter security solutions and effectively testing these technologies.

The redesign of Pennsylvania Avenue in front of the White House was a primary focus area of the NCPC overall plan. Due to world events that may pose security threats, such as the Oklahoma City bombing of 1995, Pennsylvania Avenue was closed to vehicles and undermining the symbolism of the President's house. Based on legitimate security considerations, the task force agreed that this portion of the street should remain closed to vehicular traffic, but recommended that the situation be reassessed should there be vast improvements in security technology. To reverse the effects of the street closure, the task force called for doing away with barricades and creating a new, distinguished, pedestrian-oriented public space that respects the historic integrity of the street.

The Commission invited four of the country's top landscape architecture firms to submit concepts for creating a pedestrian-oriented public space on Pennsylvania Avenue in front of the White House. Michael Van Valkenburgh Associates, Inc., was selected to create this significant precinct. In November 2004, Pennsylvania Avenue was reopened as a dignified new civic space featuring pedestrian-friendly amenities and furnishings. The redesign of America's main street has transformed the avenue from one cluttered with ad-hoc security measures to a beautiful civic area befitting one of the nation's most prominent and visited destinations. (See Figure 5.9.)

Another recently completed project brings attractive security solutions to one of Washington's most iconic structures—the Washington Monument (see Figure 5.10). Previously surrounded by a ring of jersey barriers, the monument grounds had become an eyesore along the National Mall. The new security scheme features new pedestrian pathways, sunken seating walls, upgraded lighting, granite benches, and hundreds of new trees to complement the monument's landscape setting. As evidenced by the security improvements at these two symbolic locations, NCPC's *National Capital Urban Design and Security Plan* is transforming the way that federal government secures its land and buildings in the nation's capital through continued improvements in security planning and design.

5.8

The use of bollards could be an attractive design solution that meets security needs.

5.9

The redesign to Pennsylvania Avenue in Washington, DC, in 2005 included an improvement to its look and security features.

5.10

The federal government continues to improve security and design in Washington, DC, including changes to the surrounding landscape of the Washington Monument.

SECURITY TECHNOLOGY WITHIN HISTORIC SETTINGS

"People stay away from historic buildings because they're afraid of making a mistake," says Bob Rindahl of Arrowhead Security Systems, Inc., in Duluth, Minnesota. "They think they will ruin the old building during the installation. But with wireless systems you only have to drill little holes, which do very little damage. You're not going to ruin anybody's century-old oak door jambs using wireless transmitters as a security measure (CES, 2007)."

The integration of security technology into historic settings is one of the many challenges faced by the design professional involved in this important and rewarding type of design practice. As previously stated in the Principles of Development of Security Measures for Historic Places, security information as it relates to historic settings is evolving and the methods and technologies are changing and improving daily.

An example of change can be seen in the security policies involving public access to the Statue of Liberty from the time of its closure in 2001, prior to its full reopening in 2004. Following the closure of the statue after the events of 9/11, and its subsequent reopening, the public had limited access, with visitors only allowed to access Liberty and Ellis Islands without touring the interior spaces. Visitors were also subject to a manual security screening process before boarding the ferries to the islands. Beginning in 2004, security measures were put in place that now allow anyone wanting to go to the interior spaces within the statue to do so through a second screening once they reach Liberty Island. To speed up the screening process for the many hundreds of thousands of visitors each year, backpacks, purses, and other small parcels are not allowed inside the statue. Visible signage and park rangers positioned at the entrance to the security screening area inform visitors that these items are not permitted inside the monument.

The use of security technology at historic settings is evident in the solution provided to offer a safe place for visitors to store their belongings. Visitors now store their personal items in private lockers for a minimal fee. The locker, accessed with the touch of a thumb through the use of biometric fingerprint technology, virtually eliminates the opportunity for theft, limits the owners' liability, and provides assurance that the historical setting is as safe and secure as humanly possible, all without changing the experience of visiting this icon of liberty and freedom.

ALLIED PROFESSIONS

As a member of the design team, when planning for historic settings, the interior design professional must appreciate the basic safety and security solutions undertaken by allied design professionals, such as architects (AIA) and landscape architects (ASLA). As in any safety and security–minded project, there are numerous architectural and landscape architectural design considerations that are implemented to mitigate the effects of a bombing, shootings, or acts violence. These concerns though are addressed differently when they occur at historic places, sites, or landmarks. It is the architectural and landscape architectural team member who will be addressing the building access security and perimeter security and solutions respectively, that create the initial layer of safety for historic settings.

The American Society of Landscape Architects (ASLA) became active immediately following the events of 9/11 in developing a *Security Design Coalition,* which defined a set of principles for best practices in landscape architecture and security design. The American Institute of Architects (AIA) has prepared materials on security, particularly in the areas of new building design and construction. A few engineers and architects have shown how security technologies can be placed unobtrusively in historic buildings. However, to date, discussions on security design, infrastructure protection, and similar topics have made little mention of how new security procedures and techniques can be integrated in such a manner that they do not reduce the accessibility—and the democratic symbolism—of historic places.

Detailed information about the positive measures undertaken by these allied professions in regards to historic settings, and related security design considerations, can be found for the AIA at www.aia.org, and for the ASLA at www.asla.org. In order to familiarize the interior designer with considerations made by the architectural and landscape architectural professions in safety and security solutions for historic settings. Selected examples are provided in the next sections.

Best Practices—Architecture

- Windows and structural members of buildings are made secure without altering the historic appearance.
- Use of existing walls and incorporation of upgraded permanent elements in a manner that does not detract from the appearance of the structure.
- Replacement of unsightly and inappropriate temporary features with those that fulfill security needs in an aesthetically sensitive way.
- Use of blast analysis and studies of the impacts of trucks loaded with explosives upon structures.
- Use of the array of technical security options provided by alarm systems and monitoring devices, such as CCTV.

Best Practices—Landscape Architecture

- Design landscaping and tree placement to eliminate roof access.
- Shrubs, trees and landscape features should not impede visual surveillance on the historic site.
- Increase the perimeter around historic buildings and structures.

- Control access to grounds.
- Elements: bollards, stone-clad planters, guardhouses, vehicular barriers, lift gates, and the addition of technological systems including monitoring and communications devices. These elements will incorporate the best available technology and materials to complement the existing landscape design.

CONCLUSION

The interior design professional should take into consideration that the historical and architectural character and integrity of a property must be retained, and that the risk of public use must be balanced with the value of the property and possible design solutions. Moreover, designers should note that well-planned security solutions will preserve the public's use and enjoyment of an historic resource for its intended or designed purpose. Designers must go beyond prescriptive solutions to find appropriate resolutions specific to the property and site that do not diminish its design functionality or architectural character. Within the United States, the Advisory Council on Historic Preservation and the National Park Service can provide the leadership and technical guidance to balance security requirements and public access to historic properties.

Designers play an important role in ensuring that all citizens continue to experience their authentic heritage in a secure environment. Potential threats of terrorism, natural disasters, man-made hazards, and limited budgets must be balanced against the desire for public access and a gracious and welcoming ambiance, while dealing with issues of security and protection within historic settings. The prospect of closing historic resources to the public because they may be terrorist targets, or at risk in any way, is a decision that few property owners want to make, nor is it one that most Americans want to accept.

Currently, the preservation community is facing several complicated challenges that go to the heart of operating, maintaining, and celebrating historic resources. Designers, with an understanding of and sensibility to historic settings can contribute greatly to the built environment by assessing potential risks; recommending the appropriate safety and security design solutions, with the goal of enhancing public safety and the quality of daily life; and preserving and protecting historic resources. The design profession can, and must, play a vital leadership role by understanding the unique needs of historic resources within communities and by creating appropriate security design responses in the spirit and intent of preservation of a society's historic settings.

KEY CONCEPTS

- Historic public places and buildings are preserved precisely because they inspire, educate, and uplift. Moreover, historic landscapes, approaches and entrances, and significant interior spaces contribute greatly to the public's experience and appreciation of a society.
- The National Trust for Historic Preservation is a valuable resource to the design professional regardless of a building's historical classification.
- Of importance to the design professional is the 1998, Government Services Administration's (GSA) First Impressions Program, a federal initiative to improve the architectural integrity of visitor and tenant gateways into federal buildings.
- The Secretary of the Interior's Standards for the Treatment of Historic Properties provides standards for four distinct approaches to the treatment of historic properties: preservation, restoration, rehabilitation, and reconstruction.
- The Secretary of the Interior's 10 Standards for Historic Rehabilitation, although not addressing safety and security design issues specifically, provide an overall appreciation for the philosophy of design and construction when working with historical structures.
- Conducting a security assessment within historic settings requires that designers concern themselves with the safety of visitors at historic places, who at the moment of a disaster are caught in an unfamiliar environment and often far from home.
- Within the United States, Congress established the National Historic Preservation Act (NHPA) in 1966, which mandates the active use of historic buildings for public benefit and to preserve national heritage. Cultural resources, as identified in the National Register for Historic Places, include buildings, archeological sites, structures, objects, and historic districts.
- The principles of Crime Prevention through Environmental Design (CPTED), and its key elements of natural surveillance, natural access control, and territoriality are applied to historical settings.
- The integration of security technology into historic settings is one of the many challenges faced by the design professional as security information as it relates to historic settings is evolving, although its methods and technologies are changing and improving daily.
- As a member of the design team, when planning for historic settings, the interior design professional must appreciate the basic safety and security solutions undertaken by allied design professionals, such as architects (AIA) and landscape architects (ASLA).

ASSIGNMENTS

1. Evaluate the design objective and the many challenges faced in providing security for historic facilities, whether they are public or private.
2. Discuss ideas about how to create a balance between openness and free access within historic settings, while satisfying security requirements.
3. Provide examples of transparent security design and its integration into historical interiors.
4. Provide a brief review of the varied types of historical design considerations as defined by the National Trust for Historic Preservation, the General Services Administration, and the Department of Interior's Standards for Rehabilitation.
5. List safety and security codes and regulations and their application within historical settings.
6. Identity aspects of security risk assessments as related to historic interiors.
7. Review the principals of Crime Prevention through Environmental Design (CPTED) and the relationship to the security of historic interiors and national landmarks.
8. Discuss the role of the interior designer, architect, landscape architect, facility manager, and building owner as they relate to the design of safe and secure historic settings.
9. Discuss the complex security considerations of the twenty-first century and their role within historic settings.

ACTIVITIES

1. Journaling activity: Respond in written and graphic format. Visit local and/or regional setting of historical significance to observe existing visible security measures and/or procedures. Share your experiences while generating a list; look for patterns and discuss issues within these environments deemed both successful and non-successful.
2. Visit a historical site that has implemented obvious security control measures with a required exercise in behavioral mapping.
3. Research Web sites related to historical restoration and preservation and note any related security information. Share your research results, generate a list, and look for patterns of security solutions and/or recommendations. Discuss issues within these environments toward the development of a basic programming document.
4. Create a project that requires, through site visit or photo research, the integration of security solutions within a historical setting and/or interior.
5. Collect current information related to events and policies regarding historical settings and analyze the information based on the recommendation of the National Trust for Historic Preservation (or a similar organization).

6

SECURITY IN HEALTH-CARE ENVIRONMENTS

The modern concept of disease is no longer narrowly pathogenic; instead, every disease is seen as having complex origins and effects. . . . This means that health promotion must be an integral part of facility design. The Academy is recognizing people and projects that demonstrate how the built environment can achieve this critical dimension

—Alan Dilani, Ph.D., director, The International Academy for Design and Health, 2007

OBJECTIVES

- Understand the human need for safety and security as applied in health-care settings
- Integrate design security needs in health-care settings from program to schematic design
- Reinforce an understanding of the security concerns of the twenty-first century and their impact on and interdependence within the design and management of the built environment
- Understand the complexity of health-care operations and the need for systematic integration

Healing and care are compromised when those facilities designated for the protection and enhancement of health are faced with security breaches that undermine the foundation of what a health-care facility symbolizes and aims to provide. For example, a Security Management Online 2003 report states that "a gunman entered a San Diego hospital emergency room and started shooting indiscriminately, killing two and wounding two. A man dressed in a security uniform walked into an Atlanta hospital emergency room, where he shot four people and then committed suicide. These types of incidents are weekly occurrences in emergency departments in the United States. In fact, the emergency room chief at San Francisco General reports that threats from angry patients and/or visitors occur daily, and violence breaks out at least once a week." (Security Management Online, 2003)

On July 15, 2005, a state-of-the-art infant protection system thwarted an infant abduction from Presbyterian Hospital in Charlotte, North Carolina. An infant protection system sounded an audible alarm when a baby was snatched from the hospital nursery. The high-tech "Hugs" infant protection system is part of an elaborate security management program designed to protect the hospital's patients, visitors, and staff. (Aldridge & Wells, 2005). The definition of "public access" means that all people who enter a hospital seeking treatment, or to visit a loved one, have the right of access, movement, and function. Hospitals are targets because they are open to the public 24 hours a day, seven days a week. These public access facilities have been conditioned over the years to allow scores of people from all walks of life to enter their institutions unchallenged, day or night.

CONTEXT AND EXPERIENCE

Conceptually, one would expect a health-care facility to be a place of healing for the body, for the mind, and for the spirit. In the past, health-care facilities were predominantly viewed as sacred places, and as such, any thought of encroaching on their sense of safety and security would not have been considered. This, however, is regrettably the exception, not the norm. One only has to scan the newspapers or television channels to find evidence of the ill effects of outdated, unsafe, and badly integrated facilities. One of those exceptions is a facility that has emerged literally from the ashes. Nowhere in the world do the elements of health care, green building, and human restoration intersect more vividly to create hope than two miles away from the world's worst industrial chemical accident.

The Sambhavna Clinic provides medical care to survivors of the chemical leak that occurred in Bhopal, India, in 1984. *Sambhavna* is a Sanskrit/Hindi word that means "possibility." The clinic was founded in 1996 in response to the overwhelming medical need in the area; in 2007, a new clinic facility was unveiled. From the start, the building was designed with one goal in mind: to be a place of healing, where people could come to receive care and also benefit from the space, tranquility, and natural vegetation. Sambhavna Clinic was built using green building and design techniques similar to those embodied in *The Green Guide for Health Care,* and today, the clinic stands as a powerful symbol for a new "architecture of healing" (Stephens, 2006). In its symbolism, and in its actual offering of a comprehensive integrated system of care, the Sambhavna Clinic responds to security issues in the same seamless fashion as it does to the culture it's situated within.

Health care encompasses hospitals, hospices, clinics, physicians' surgeries, and rehab facilities. Health-care facilities in general present a unique security environment. Those are the environments that are symbolically and physically meant to be open to all individuals who are in need of, or seek, health care. In such facilities we anticipate a place where causes of pain and illness are addressed in a clean, healing, and safe environment. Just as the design of a health-care facility reflects its philosophy of care, so does the way security is addressed in that facility. However, from the few examples listed earlier one can see that balancing a strong security approach and facilitating a non-invasive, comfortable, manageable level of openness for patients, visitors, and staff is the challenge. The complexity of a health-care setting and its challenging security stems from the realities of what a hospital or health-care facility is, and includes:

- The variety of people who make up the typical hospital environment: patients, staff, vendors, physicians, visitors, and even their enemies.
- Realities of the place: Many different rooms and spaces, high-value equipment, accessibility to drugs, many entrances, and ease-of-movement around the building and premises.
- Management and autonomy: An open feeling, many managers, politics, and autonomous physicians.
- Daily routines and realities: Life-threatening situations, specialist facilities and equipment, access to medicines and drugs, and areas where emotions run high.

The health-care facility conveys a message to patients, visitors, volunteers, vendors, and staff. The facility also communicates an overabundance of clues about the organization and the medical care being provided there. According to Robert Carr, "The clues start at the approach to the facility, the drop-off area, the parking lots, and the street signs. Ideally, that message is one that conveys welcoming, caring, comfort, compassion, and commitment to patient well-being and safety, where stress is relieved, refuge is provided, respect is reciprocated, competence is symbolized, way-finding is facilitated, and families are accommodated" (2007). Providing a consistent message from the exterior and all throughout the interior of the facility regarding quality, access, safety, and security within the environment is central to creating and managing responsive proactive design solutions.

The design of the facility also influences employee service attitudes and behaviors. Finishes, signage, and artwork must be carefully selected, well-coordinated, and integrated in a manner that does not overwhelm an employee physically or psychologically, or detract their attention from important environmental information such as possible circulation hazards (See Figure 6.1). "Security can include balance with some features apparent to patients/visitors, while conveying a message of safety. Thoughtful design can help ensure the proper first impression is created and sustained" (Carr, 2007). The complexity of health-care settings demands a fresh, layered, appropriate, and manageable approach to security. For a health-care facility to be safe in today's world everyone coming into and going out of the facility has to be identified and the path of circulation controlled. This is essential to prevent unauthorized people from entering a facility to cause harm, which also means controlling egress.

Previously, misunderstanding and strict enforcement of fire codes has prevented hospitals from securing fire doors that lead to the outside. An unsecured fire door, leading to the outside, provides an escape route for anyone that comes into the facility for the purpose of committing a criminal act against it or its users. Newer fire codes and better fire code education are being activated; the new codes will allow fire exits to be locked and alarmed by a time-delay lock and alarm system. This type of "lockdown" capability can prevent unauthorized people from entering or leaving the health-care facility undetected. Other means of maintaining control over egress such as visibility from nurse's stations or other managed areas may be employed. Retrofitting older facilities, specifically older hospitals with characteristic open design is not only very costly, but often creates disastrous consequences related to zone segregation, wayfinding, and usability of the facility.

6.1 Trellis design can create a feeling of openness, without causing a sense of fear or exposure.

Complex functionalities, diversity of user groups, and physical relationships between functions, which determine the configuration of the overall environment and how it is communicated, all contribute to the complexity of security in health-care settings. (See Figure 6.2). At all levels, health-care facilities must respond to the variety of risks and threats in ways that reduce the potential of those risks and mitigate their impact by incorporating physical security, access control, and staff and stakeholder awareness and education.

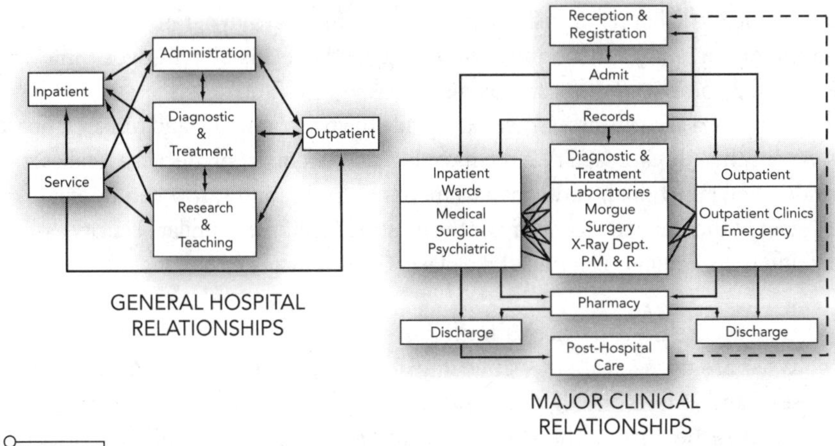

6.2 The configuration and functionalities in the health-care environment affect and contribute to the complexity of security.

VULNERABILITIES AND THREATS

The complexity of health-care operations physically, psychologically, and economically, and the overlapping of private and public zones all contribute to the critical nature of health-care security analyses. Coupled with compliance to the security and safety standards for health-care environments stipulated by the U.S. Department of Health and Human Services—Centers for Medicare and Medicaid Services (CMS) and the Joint Commission on Accreditation of Health-care Organizations (JCAHO), new standards of care, codes, and design philosophies about healing must be integrated to allow for a seamless and comprehensive address of security needs in health-care settings.

When analyzing the potential threats in any environment, but specifically in health-care settings, one must be cognizant of the variety of possible risks associated with function, access, and management of such environments both accidental as well as premeditated. Main threats in health-care environments are chemical/biological/radiological hazards, theft, violent patrons such as gang members or intoxicated patients in emergency departments, threats against patients or staff throughout the facility, and crimes of opportunity, such as those related to access to controlled substances.

Security Assessment and Management Plan

Security is a system concept that requires ongoing training, corroboration, monitoring, and swift attention to problem identification. In an integrated system that is the built environment, the components of the system influence one another, and it is their collective integration that we experience as designed environments. As stated earlier in Chapter 2, risk, threat, and security are dynamic entities which pose the opportunity for modification and growth of this system over time, and the renewed commitment for its sustainability.

Conducting a security assessment alongside the programming and research phase for any new health-care facility is the most logical plan of action because it takes into consideration functional, code, management, aesthetic, and safety conditions from the outset of the project. However, for the existing facilities, a similar security assessment and management plan must take place. Questions posed will include:

- How secure is the particular facility?
- What are the security measures in place that ensure the security of patients, staff, and visitors and that meet national norms, JCAHO, and CMS standards?
- What is the hospital/health-care facility doing to prevent infant abductions and mother/baby mix-ups?
- How well does the facility manage and address emergency department, pharmacy, and pediatric security issues?

According to Jeff Aldridge, President of Security Assessments International and a principal consultant on health-care security, "If you find these questions troubling, you may need to invest in a security assessment" (Aldridge, 2007).

FYI: "The mission of the Joint Commission is to continuously improve the safety and quality of care provided to the public through the provision of health care accreditation and related services that support performance improvement in health care organizations."

—JCAHO, 2007

Each year, health-care providers must meet the requirements of the Joint Commission's National Patient Safety Goals as part of the accreditation process. In 2005, nine goals and sixteen requirements were identified and the compliance assessment results are listed here. "Compliance" means consistent performance of the requirement. When an organization is found to be "noncompliant," it does not mean that the organization is failing to do what is required at all; it means that the organization is not meeting the requirement consistently. The goals, as well as the overall approach, address security of people, place, and information as an integrated system (see Figure 6.3). The nine goals are:

Goal 1: Improve the accuracy of patient identification.
Goal 2: Improve the effectiveness of communication among caregivers.
Goal 3: Improve the safety of using medications.

6.3

A health-care facility must be designed to keep people and information safe and secure.

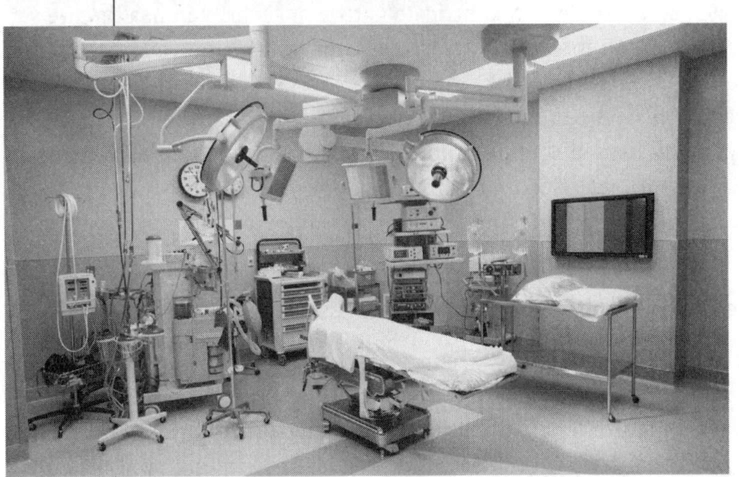

Status Codes

A-Available
B/A-Assigned
D/C-Discharge O
D/L - Likely
D/P-Pending
D/T-Transfer
ES-Cleaning

NS - No Staff
NIS - Not in Svc
PW - Pt Waiting

O-Occupied
OM-Over Matrix
P - Ped

ED		ICU 2nd flr		L&D		NICU	
Rm	Status	Rm	Status	Rm	Status	Rm	Status
1	O	201	O	301	NIS	1	O
2	A	202	O	302	NIS	2	O
3	O	203	O	306	O	3	O
4	O	204	O	307	NIS	4	O
5	O	205	A	308	A	5	O
6	O	206	O	309	O	6	A
7	O	207	O	310	NIS	7	A
8	O	208	O	311	O	8	A
9	O	209	O	312	A	9	A
10	O	210	O	314	O	10	A
11	O	211	O	315	A	11	A
12	O			316	A	12	A
14	O			317	O	14	A
15	O			318	A	15	A
16	O			319	O		
17	A			320	A	**Nursery**	
18	A			321	A		8
19	A			**PACU**			
21	A			303	A		
22	A			304	A		
				305	A		

Mom Baby		4th Floor		Tele - 5th		Surg - 6th		Medical	
Rm	Status	Rm	Status	Rm	Status	Rm	Status	Rm	Status
351	A	401	O	501	O	601	O	701	O
352	A	402	DP	502	O	602	O	702	O
353	NIS	403	O	503	O	603	O	703	O
354	NIS	404	O	504	O	604	O	704	O
355	NIS	405	O	505	A	605	O	705	O
356	NIS	406	O	506	A	606	O	706	O
357	A	407	A	507	O	607	O	707	DP
358	A	417	A	508	A	608	O	708	O
359	A	418	O	509	O	609	O	709	O
360	A	419	O	517	O	610	O	710	O
361	A	421	O	518	A	611	O	711	O
362	A	422	O	519	A	612	O	712	O
363	A	423	O	520	O	614	O	714	O
364	O	424	A	521	O	615	O	715	O
365	A	SITTER		522	DP	616	O	716	O
366	A	1	A	523	O	617	O	717	O
367	O	2	A	524	O	618	O	718	O
368	A	3	A	525	O	619	O	**Peds**	
369	A			526	DP	620	O	719	P
370	A			527	A	621	O	720	A
371	O					622	O	721	P
372	A	**PCU**		**CPC**		623	O	722	A
373	O	408	A	510	A	624	O	723	P
374	A	409	O	514	O	625	O	724	A
375	A	410	NIS	515	O	626	O	725	A
376	O	414	O	516	O	627	O		
377	O	415	O						
378	O	416	O						
379	A								
380	A								
381	A								
382	A								

Updated
10/04/06
09:05

Hall	O
Rack	0

Infusion Center	8
CAH	0

Legend

Available	A
Discharge	D/C
Occupied	O
Med or Ped	

Bed Census

													Tele - 5th				Medical		Total %	
% Open	6	30%	1	9%	10	83%	9	64%	21	75%	7	44%	6	30%	0	0%	0	0%	60	37%
% Reserved	0	0%	0	0%	0	0%	0	0%	0	0%	0	0%	0	0%	0	0%	0	0%	0	0%
% Occupied	14	70%	10	91%	6	38%	5	36%	7	25%	9	56%	14	70%	26	100%	17	100%	103	63%
Number of Beds	20		11		20		14		32		17		20		26		17		173	
Staffing AM	3		5		3		3		3		3		3		4		3		34	
Staffing PM	3		5		3		3		3		3		3		4		3		37	

	PCU		CPC		Peds	
% Open	1	25%	1	25%	4	57%
% Reserved	0	0%	0	0%	0	0%
% Occupied	3	75%	3	75%	3	43%
No. of Beds	5		4		7	
Staffing AM	2		2		3	
Staffing PM	2		2		3	

Legend

Occupied>=80%	87%
>90%	91%
100%	100%

Goal 4: Eliminate wrong-site, wrong-patient, and wrong-procedure surgery.
Goal 5: Improve the safety of using infusion pumps.
Goal 6: Improve the effectiveness of clinical alarm systems.
Goal 7: Reduce the risk of health care-associated infections.
Goal 8: Accurately and completely reconcile medications across the continuum of care.
Goal 9: Reduce the risk of patient harm resulting from falls (The Joint Commission, 2008).

This list is just an example of the intricate nature of security in health-care settings and the need for an integrated, layered system of security. The new JCAHO standards require hospitals to collect information about security deficiencies and provide corrective action to improve the environment of care. Similarly, CMS's "Conditions of Participation" require information gathering from the perspective of managers, directors, and security administrators in addition to medical staff, patients, and the general public. The focus on proactive and corrective action is exciting as it positions design and ongoing evaluation at the forefront.

The Purpose of the Health-care Security Assessment

The purpose of a health-care facility security assessment is to assist in the protection of patients, employees, and visitors by methodically and holistically identifying spatial and organizational strengths and weaknesses in physical protection and security practices. The security assessment analyzes existing protocols, policies, and procedures, in addition to evaluating physical security vulnerabilities and threats. Findings are analyzed and evaluated, and written recommendations are made to control these threats.

All security design and management programs should be developed using the security assessment concept from the broadest perspective possible, including contextual parameters that are grounded in the location, culture, and philosophy of care. A health-care security program should be designed to teach, implement, monitor, assess, and improve components that are part of the health-care facility's existing program, from both a theoretical and a hands-on perspective. The assessment should be designed to identify environmental deficiencies, hazards, and unsafe practices. The security assessment should evaluate JCAHO standards as well as compliance issues that require:

- Hospitals to collect and analyze information to identify safe patient practices and implement changes to reduce the risks
- Changes to be made and evaluated to ensure that expected outcomes are successful
- Programs to be monitored for effectiveness

The hospital-security assessment should evaluate a facility beginning in the parking lot and continuing all the way to the roof. Some of the components that should be considered (related to people, place, and information) are:

- Geographical location (inner-city, suburb, rural)
- Physical design and layout of the health-care campus and surrounding property
- Number of uncontrolled access points into and out of the facility
- Criminal demographics surrounding the hospital and campus
- Security incident data within the hospital as well as incidents on campus
- Level of physical security protection
- Health-care-related or relevant sentinel security events that are identified by stakeholders and management
- Quality of the security department and security management program
- Employee security awareness associated with ongoing educational programs
- Administration and management support
- Patient, staff, employee, vendor, and visitor identification
- Emergency department security
- Violence in the workplace issues (clinical and other locations)
- Birthing-center security
- Pediatric security
- Pharmacy
- Employee education
- Patient education

User-Centered Design Perspective

User-centered (i.e., expert-driven) and participatory (i.e., user as coauthor) design processes (see Figure 6.4) are necessary problem-identification, data-gathering, and design-process approaches that can lead to more context-appropriate solutions. In experiential-based projects, as well as in context-based design projects, a User-Centered Design approach is a must. This approach utilizes visual and oral narrative to solicit information, reiterate the meaning of the information, and evaluate it in specific areas. One would expect that with the complexity of health-care settings and the multiple categories of users, such an approach might afford a greater depth and breadth of programming and usability information gathered. The questions posed usually include:

- Who are the users of this space/product/service? For example, patients, physicians, nurses, guests, support staff, other?
- What are the users' tasks and goals? May include care, socialization, teaching, or healing.

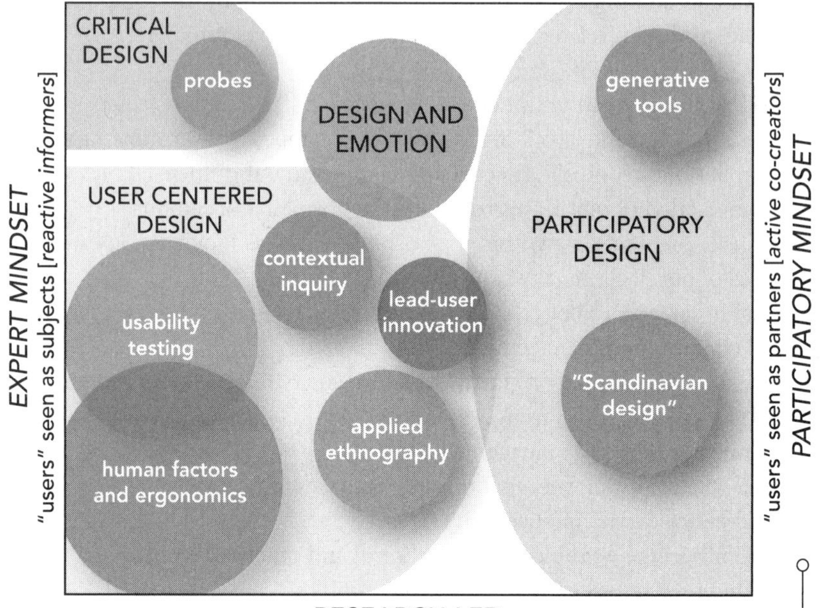

6.4 User-centered and participatory designer processes.

- What are the users' experience levels with this space/product/service, and spaces/products/services like it? Familiar, unfamiliar, restricted?
- What functions do the users need from this space/product/service? Immediate care, biological, psychological, cultural/spiritual, visual, immediate, or restricted?
- What information might the users need, and in what form do they need it? General questions include what, why, how, when, and where.
- How do users think this space/product/service should work? Feedback, memory, cognition, perception, frustration, intuition?
- How can the design of this space/product/service facilitate users' cognitive processes? This is a very complex question, which necessitates the need for other facets of design, such as environmental psychology, cultural perspective, and universal design, be integrated.

Security-sensitive Areas

In addition to an overall security management plan, the Joint Commission requires that health-care facilities identify security-sensitive locations within the hospital that may require unique security protection. Sensitive locations require special training, additional physical protection, and policies or procedures specific to the location identified.

FYI: Common-sense perspective: sensitive locations within health-care environments, include, but may not be limited to:

- Birthing Center (Maternity, Nursery, L&D, Postpartum)
- Pediatrics
- Emergency Department
- Psychiatry (Inpatient)
- Psychiatry (Outpatient)
- Radiation Therapy
- Nuclear Medicine
- Pharmacy
- Medical Records
- Information Services
- Human Resources
- Surgical Services (Operating Room)
- Food Services

Per health-care and security standards, sensitive areas should be identified with a Risk Value Rating 1–5, where:

1 = No Risk or not applicable
2 = Minimal Risk
3 = Moderate Risk of injury/theft (**premise liability**)
4 = Significant Risk without history of injury/theft
5 = Significant Risk with history of injury/theft (premise liability)

CPTED in Health-care Environments

The CPTED principles and guidelines provide us with a framework that can be integrated into the design process and simultaneously afford us opportunities to draw upon the interior design body of knowledge. CPTED 3-D approach mentioned in Chapter 2 can be the overarching umbrella for security consideration within any context. The 3-Ds as applied to health-care settings are (see Figure 6.5):

- *Designation.* What is the purpose or intention that the space is used for? For example, patients' rooms located away from main public waiting areas because each is designated for a specific functionality and occupancy.

- *Definition.* How is the space defined? What are the social, cultural, legal, and psychological ways the space is defined? Are walls with restricted entry necessary or would partitions, future arrangement, and lighting define the various territories of the space and imply restricted access?
- *Design.* Is the space defined to support prescribed or intended behaviors? For example, are the nurses' stations designed with visibility and direct access to patients care in mind while simultaneously securing patients records?

FYI: **Security in health-care settings based on CPTED Principles**—if integrated appropriately, it allows for nonprescriptive, organic, sustainable, and project-specific attention. CPTED principles include:

- Natural Access Control: Access and egress control, emergency locks and alarms
- Natural Surveillance and CCTV/camera surveillance
- Territoriality/territorial reinforcement
- Management
- Target hardening

Due to the complexity of health-care settings each of the CPTED principles and application in health-care settings will be outlined at length in the following sections.

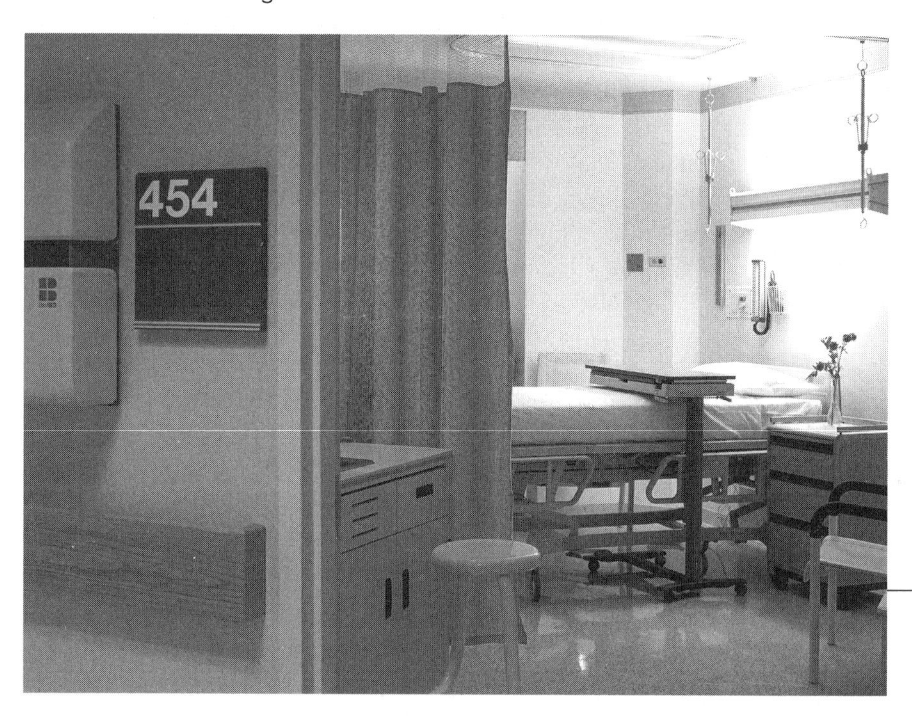

6.5

A designer considers the scale, use, and approach to CPTED designation, definition, and design when planning a space.

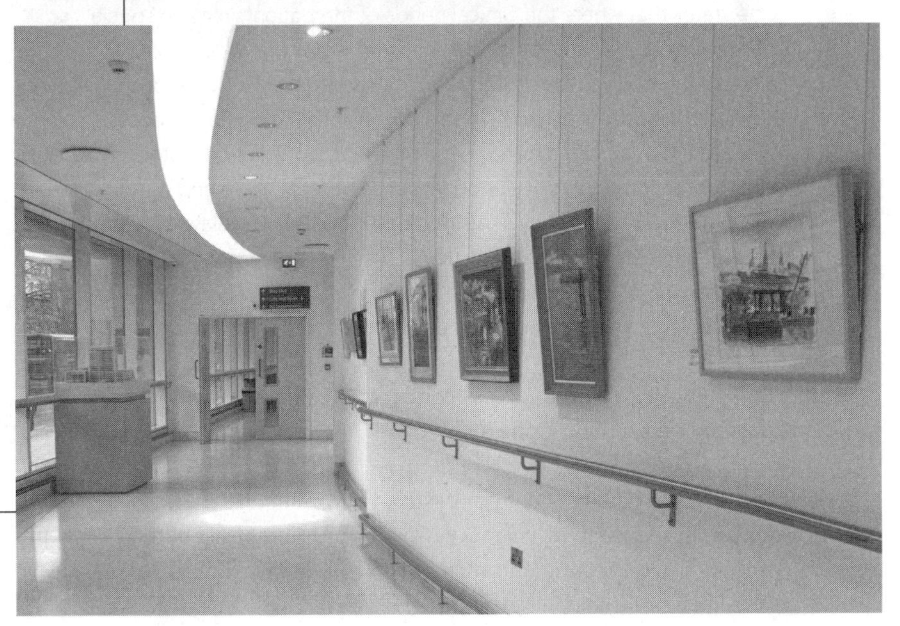

Natural Access Control

A large percentage of assaults that occur within health-care environments are perpetrated by people not authorized to be there. Access control is designed to ensure that only authorized people are allowed to enter and leave the particular health-care setting. Unauthorized people perpetrating acts of crime in health-care settings including criminal assaults, infant abductions, rape, murder, and theft will immediately look for the closest escape route, which is usually an unlocked emergency egress. Access control takes on several layers that together provide an integrated system of access. The public should be directed to use an entrance that is dedicated to patients, visitors, and guests. A separate entrance, not as prominently placed as the public access entry, should be dedicated to employees and staff displaying identification badges, and controlled by use of card access.

It is just as important to prevent unauthorized egress from the facility as it is to prevent unauthorized access into the facility. An uncontrolled, unlocked emergency exit provides an escape route for a fleeing criminal. Uncontrolled, unlocked exits also encourage patients to leave the hospital against medical advice (AMA). However, in cases of emergency egress need, such as when evacuating a whole facility, egress must provide the safe route for evacuees.

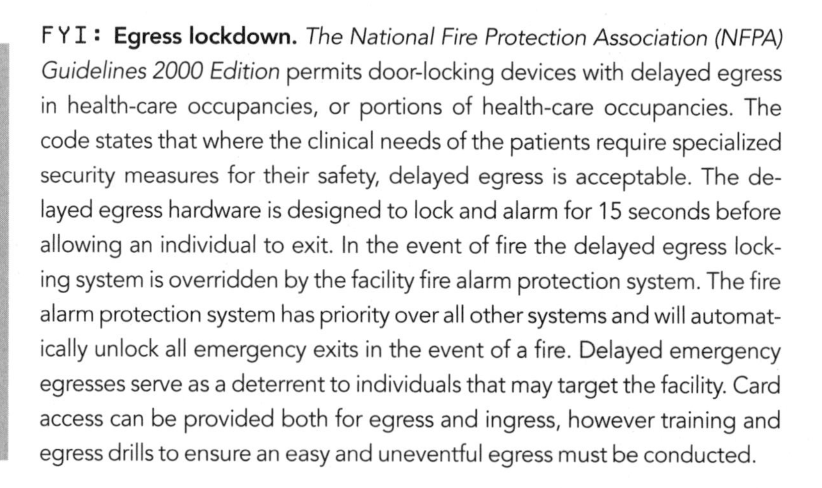

FYI: **Egress lockdown.** *The National Fire Protection Association (NFPA) Guidelines 2000 Edition* permits door-locking devices with delayed egress in health-care occupancies, or portions of health-care occupancies. The code states that where the clinical needs of the patients require specialized security measures for their safety, delayed egress is acceptable. The delayed egress hardware is designed to lock and alarm for 15 seconds before allowing an individual to exit. In the event of fire the delayed egress locking system is overridden by the facility fire alarm protection system. The fire alarm protection system has priority over all other systems and will automatically unlock all emergency exits in the event of a fire. Delayed emergency egresses serve as a deterrent to individuals that may target the facility. Card access can be provided both for egress and ingress, however training and egress drills to ensure an easy and uneventful egress must be conducted.

In short, key points related to access control in health-care facilities and manifesting the layered onion philosophy include:

- Control access to the facility by pedestrian and vehicular traffic.
- Minimize the number of entrances to the interior of a building with the function of the remaining entrances clearly identified. Entrances should be secured when not in use.

- Provide keyed access to vulnerable areas such as laundry rooms, storage areas, elevators, and bathrooms.
- Know the users of the facility and the potential for unauthorized egress.
- Avoid prominent locations and high visibility of doors to spaces which patients should not enter when designing for dementia patients.
- Restrict emergency stairs and exits to their intended use by equipping them with alarm panic bars with timed egress delays and no exterior door handles, however this will pose another possible risk by trapping individuals in the stairwell.
- Install barriers on vulnerable openings such as ground-floor windows, exterior fire stairs, roof openings, and skylights. Fence off problem areas to prevent unauthorized access and funnel movement along desired paths.
- Provide lockable security areas for items which are stored in low-surveillance areas or items that are easily portable.
- Control access for servicing and deliveries.
- With a potentially very large number of cardholders, electronic access offers physical security and freedom of movement for authorized cardholders as well as an assurance of personal safety. CCTV provides a means of keeping watch over movements, particularly in public, open areas.
- Access to an operating theatre cannot be jeopardized. CCTV footage of individuals visiting babies must be available. Security systems must always be operating, and there can never be "down time."
- Control of access to hazardous spaces.
- Unique policies include, but may not be limited to: access control, visitation, identification procedures, information security, and patient privacy.

In relation to access control, other CPTED principles come into play. Such principles include surveillance as a means of monitoring access, territorial reinforcement as a means of designating areas for access, and management such as exit drills. Physical protection may include but is not limited to: CCTV, time-delay lock and alarm systems, panic alarms, special locks, protective barriers, security presences, and dedicated security patrols.

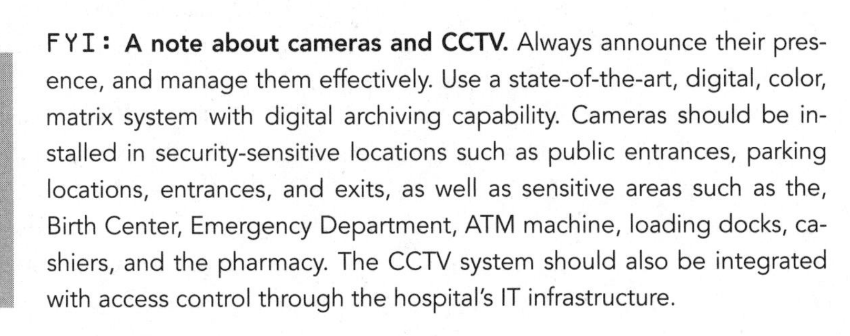

FYI: **A note about cameras and CCTV.** Always announce their presence, and manage them effectively. Use a state-of-the-art, digital, color, matrix system with digital archiving capability. Cameras should be installed in security-sensitive locations such as public entrances, parking locations, entrances, and exits, as well as sensitive areas such as the, Birth Center, Emergency Department, ATM machine, loading docks, cashiers, and the pharmacy. The CCTV system should also be integrated with access control through the hospital's IT infrastructure.

Surveillance: Natural and Otherwise

The second CPTED principle is Natural Surveillance. Increasing the risks associated with committing a crime contributes to crime prevention or deterrence by improving the probability that the criminal will be observed, identified, and arrested. Criminals commit crime because they believe they will not get caught. Ways to increase the risk of detection include entry and exit screening, formal surveillance, increasing surveillance capabilities by employees, and improving overall natural surveillance by various stakeholders in the health-care facility.

The ability to integrate Jane Jacobs's "eyes on the street" within the health-care environment appears to be both integral to how health-care facilities operate, and at the same time very contradictory to privacy and possibly wayfinding issues. What complicates the problem even further is the need for facility, which then interferes with the surveillance mechanisms set in place originally. Take for example the Wesley Medical Centre, near downtown Wichita, Kansas, which grew from a humble, 30-bed beginning in 1912 to a three-and-a-half city block campus that provides 760 beds and 102 bassinets, and is a designated full-service medical and Level 1 Trauma Center (*SourceSecurity,* 2007). As the campus continued to expand to meet statewide medical needs, so did the security challenges. New facilities obstructed installed camera views, requiring cameras to be added or repositioned. Trauma helicopters landed on the rooftop helipad and employees walked underground from the Birth Care Center to the main hospital, both out of camera view. The medical center also needed to ensure the safety and care of patients and staff during the occasional admission of local gang-related injuries and bar fights. The complexity of the setting and the difficulties due to old and new features demanded a systematic approach to ensure overlapping surveillance, through the presence of architectural and interior design features, as well as cameras and security personnel. This scenario and security challenge is not unique to Wesley Medical Center.

Within health-care and senior citizens' settings, intelligent video is being used to detect events and alert personnel to safety issues. With its network capabilities and analytics, intelligent video is a solution to a variety of serious issues, including patient and resident falls, and injuries that result from falls. The Joint Commission of Accreditation of Health-care Organizations (JCAHO) named the reduction of risk of falls, and implementation of a fall-reduction program, among their 2007 Assisted Living National Patient Safety Goals (The Joint Commission, 2008). The financial impact of fall injuries is staggering. In 2000, the Center for Disease Control (CDC) reported that direct medical costs for all fatal and non-fatal falls totaled $19.4 billion. This is expected to rise to $32.4 billion by 2020 (www.securityinfowatch.com). Intelligent video is currently being used in health-care settings to help with the care of patients whose movements or activities must be confined in hopes of reducing and mitigating falls and injuries. Security cameras are strategically mounted in the rooms for wide coverage and digital areas of interest are created around the patient beds using the Intelligent Video System (IVS) analytics software. If a patient gets out of bed or slips, falls, or wanders away, the IVS detects this event as abnormal behavior and immediately alerts the personal hand-held communication device (the Nurse Call Station, PDA, or smart phone) of the on-duty staff (www.securityinfowatch.com, 2006).

The following surveillance strategies may also be applicable:

- Use screening devices when appropriate to allow legitimate building users and guests access. Employee screening should be separate with use of badges or IDs.
- Formal surveillance uses security personnel and hardware such as CCTV and intrusion detection systems. It is imperative to clearly, visibly, and legibly announce the use of such devices in public areas. Informal surveillance by use of the facility employees uses the existing resources of nurses' stations, maintenance workers, and administrative assistants/staff to increase site surveillance and crime reporting.
- Allow easy visual supervision of patients by limited staff. Nurses' stations on inpatient units should be designed to provide maximum visibility of patient areas.
- Improving natural surveillance by careful placement of windows, doors, lighting, and controlled landscaping and plantings.
- Interior lighting enhances opportunities for casual or formal surveillance in spaces visible through doors and windows. Lighting should be even without deep shadows and fixtures should be vandal proof.
- Eliminate when possible interior blind spots such as alcoves and dead-end corridors that can create vulnerable entrapment areas.
- Clearly defined regulations and signage reduces potential of accidental misunderstanding and prevents offenders from excusing their crime with claims of ignorance or misunderstanding.

Territoriality/Territorial Reinforcement

Oscar Newman (see Chapter 2) used the term "territoriality" to mean the subdivision of an environment into zones that may be influenced by users or managers. As a CPTED principle, territoriality and territorial reinforcement denotes demarcated areas within which exercise of proprietary "ownership" of public or semipublic space (through personalization, use, maintenance, surveillance, etc.) is expected. (See Figure 6.6.) Design configurations that help users adopt or extend a sphere of influence can deter crime. In health-care environments, territorialities range from clearly designated territories to less obvious demarcations. The designer's

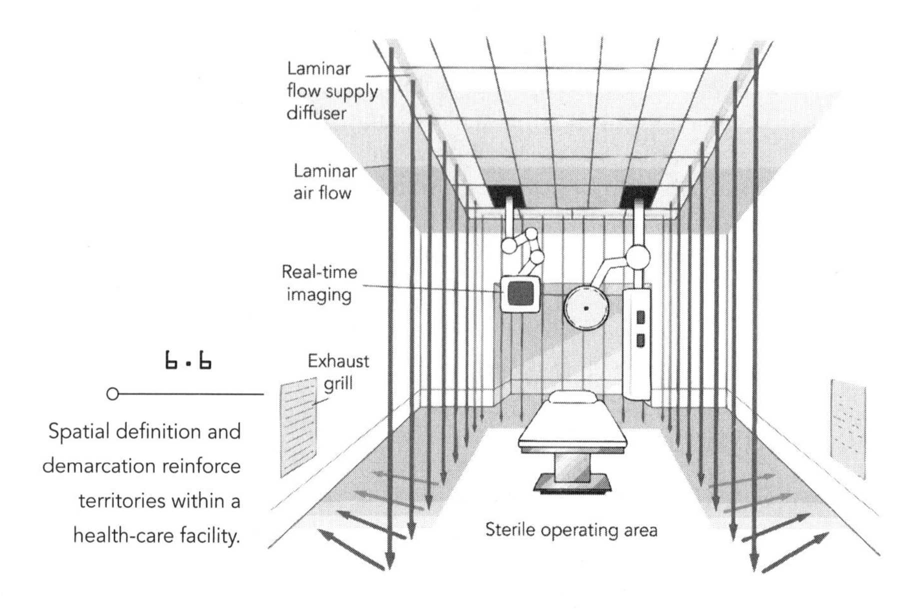

6.6

Spatial definition and demarcation reinforce territories within a health-care facility.

responsibility is to provide congruent and evident expression of territories, and thus facilitate appropriate users and usages within the space. Issues related to security and territorial reinforcement include:

- Dividing interior and exterior spaces into small, easily identified areas that are associated with a specific group of individuals or users.
- Having detection devices easily visible to increase the perceived risk to the offender and posting signs advertising the use of such devices.
- Utilizing environmental cues in the built environment to designate settings for specific territories, ranging progressively from most public to most private.
- Affording primary users the most control of their territories for an enhanced sense of safety and security.
- Making spatial demarcations consistent and not contradictory (i.e., openness and lighting state the same message).
- Applying new HIPAA (Health Insurance Portability and Accountability Act) regulations to address the security and privacy of "protected health information" (PHI). These regulations put new emphasis on acoustic and visual privacy and may affect location and layout of workstations that handle medical records and other patient information, both paper and electronic, as well as patient accommodations. When designing for territorial reinforcement, this acoustical and visual privacy must be reconciled with the need for visibility.
- Using multiple cues from building elements, colors, texture, pattern, and artwork, as well as signage, to help residents understand where they are, what their destination is, and how to get there and back.

- Identifying frequently used destination spaces by architectural features and landmarks which can be seen from a distance, as well as symbols, signage, art, and elements such as fish tanks, birdcages, or greenery.
- Using non-reflective and non-slip floors to avoid falls.

A health-care facility is a complex system of interrelated functions and territorialities, requiring constant movement of people and goods, some of which must not come into contact with each other. Much of this circulation, similar to territorialities, should be clearly demarcated and controlled. Some ways to control circulation are:

- Outpatients visiting diagnostic and treatment areas should not travel through inpatient functional areas nor encounter severely ill inpatients.
- Typical outpatient routes should be simple and clearly defined.
- Visitors should have a simple and direct route to each patient nursing unit without penetrating other functional areas.
- Separate patients and visitors from industrial/logistical areas or floors.
- The outflow of trash, recyclables, and soiled materials should be separated from movement of food and clean supplies, and both should be separated from routes of patients and visitors.
- Transfer of cadavers to and from the morgue should be out of the sight of patients and visitors.
- Dedicated service elevators for deliveries, food, and building maintenance services are needed.

Management

The best security design may be in place, however, without proper management, updates, and communication the security system will be compromised. The written **Security Management Plan** (**SMP**) is designed to provide a proactive, timely, and vigorous approach in the protection of patients, visitors, staff, and health system assets. This is accomplished by identifying security threats in all areas of the facility which could have an adverse impact on people and property by employing the security-assessment protocols addressed earlier in this chapter. Those security assessment protocols are also designed to reduce the occurrence and severity of security incidents and promote security education and training for hospital employees and staff.

Jeff Aldridge (2007), as well as other health-care and security experts, stipulates that within the Security Management Plan (SMP), important issues to be raised include the following:

- Development, implementation, maintenance, and evaluation of comprehensive facility-wide security management program, from location/site to hardscaping and landscaping, building envelopment and structure, interior layout and occupancy, access, egress, visibility, and overall management.

- Identification, development, implementation, and evaluation of written policies and procedures that are designed to enhance security.
- Promotion and maintenance of ongoing hospital-wide hazard surveillance program to detect and report security hazards related to patients, visitors, staff, and property.
- Establishment of a system for reporting security occurrences and security hazards which involve patients, visitors, staff, and property.
- Reviewing and monitoring of data to identify trends and measure the effectiveness of the SMP on an annual basis.
- Maintenance of and familiarity with current reference documents and publications related to health-care security, including federal, state, and local regulations and resources provided by various regulatory and private agencies that impact the health-care system.
- Implementation, training, and monitoring of security staff charged with enforcing the health-care facility's security policies, protocols, and procedures.
- Development of policies and procedures for the security department to assure that the SMP enhances the overall security operations of the facility.
- Providing an identification system appropriate for employees, staff, vendors, and visitors, as well as access control to various areas within the facility and on the hospital grounds to include access control to sensitive areas as deemed appropriate by the institution.
- Maintenance of the facility parking plan to include patient, visitor, and staff access to the facility. The program should include traffic control at sensitive location such as the emergency department. All parking rules and regulations should be enforced so as not to promote lax enforcement of security plan.

Target Hardening

Highly sensitive areas must be hardened, by using strong, highly visible defense systems to reduce crime opportunity and deter breach of security of areas such as pharmaceutical centers or radiology wings. Provision of secure spaces to safeguard facility supplies and the personal property of residents and staff is an example of target hardening within a health-care facility. Target hardening alone will not solve security problems, although it may assist in decreasing the incidents of criminal activity. Designers must be aware that in some cases, target hardening may cause a change in the profile of the crime or its context, displacing the criminal behavior, its location, time, or nature.

An example of target hardening and integration within a CPTED approach is the renovation of the Radiosurgery Center on the campus of Riverside Regional Medical

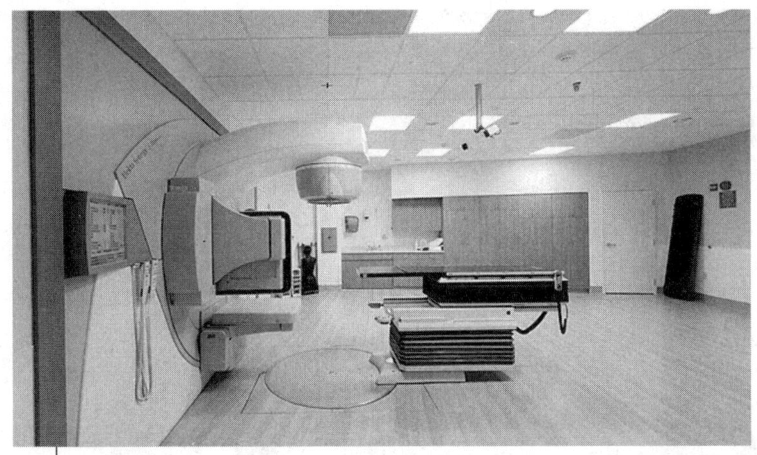

6.7 The renovated Radiosurgery Center in Virginia incorporates target hardening.

Center (See Figure 6.7), with a design completed by architecture and interior design firm Paul Finch & Associates P.C. (PF&A). The center was developed to house both a Gamma Knife and Synergy System experience. The Gamma Knife suite involved reinforcing the concrete floor inside the existing vault in order to support the 50-ton weight of the Gamma Knife equipment and source loader. The structure of the existing corridor was not sufficient to support the weight of the equipment; therefore, an exterior radiation-shielded door was installed to provide an entrance for the Gamma Knife equipment. Additionally, finding the optimal orientation for the equipment within the vault in such a way to minimize the additional shielding required was necessary. By rotating the unit, the additional lead-brick shielding was reduced to three locations. Consistent with the need for redundancy, the high-radiation areas of the room were indicated by using a distinguishable floor pattern.

EMERGING ISSUES AND BEST PRACTICES

Physical relationships between bed-related inpatient functions, outpatient-related functions, diagnostic and treatment functions, administrative functions, service functions (food, supply), and research and teaching functions determine the configuration of the health-care facility. Certain critical relationships between the various functions are required and designate a systematic configuration and communication of people, materials, and waste.

Innovative approaches in health-care design capitalize on integration of practices and perspectives related to wellness (physical, social, psychological, and mental), along with security, sustainability, economy, and workplace culture. In large health-care settings, the form of a typical nursing unit becomes a principal element of the overall design configuration. Regardless of their location, size, or budget,

6.8 The Ronald McDonald Children's Hospital at Loyola University Medical Center in Illinois is a state-of-the-art user-centered hospital that offers a welcoming environment.

all hospitals have certain common attributes, modified by context and stakeholders. Stakeholders' input for example has been instrumental in creating a state-of-the-art hospital with a safe and welcoming environment for the Ronald McDonald Children's Hospital at Loyola University Medical Center in Maywood, Illinois (See Figure 6.8).

For the remodel, HDR Design Team established an Interior Design Theme Committee, including physicians, nurses, social workers, child-life specialists, administrators, parents, and designers, and held a retreat to brainstorm ideas for a hospital-wide theme that afforded a sense of safety, security, and place. The group also enumerated patient/family requirements, ranging from interactive art and wayfinding assistance to an in-hospital school room and a quiet room for parents. The use of Illinois-themed imagery to create a child-friendly environment, artfully blending entertainment with enlightenment and technology assisted in connecting the health-care environment to a familiar place for stakeholders. The design established a clear demarcation of territorialities, an intuitive system of wayfinding, and integrated access control and natural surveillance. The Illinois experience begins upon arrival at this hospital-within-a-hospital, where people find themselves at an old-fashioned elevated train stop. A 3-dimensional depiction transforms the elevator cabs into "Loyola Transit Authority" trains, patterned after the Chicago Transit Authority, with a life-size Ronald McDonald sitting on the bench across from the elevator. The transportation theme continues with a neon chasing-light airplane on the ceiling and a painting of air balloons, kites, and airplanes in a vaulted light cove. Footprints of well-known McDonald's characters are boldly displayed on the floor, each leading to specific destinations such as the monitored unit, north and south patient rooms, and the pediatric intensive care unit (PICU). Natural surveillance is enhanced with the location and character of the Central Reception Nurse Station, themed after Chicago's Loyola Loop, utilizing light oak materials and features tiles depicting art created by local schoolchildren, patients, staff, and families. On the floor is a terrazzo map of Illinois and neighboring states.

Emergency Department Threats and Protection

A 1997 Justice Department study revealed that hospital emergency departments across the country treat more than 1.4 million people a year for injuries caused by violent attacks, an increase of 250 percent over previous government estimates. More recent studies show the same pattern. A study by Erickson and Williams-Evans (2000) reveals that nurses are the frequent targets of assault and the greatest number of assaults (25 percent) occurred in emergency departments; of the 51 homicides recorded, 23 percent occurred in emergency departments. The physicians and nurses who staff emergency departments are demanding greater protection by hospitals. The Emergency Nurses Association, representing more than 21,000 nurses, recently enacted a resolution calling for legislation to increase the safety and security of emergency department health-care workers. The resolution also called for collaboration and liaison with other organizations to develop security and safety protocols, to develop educational programs, and to develop position statements, including minimal safety standards for personnel and for the physical plant.

Emergency departments across the country are becoming the scenes of violent attacks by random individuals, patients, relatives, or their friends, often involving knives and guns, and in some instances involving hostage-taking situations. Especially after the events of September 11, 2001, hospitals are beefing up security to prepare for mass causalities in the event of a bioterrorism attack. Hurricane Katrina in 2005 presented us with a glimpse of a mass casualties scenario. With these increasing trends health-care providers are facing serious liability and the charge is usually, without exception, inadequate security.

On another level, patients and visitors are being found in possession of knives and guns on a daily basis in the patient treatment areas. Weapons need to be detected before they enter the patient treatment area in emergency departments, where they may be abused under increased levels of stress. Despite their intrusive appearance and nature, metal detectors and scanning devices are the primary methods for detecting unauthorized weapons brought illegally into the emergency department. Although health-care facilities, specifically hospitals, may be inclined to consider installing a metal detector at the entrance to the emergency department to screen all people that attempt to enter with unauthorized weapons, it is imperative to consider the functional fit of the unit, and the costs associated with not only the installation of screening devices, but also management and personnel needs.

Every hospital that has an emergency department must assess its own specific vulnerabilities and apply necessary security measures to maintain a reasonably safe and secure department. The number of patients, the types of patients and visitors, the area's crime rate, and the layout and design of the ER are among the chief security assessment considerations. Extreme mental and physical factors, acute psychiatric manifestations, drug and alcohol abuse by patients and visitors, the mix of patients and providers outside the medical staff (i.e., spiritual counselors, police, fire, ambulance, or coroner), and often chaotic circumstances combine to produce a unique environment. Disruptive behavior is predictable, and it can be managed to minimize the risk in providing safety for all concerned. A variety of physical security safeguards can be used when securing the emergency department. These safeguards include card-access equipment, bullet-resistant glazing, duress (panic) alarms, CCTV, signage, secure storage containers including gun lockers, and metal detectors. The security layout and design of an emergency department can be viewed as compartments that must have clearly defined control points. The first of those control points is access control for both walk-ins and ambulance entries, with a clearly marked communications station that affords visual observation or CCTV that is managed properly.

The ambulatory or walk-in entry point is usually not locked, but it could be, depending on the vulnerability. It is recommended that this entry be equipped with a lock even if the entry is always open. The purpose of this lock is to have the means to lock down in the case of an unanticipated emergency condition. In most cases, the first person the patient and visitors encounter is a receptionist or triage nurse. It is imperative this point be staffed at all times to greet those who enter. It is recommended that the receptionist or nurse sit inside an enclosed booth with a service window. The enclosure should make it difficult for someone to grab the receptionist or to jump over the counter. The degree of enclosure depends on the assessed vulnerability and overall context.

The use of protected or controlled areas is a key concept of emergency department security (see Figure 6.9). The following areas should be protected and separated:

- Walk-in areas (waiting rooms and admissions): Many security incidents involve visitors and occur in the walk-in area. Providing washroom, vending equipment, and access to information and effective communication with staff while waiting are crucial to minimize risks and security incidents.

DESIGN AND SECURITY

In the twenty-first century, security has become a paramount concern within the built environment professions. Security and safety are among the most basic and central of human needs and rights. One of the initial steps to take, as students of design, and design professionals, is to become more familiar with the security concerns at hand and to proactively initiate security dialogues with clients and professional peers. For the built environment to be effectively safe and secure, it has to communicate with a global voice, User-Centered Design, and contextual sensitivity.

In the absence of more physical (fortress-like) security measures, technology faciliates a high level of security and control, while allowing flexibility. There are numerous examples worldwide, where this approach is being adopted to create an open, welcoming, and safer environment for learning. Within a fortress school, (a school requiring security clearance upon admittance), the design challenge is to balance security with a culture of openness and agility. Inevitably this leads to a zone of interface where the "inside" and "outside" meet, requiring careful design. In this context, a welcoming message at the entry, offered at "reception," without compromising tough security protocols, is crucial in giving the community a sense of ownership and engagement. In the twenty-first century, integrated security approaches have created vibrant designs that are bright, open and accessible, and secure.

Historic public places and buildings are preserved because they inspire, educate, and contribute to our experience and appreciation of society. The design community can play a valuable role in ensuring that the architectural integrity and historic character of those properties are retained, respected, and preserved when adding required security measures.

06

Personnel access control is fundamental to a sound security program and greatly influenced by the facility design. A balance must be achieved between the aesthetics of the lobby and its ability to provide a natural flow of personnel past the security or reception desk.

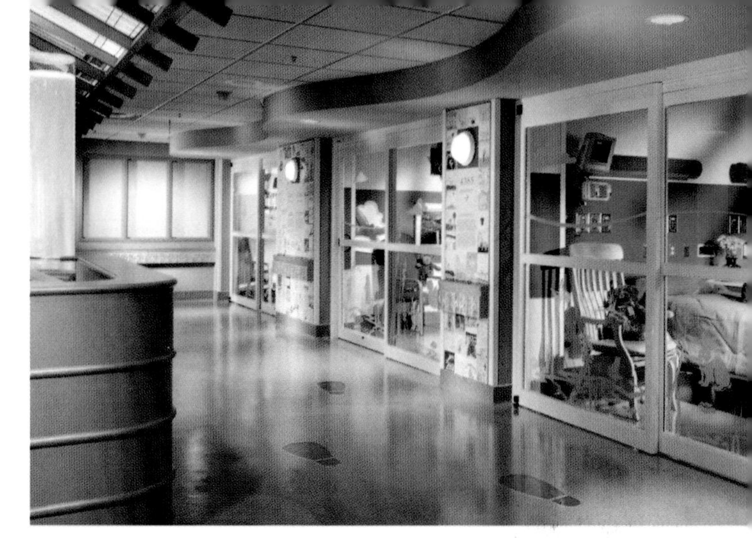

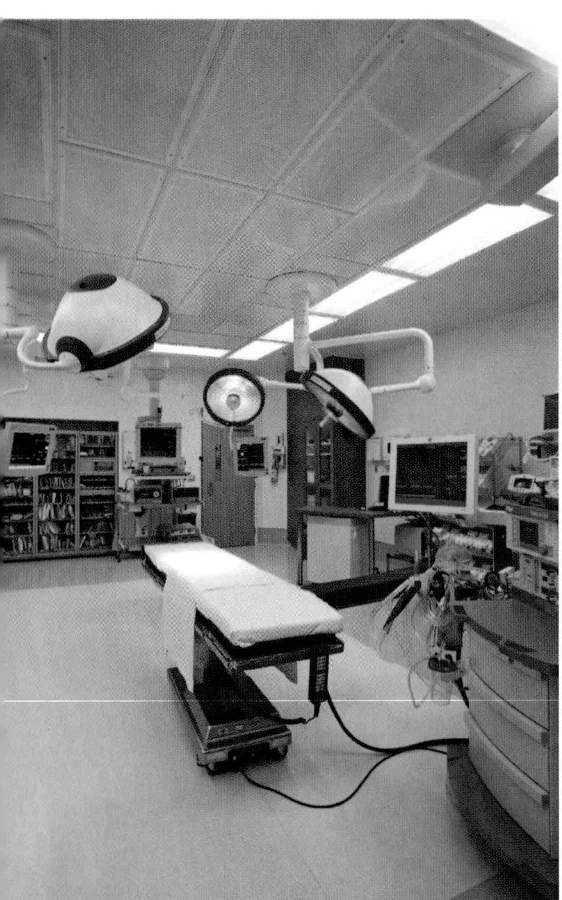

A health-care facility is a complex system of interrelated functions and territorialities, requiring constant movement of people and goods. Innovative approaches in health-care design capitalize on integration of practices and perspectives related to wellness, along with security, sustainability, economy, and workplace culture. The complexity of health-care operations, and the diversity of philosophies and approaches of care, demand a conceptually congruent fresh perspective in addressing security needs within the facility. Flexibility is a basic feature of any new health-care facility that integrates security within its systems to keep it from rapid obsolescence in the face of changing needs and technologies.

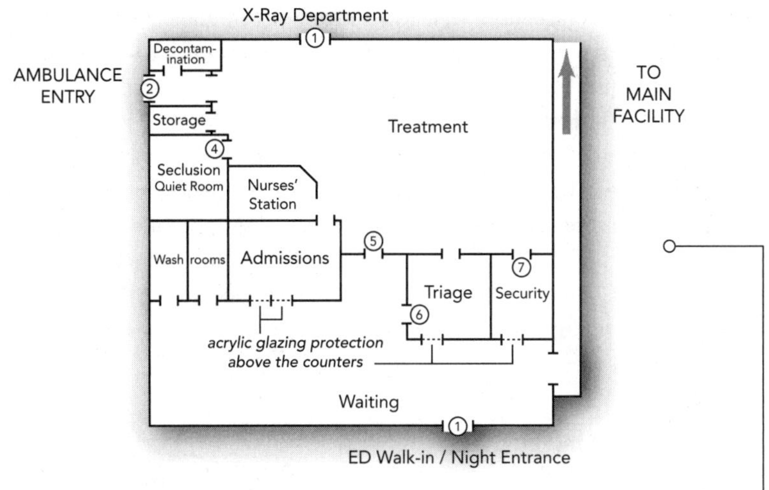

6.9 The emergency department should have protected and controlled areas.

- Triage areas: Should be separated from the walk-in area, which is necessary for security and patient confidentiality during the admission process, and have controlled access into treatment areas.
- Treatment area: Must be separated from the walk-in area, and simultaneously have the exit door controlled as well.
- Quiet (seclusion) rooms: A secured space within the treatment area to administer care to the combative patients, may be stripped of objects for security purposes, or may be padded with tamper-proof hardware items. Seclusion rooms generally have an observation window and/or a television monitoring system.

Safe Room

The concept of a safe room, primarily in emergency departments, has recently emerged as another safeguard in managing workplace violence. A safe room merely means a designated room that can be locked from the inside, as a place for staff, patients, and even visitors to "hide" due to an immediate threat of danger. The typical safe room is a room usually utilized for day-to-day activity and equipped with telephone and/or radio communications equipment. It should be easily accessible and somewhat centrally located within the department. It is most often a regular treatment room, which may be a distinct advantage if patients are present when the safe room is actually being utilized as such. The safe room may be put in use to protect a patient from others who may want to induce harm, or a staff member, or to actually isolate a patient.

The term "patient watch" is sometimes used to describe the activity of standing by to watch a particular patient. Officers are generally asked to perform a patient watch when a patient causes staff to feel fear, anger, uneasiness, potential danger, or when there is an indication that the patient may attempt to leave prior to proper medical evaluation or treatment. Staff members must recognize the considerable range of these feelings and assess the gravity of the risk they perceive. Many incidents of emergency department violence could have been avoided if personnel had erred on the side of being overly cautious. However, the risk of disruptive or harmful behavior could be escalated if inappropriate steps are taken. The overall goal is to maintain safety for everyone involved, including the patient (Aldridge, 2004). The American College of Emergency Physicians along with JCAHO and OSHA have developed a dangerous subject protocol, which involves the following three levels of security alert:

- *Level I.* Patients who are potentially violent but cooperative and responsive and who require close and continuous observation while being evaluated or treated
- *Level II.* Patients who are obviously dangerous, uncooperative, unresponsive, or expressing violent behavior
- *Level III.* Armed patients with the same characteristics as Level I–II, they generally require police or security intervention

Forensic patients are often treated in the same health-care facilities with the general public when needed. According to Pamella Carter, co-founder of the Security Assessment International, nursing and other hospital staff caring for forensic patients must continually negotiate the boundaries between the cultures of custody and caring. Hospital security staff should maintain a daily list of all forensic patients in their facility. However, no forensic patient should be listed in the hospital's patient information listing or posted by the patient's room door. Care must be taken to strip the patient's room of all objects that could become a weapon, and active surveillance should be put in place (2005).

Emergency Signals

The emergency department should have a system of alerting other staff members of an emergency situation that requires immediate help. These systems are used primarily to summon additional medical assistance, but they may also serve as an element of the security system. Wall buttons, pull chains, and foot or other activation devices should be strategically located within the department, with particular attention given to isolated areas. The device must be placed so that staff members can easily access it, but it does not invite improper activation by patients, visitors, or even staff: There are also available devices that the caregiver can carry (as a pendant or clip-on device) to summon assistance. These devices are more costly than fixed location devices, as the equipment must be able to track the movement of the person to fix their location when the device is activated. As with all electronic devices, the system should be periodically tested.

Infant Electronic Protection

Health-care facilities must take the threat of infant abductions seriously. They have a responsibility to take reasonable action to prevent foreseeable harm to those in their care. Hospitals have been found negligent for not providing reasonable security for their maternity and pediatric units.

FYI: Statistical data from the FBI and National Center for Missing & Exploited Children show that there have been 248 infant abductions since 1983 by non-family as well as family members. Close to one half of all abductions have been from acute care facilities with the majority of these [57 percent] occurring directly from the mother's room. The remaining infant abductions have taken place from the mother's home and other locations of opportunity.

A physical security assessment should identify any need that may exist for security cameras, electronic controlled access, locks and alarms, and infant electronic protection. Electronic security measures, including access control, security cameras, and an infant alarm system, can assist nursing personnel in maintaining a constant watch over infants. However, physical security systems are not enough alone to prevent an infant abduction. While health-care facilities have been making strides in combating infant abduction from the facility, those abductions have shifted to the home. Hospitals have a responsibility to provide a safe and secure environment for their new mothers and their baby. A minimally obtrusive electronic security system, clearly defined security policies, reenforced with education and training for hospital employees, staff, and, most importantly, new moms, will go a long way toward minimizing abductions while, at the same time, providing a warm friendly environment (Aldridge, 2007).

Concerns about wandering patients and infant abductions have been a common fear among hospital administrators for some time. These concerns have brought renewed interest in electronic tracking of patients and infants. Litigation continues to be brought against hospitals and birthing centers with charges of inadequate protection against infant abductions. As a result, this phenomenon has sparked a myriad of manufacturers and vendors to develop a variety of systems designed to foil abduction attempts and locate wandering patients. In addition to surveillance by high-cost tech equipment, logical pathways, visible centers of activity, territorial markers in spaces denoting their occupancy and alerting medical staff to any potential breach of those territories; and control of one's environment combine to provide a more safe and secure environment. An interdisciplinary team of stakeholders

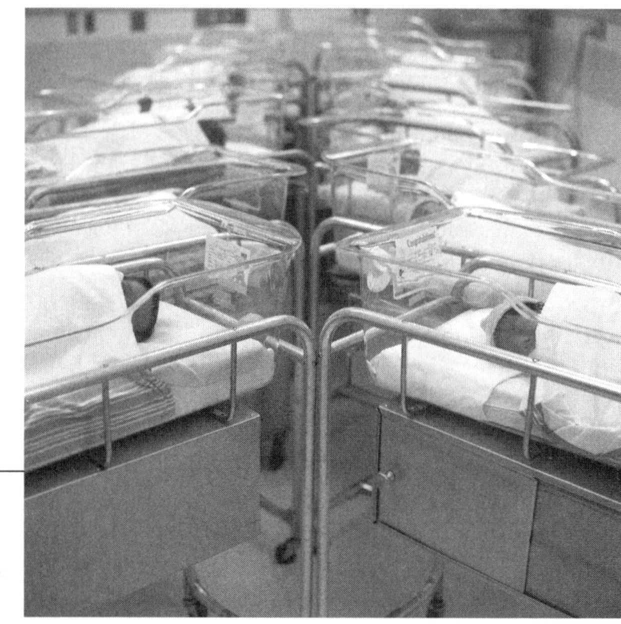

6.10

New parents look for hospital facilities that will keep their infants safe.

can best formulate a security management plan for sensitive areas that utilizes the assets of the facility in a most integrated fashion (see Figure 6.10).

IT Security

Juxtaposition of technological advances and the need for change can be seen clearly in the information technology (IT) sector of health-care systems. The health-care industry is embarking on a new era of development. Faced with imperatives to change in areas such as federal regulations and patient safety, health-care providers are increasingly viewing IT as a way to address many of their ongoing challenges. In the past, most health records were kept on paper. However, new medical devices, clinical applications, and inexpensive wireless technology have caused significant changes in the IT landscape. As the ultimate goal of every health-care provider is to provide quality patient care, systems that keep electronic records and data—and manage critical aspects of patient care—must be kept secure. HIPAA has spelled out important security and privacy requirements that provide a strong foundation for a comprehensive, risk-based information security program. Top security issues are emerging in this new landscape. IT security means a secure network, secure data transmission, and the protection of patients' confidential information. This aspect of IT security is now of paramount importance to hospitals and health-care affiliations because of HIPAA mandates. In place of patients' medical files being left in a public location, health-care facilities managers now worry about hackers and wireless "insecurity," in addition to compatibility with environmental control systems and IT needs. Imagine what would happen in cases of mass emergencies, or in case of a fire and sprinkler system incident in the server zones.

Prospective patients and families are increasingly evaluating hospitals not only for the quality of care a hospital provides, but also now, more than ever, for the level of security available during and following the patients stay. With this in mind, it becomes increasingly essential for health-care providers to offer state-of-the-art security protection for their patients, staff, and visitors.

Psychiatric Facilities

Psychiatric facilities are among the most prominent of facilities that have suffered disastrous consequences from ill-conceived safety, security, and protection ideas of the past. Examples of psychiatric wards or units set in dehumanizing conditions, where structures or units are set in isolation of their context, and where patients were treated as prison inmates were common. In those examples of the past, security was arguably met by maintaining segregation and isolation, often utilizing fortress-like facades and reinforcing the larger community's stigma of the mentally ill. The prevalence of such care, despite the ethical implications and ill effects on stakeholders within the facility and in the surrounding context, undermines not only the competence of the patient, but elevates security risks due to stress. Researchers have extensively investigated institutions such as psychiatric facilities and their possible negative effects on mental health. Robert Bechtel, Gary Evans, Kathryn Anthony, M. McCormick, Rudolph Moos, Roger Ulrich, and others have investigated impact of the physical environment on patient and staff stress and subsequent reaction to that stress.

Psychiatric facilities are public buildings that may have a significant impact on the environment and economy of the surrounding community. As facilities built for "caring," it is appropriate that this caring approach extend to the larger world as well, and that they be built and operated "sustainably." Often, emergency psychiatric patients are treated in the same area as other emergency patients. The potential suicide of patients is a special concern of psychiatric facilities, thus the facility must not unwittingly create opportunities for suicide. Nicholas J. Watkins and Kathryn H. Anthony qualitative research on Design of Psychologists' Offices from an Environment-Function Fit perspective (2007) revealed that although psychologists' offices serve as workspaces laden with the territoriality and symbolism associated with other office environments, "some mental health facilities force psychologists to work in deplorable offices that inhibit personalization and territoriality" (Watkins & Anthony, 2007). The authors suggest in their conclusion that psychologists need to be trained on how to employ design to create a safe haven that affords them a sense of control over their environment and work.

Designs to address safety and security issues in psychiatric built environments include:

- Plumbing, electrical, and mechanical devices designed to be tamper-proof
- Use of breakaway shower-rods and bars, no clothes hooks
- Elimination of all jumping opportunities
- Control of entrances and exits by staff
- Provision for patient bedroom doors to be opened by staff in case of emergency
- Laminated glass for windows in inpatient units
- Fiber-reinforced gypsum board for walls
- Special features in seclusion rooms to eliminate all opportunities for self-injury, including outward opening door with no inside hardware
- Careful consideration of appropriate locations for grab bars and handrails (where they must be used in unsupervised spaces, and a patient profile justifies extra care, special designs are available that preclude their use for self-injury).
- Elimination of door knobs and handles
- Solid material–specified ceilings

Infection Control

Construction of new health-care environments, as well as additions and renovations, has been occurring at a rapid pace over the past few years in response to population growth and new health and safety standards. These buildings have to adequately address infection control measures—a due diligence process that begins in the design and construction phases of these projects. According to the Centers for Disease Control, a patient has nearly a 1-in-20 chance of contracting a nosocomial infection, or one that is contracted in a hospital. Similarly, with biological hazards, airborne pathogens, and possible risk of environmental contamination, infection control takes on heightened levels of attention. New standards and guidelines for 2006 have been developed for infection control in the *Guidelines for Design and Construction of Hospital and Health Care Facilities*; a reference tool published by the American Institute of Architects every five years and used by the American Society of Health-care Engineers. The new 2006 standards provide new material on infection-control risk assessments (ICRAs) and infection-control risk mitigation recommendations.

Health-care administrators and the construction industry must be cognizant of these standards before they budget for new construction or a renovation. Unless they understand and follow these standards, patients and staff could be placed at greater risk. There are a number of important ways for administrators, architects, engineers, and construction managers to ensure control standards are being applied during hospital construction or expansion, including:

- The building team members should collaborate to complete an ICRA by defining the level of patient susceptibility and applying the proper confinement strategies according to the new standards. The new rules require that the ICRA be conducted by a panel with expertise in infection control, risk management, facility design, construction, ventilation, safety, and epidemiology. The ICRA will be incorporated into the contract documents.
- Preplan the construction phases to accommodate proper patient and staffing levels to minimize the number of hospital services interrupted. For instance, schedule phases to keep a minimum number of examination and trauma rooms open so an emergency department can remain operational.
- Plan a construction schedule that ensures all required infection-control partitions can remain in place properly through each phase.
- Provide negative air pressure within the construction space to ensure building material particulates don't leak into hospital wings that are operational.
- Constantly and vigilantly monitor walk-off mats leading to and from construction areas.
- Use manometers to check the air pressure around infection-control partitions and entrances and exits from construction areas.
- Complete a preconstruction air sampling, as well as periodic monitoring throughout each phase.
- Make sure every construction worker understands the absolute requirement and necessity of infection-control measures prior to setting foot within the construction area and within patient care areas.

Healing Environments

In the past, communicable diseases were the major health problem, and sanitation or cleanliness was the main characteristic of a healing or therapeutic environment. Cleanliness remains extremely important, but there is increasing recognition of the value of a pleasant, easily understood, and non-threatening environment for patient recovery. For example, the Planetree philosophy of patient-centered care and "demystifying medicine" emphasizes such a physical environment as part of its approach (Planetree, 2007). Good design in the health-care setting starts by recognizing the basic functional needs, but does not end there—it must also meet the emotional needs of those who use such facilities at times of uncertainty, dependency, and stress. Some of the key emerging issues include:

- Increasing emphasis on security, especially in large public facilities, and the need to balance this with the desired openness to patients and visitors.
- Promoting patient dignity and privacy by visual screening within exam rooms and sound insulation between exam and consultation rooms and other spaces.
- Encouraging patient independence by a patient-orientated layout, with clear and uncomplicated patient routes, visual cues, and clear signage, while simultaneously providing territorial reinforcement, access control, and natural surveillance.
- Providing quiet areas for meditation/spiritual renewal, such as, in larger facilities, quiet rooms, and meditation gardens, thus reducing stress and volatile incidents.
- Ensuring grades are flat enough to allow easy movement, and sidewalks and corridors are wide enough for two wheelchairs to pass easily and to minimize risks of falls and injuries.
- Protecting clinic property and assets, including drugs.
- Protecting patients, including incapacitated patients and staff.
- Safely controlling violent or unstable patients.
- Recognizing that large, prominent, publicly-owned clinics may be potential terrorism targets.
- Making entrances easy to enter, visible, and well-identified entrance, with a clear route from parking.
- Allowing easy visual supervision of patients by limited staff.
- Providing an efficient logistics system, which might include elevators, pneumatic tubes, box conveyors, manual or automated carts, and gravity or pneumatic chutes, for the efficient handling of food and cleaning supplies and the removal of waste, recyclables, and soiled material.
- Providing optimal functional adjacencies for maximum security benefits, such as locating the surgical intensive care unit adjacent to the operating suite. (These adjacencies should be based on a detailed functional program which describes the hospital's intended operations from the standpoint of patients, staff, and supplies.)
- Remaining operational during and after disasters.
- Requiring state-laws-mandated earthquake resistance, both in designing new buildings and retrofitting existing structures.
- Balancing increasing attention to building security with openness to patients and visitors.

FYI: **Innovations: The Pebble Project Research Initiative.** Launched in 2000, the purpose of the Pebble Project is to create a ripple effect in the health-care community by providing researched and documented examples of projects that have created healing environments for patients, families, and staff. In Best Practices within the Pebble Project, security became an integral part of the healing environment, not a separate entity. The primary initiator of the project is The Center for Health Design, which is a non-profit research and advocacy organization whose mission is to transform health-care settings into healing environments that contribute to health and improve outcomes through the creative use of evidence-based design.

St. Charles Medical Center in Bend, Oregon, is a leader in patient-centered care (See Figure 6.11). The planning, architecture, and interior design services for the expansion were provided by Callison Architecture, Inc., in Seattle, WA. In this design, the nursing unit of the future centers on enhancing the patient and care-team experience with added amenities for each. According to Health-care Design Architectural Showcase (2005), the design addresses physical and psychological needs of patients and medical staff alike; and consequently improves patient safety, thus allowing nurses to stay focused on the patients. Based on an innovative plan designed to improve the work environment for care teams, the unit design addresses five major factors that affect patient care and safety. A variety of strategies combine to provide strong support for care teams and families, while granting more patient control, eliminating environmental stressors, offering positive distractions, and providing access to nature. Functions not related to direct patient care, such as the staff lounge and elevators, were located away from the core, creating a central care-team work area with satellite nurses' stations to reduce fatigue. This planning solution cuts down on nurses' travel time without isolating them. Although the current industry standard is to disperse nurses' stations to reduce fatigue, this isolated them from their colleagues, causing increased stress levels.

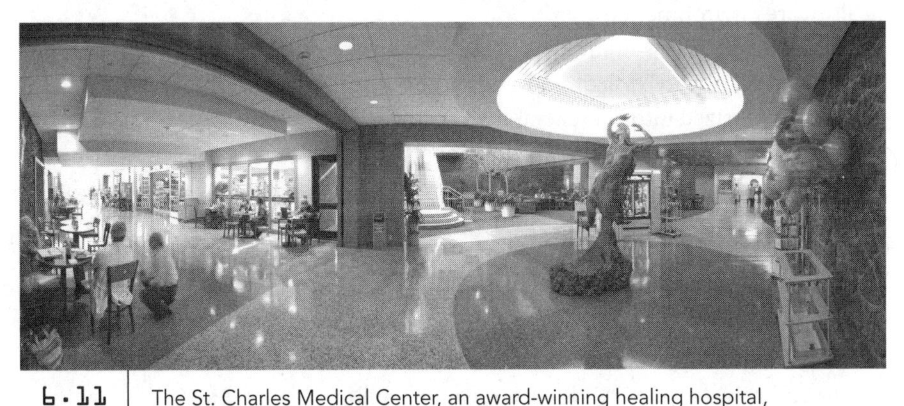

6.11 The St. Charles Medical Center, an award-winning healing hospital, provides design solutions that address the physical and psychological needs of the patients and staff.

The Birthing Suites in Morris Hospital in Morris, Illinois, is another exemplar facility that has been recognized by the Center for Health Design (2006). The Design Group's Columbus, Ohio, team's mission was to create an evidence-based design that fostered a healing and supportive environment through the use of sound, light, warmth, comfort, and privacy. "The soothing sound of a granite water fountain fills the two-story volume of the dynamic, transformed lobby. The gentle curve of the exterior glass wall and the warmth of the light-filled connecting corridor beckon patients toward the Birthing Suites. An expectant mother and her family arrive at their destination without experiencing the feeling of being in a 'hospital' environment" (*Healthcare Design* magazine, 2006). The term security was not expressively used in concept or project description, however notions of physical and psychological safety and security were afforded through the overall experience in the place, facilitating clear and confidence-evoking access control; visibility and wayfinding; territorial reinforcement; and decentralized nursing.

CONCLUSION

Security is a system concept; it requires the agile attention of various design and management team members.

The complexity of health-care operations physically, psychologically, and economically, and the diversity of philosophies and approaches of care, demand a conceptually congruent fresh perspective in addressing security needs within the facility. Contextual threat assessment, coupled with operational safety and security standards stipulated by the US Department of Health & Human Services, Centers for Medicare and Medicaid Services (CMS), and the Joint Commission on Accreditation of Health-care Organizations (JCAHO), new standards of care, and codes can be addressed from within the design and care philosophies about healing in health-care environments.

According to NBBJ, an internationally leading design firm, the firm's philosophy related to health-care design and integration of security into the design process can be summarized into a few sentences: "For over six decades, our teams of architects, designers, and health-care professionals have passionately believed that form follows human need so our process for developing ideas differs from other firms: we delve deeply into the values, cultures, and actions of staff and patients to weave the activities of everyday life into the health-care experience. We have proven time and again that flexible design that promotes healing is also good for the bottom line" (NBBJ, 2007). Those were not empty words; the Banner Estrella Medical center in Phoenix, Arizona, is a 172-bed full-service facility designed by NBBJ that features all private rooms with a degree of flexibility of adaptable rooms, living areas for families, electronic medical records with computer-assisted physician order entry, and state-of-the-art clinical systems that ensure and communicate safety of people, property, and information. The advances and special considerations related to security in health-care settings should not be seen as compartmentalized areas of focus, rather, they should be seamlessly and systemically integrated with all the other programmatic and contextual issues of the project at hand.

The entire health-care system is under great pressure to reduce costs, and at the same time, be more responsive to customers, so security may take a back seat in how it is addressed, and attention may be placed on the immediate situation. To afford a dynamic system of security, flexibility must be a basic feature of any new health-care facility that integrates security within its systems to keep it from rapid obsolescence in the face of changing needs and technologies.

KEY CONCEPTS

- Health-care environments pose a unique dilemma for designing for safety and security due to apparent contradictions related to context, public image, experience, and accreditation standards.
- Health-care environments are complex functionally; this complexity demands a deep level of understanding and a systems-thinking approach.
- There is a significant need to integrate and apply design security perspectives in health-care settings from program to schematic design, utilizing several methods of data collection, User-Centered Design perspective, and stakeholders' engagement.
- Regulatory bodies provide guidelines and mandates related to security and safety standards in health-care environments, identifying **security sensitive areas** (areas that may require unique security protection), occupancies, and adjacencies, as well as protocols for mitigating contamination and security breaches.
- An up-to-date and reflective Security Assessment and Management Plan is a necessary component of design and security, as well as a requirement for health-care compliance review.
- Health-care security concerns of the twenty-first century present complex scenarios with seemingly competing concerns and issues.
- CPTED in health-care settings represent potentials for grounding design solutions in context.
- Systematic integration affords opportunities to address design and security in health-care settings with a focus on healing and wellness for all facility users.

ASSIGNMENTS

1. Provide examples of how to integrate security needs in health-care settings from program to schematic design.
2. Discuss the security concerns of the twenty-first century and the impact they have on the built environment.
3. Discuss health-care operations and the need for systematic integration.

ACTIVITIES

1. Journaling activity: wayfinding and cognitive mapping of health-care facilities visited in the last year for ease of recall. Analyze annotated diagrams and maps form an integrative perspective: looking at image-ability, sensory stimuli, psychological and physical attributes, and security-related features.
2. Look at some examples of health-care design, note when and in what context security is addressed, and discuss the implications of such approach.
3. Select a particular health-care setting to be the vignette for this assignment. Work in small teams (three to five students); each team is to prepare a scenario related to the same health-care setting from the perspective of a particular group of stakeholders: emergency doctors, nurses, patients, visitors, manager/director/administration, janitorial staff, etc. Overlay the various scenarios and discern points of conflict and similarities, and arrive at a possible conceptual security plan.
4. Work on a project that requires, as a component of the programming and design process, the integration of security needs/theories in identifying and articulating design problems.
5. Visit a site that has implemented obvious security control measures with a required exercise in behavioral mapping.
6. Collect current accreditation standards related to health-care facilities, fire code, and planning standards, and then prepare a report on significant issues pertaining to security in health-care settings.
7. Linking research and development: After investigating possible research topics in health-care security, visit product representatives and discover new security technologies, their benefits, and possible pitfalls.

.072965834

7 DESIGN FOR SECURITY IN PUBLIC ENVIRONMENTS

So-called "undesirables" are not the problem. It is the measures taken to combat them that is the problem. . . . The best way to handle the problem of undesirables is to make the place attractive to everyone else.

—William H. Whyte

OBJECTIVES

- Further develop an understanding of the human need for safety and security in public environments.
- Investigate the designer's role in fostering an integrative security paradigm in the built environment.
- Appreciate the complexity and ethical dimensions of security in public environments.
- Integrate security needs in a variety of public settings from program to schematic design.
- Understand the reciprocal relationship between the public environment, security solutions, experience, and behavior.
- Reinforce an understanding of the security concerns of the twenty-first century and their impact on the built environment.
- Understand the complexity of mixed use and public facilities and the need for systematic integration.
- Develop context-based security-minded application and integration strategies.

As cruel as the quotation above may be, it points out a key strategy that connects place membership, sense of ownership, and security. Public spaces are no strangers to crime and violence. Take the few examples here and ponder the events, context, and possible environmental design attributes and consequences in each case.

The *Seattle Post-Intelligencer* reported November 21, 2005, "A routine day of shopping turned into a terrifying scene at the Tacoma Mall Sunday, witnesses said, when a young man in a shirt and tie opened fire with an assault rifle, then kept three people hostage for hours before surrendering to police. At least seven people were injured—one critically—and the mall was locked down Sunday afternoon as frightened shoppers scrambled for safety" (Ellison, Frey, & Chansanchai, 2005).

The August 31 issue of the *New York Post* reported "A chambermaid made a grisly discovery while cleaning a Times Square hotel room yesterday—the corpse of a young woman, bundled in black garbage bags and abandoned under the bed. Police tentatively identified the woman as a 22-year-old tourist from Washington, D.C. . . . Police said the death is classified as suspicious" (Liddy & Luckner, 2007).

"The '**force-protection**' barriers at Grosvenor Square were placed to counter attacks by vehicles bearing conventional explosives. A close study revealed, however, that in some situations the US embassy would withstand a modest vehicle-borne explosion while the neighboring Bahrainian high-commission building would be completely flattened. As significant, the barriers' very visibility is deemed by security agencies to have a strong deterrent effect. Thus, the embassy needs to broadcast its protective measures in order for them to be effective, radiating force and maximizing visual presence. The arguments for security and for the projection of new, exclusive architectural features into public space are here linked" (Petersen, 2006).

In one of The United States Department of State research archival documents, kidnapping from an open public space was the concern. "Kidnapping can take place in public areas where someone may quietly force you, by gunpoint, into a vehicle. They can also take place at a hotel or residence, again by using a weapon to force your cooperation in leaving the premises and entering a vehicle. The initial phase of kidnapping is a critical one because it provides one of the best opportunities to escape. If you are in a public area at the time of abduction, make as much commotion as possible to draw attention to the situation. If the abduction takes place at your hotel room, make noise, attempt to arouse the suspicion or concern of hotel employees or of those in neighboring rooms minimally, the fact that an abduction has taken place will be brought to the attention of authorities and the process of notification and search can begin. Otherwise, it could be hours or days before your absence is reported" (ERC, 2007).

CONTEXT AND EXPERIENCE: BALANCING SECURE AND WELCOMING ENVIRONMENTS

Public environments are those environments that are neither residential environments nor privately owned and used. This means that public environment is a broad term denoting mixed diverse types of settings and environs, including hospitality, retail, mixed use, multi-family real estate, offices, health-care, institutional, recreational, and other contract design environments. The term "public" is also used in an effort to designate the types of environments this specific chapter deals with; those that are symbolically and functionally open for use by everyone; at least from a linguistic perspective those environments afford freedom of access and action and their occupancy and use are not restricted. The variety of settings, patrons, and activity/behavioral settings within such environments can only hint at the diversity of experiences expected. Our design decisions have the potential of creating vibrant destinations and public centers of action and interaction, or spaces and facilities that lack life (see Figure 7.1). In this chapter, although some overarching principles may be applied to any commercial public environment, the focus of more in-depth discussion will be on four specific components of the commercial public environment: the lobby/first impression experience, the mixed-use facility, the large-scale retail environment, and the specialty public facility of a courthouse.

The bombing attacks of July 7, 2005, in London, England, have affected the lives of many thousands of people who live, work, and study in the city. But, as Jan Petersen, British architect and founder of Specialist Operations—an independent institute setting new connections between architecture and contemporary culture in the UK—states "the imprint of 7/7 on the lives of people not directly touched by the attacks is more than just personal or psychological" (2006). This imprint is seen through the increasing significant architectural and design changes in public and commercial environments designed to avert or minimize the threat of terrorist attack. "The purpose may be justified in terms of protecting citizens; but the effect of many of these innovations is to monitor, channel, and control the free movement of Londoners" (Petersen, 2006).

Thom Mayne, AIA, stated, "Barricading is not an acceptable response to fear ... public architecture must remain open" (AIA National Conference, 2003). Similar reactions to how security is implemented in the design and management of commercial and public spaces in England faces us here in the United States. "What happens to a city when much of its architecture and planning becomes subject to a political, counter-terrorist imperative? What is the impact on citizens of the securitization of public space? Are these processes compatible with the life of the city as a healthy, confident civic space—one of the foundations of a modern democracy?" (Petersen, 2006). The need for a deeper level of discussion and a sensitive,

7.1 The Living Arts Center in Canada and the Middle Republic Square in Texas are examples of successful safety and security design decisions for public spaces.

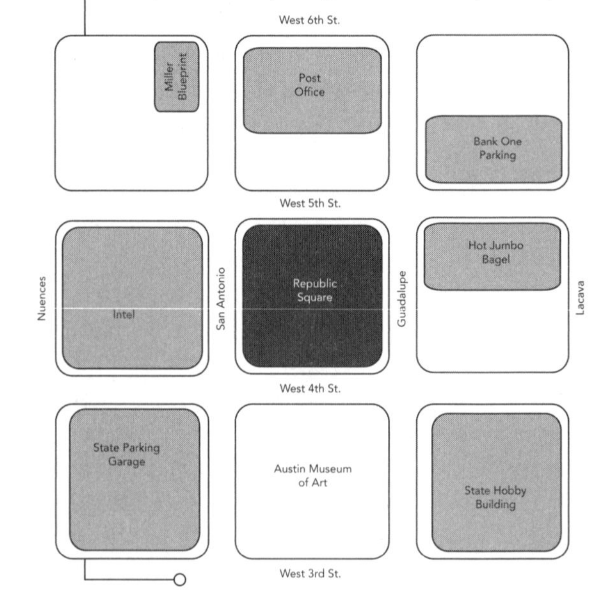

context-based security solution that has been the result of public dialogue, debate, and choice as well as administrative decision is paramount.

> **FYI:** "By controlling the public spaces in which true human interaction occurs, planners and policymakers are challenging the fundamental desires of groups to forge social bonds and enhance their own sense familiarity with the environment. Security is not merely achieved through an understanding of territory but through acknowledgement and confrontation with individuals or groups maintaining diverse perspectives on the world."
>
> —J. Nemeth, J. (Fall 2004)

VULNERABILITIES AND THREATS

The public generally feels safe in their homes or at work, where they are in a familiar place, where they feel most in control, and in a building they do not expect to collapse. When in public and commercial buildings (government office, museum, retail establishments, medical facilities, etc.) and other unfamiliar or infrequently visited places, the public may not think, as a matter of "normal" expectation, of their safety if a crisis situation such as an earthquake or a shopping mall shooting were to occur, and consequently may not know what to do, leading to possible injuries from running, hiding, or exiting spaces. Similarly, building owners and managers may not be consistently vigilant about the safety of regular occupants as well as visitors, and may not include the needs of visitors in their emergency planning, from a proactive perspective.

Evacuation procedures, crisis management, and casualty care may be the most paramount in security breach incidents, but the daily operations and safety and security in everyday practices and scenarios should not be undermined. All public and commercial facilities face certain levels of risks associated with natural events, accidents, or intentional acts to cause harm. Building owners and managers have the responsibility to limit and mitigate risks from various threats. Since there is no unified set of requirements outside of the federal government's Interagency Security Committee (ISC) Security Design Criteria for federally owned and operated buildings, it is imperative to systematically assess those risks. "The application of the Security Design Criteria is based on a project-specific risk assessment that looks at threat, vulnerability, and consequences, three important components of risk . . . The building's specific security requirements should be based on a risk assessment done at the earliest stages of programming" (ISC Security Design Criteria, 2005). Also, the National Safety Council offers a series of questions useful in assessing the vulnerability of an environment to violence (Lack, 1997, p. 375).

Now we see that security measures, such as setbacks, bollards, protective glazing, and structural hardening, are incorporated into the design of the new

Oklahoma City Federal Building, located north of where the former Alfred P. Murrah Federal Building once stood, and in numerous other federal buildings. The Department of Justice sponsored a study called "Vulnerability Assessment of Federal Facilities," conducted in response to a presidential directive and issued one day after the April 19, 1995, Oklahoma City bombing, which produced recommended minimum standards for security at federal facilities. The study divided federal sites into five security levels ranging from Level 1 (minimum security needs) to Level 5 (maximum), listing 52 standards that covered many site and structural elements ranging from parking, lighting, physical barriers, and Closed-Circuit Television monitoring. Following the September 11, 2001 terrorist attacks, many federal agencies responding to public and political security concerns adopted an overarching philosophy to provide appropriate and cost-effective protection for building occupants. Although it may be cost prohibitive to design a facility to a worst-case scenario, decision makers should strive to make smart choices and investments that will lessen the risk of mass casualties resulting from terrorist attacks.

Some federal agencies have issued their own security design standards. There are currently no universal codes or standards that apply to both public and private sector buildings. However, at least conceptually, most designers agree that security issues must be addressed through a comprehensive approach (threat assessment, vulnerability assessment, and risk analysis) in concert with other design objectives and integrated into the overall building design throughout the process to ensure a quality building with effective security. This concept is known as multi-hazard design.

Types of attack and threats to consider include:

- Unauthorized entry (forced and covert)
- Insider threats
- Explosive threats: stationary and moving vehicle-delivered, mail bombs, package bombs
- Ballistic threats: small arms, high-powered rifles, drive-by shootings, etc.
- Weapons of mass destruction (chemical, biological, and radiological)
- Cyber and information security threats

How to control and mitigate these threats is addressed under CPTED criteria later.

User-Centered Design Perspective for Commercial Public Facilities

For commercial environments where the tenants are known and functions are well established, a User-Centered Design approach may be easily achieved. One can define the needs, desires, perceptions, assets, and risks associated with diverse functions, contextual parameters, and stakeholders. However, when designing and managing a commercial environment that will host a multitude of occupants, functions, and users over its lifespan, such a User-Centered Design may seem less

7.2

Visible surveillance and gatekeeping are incorporated in this Privately-Owned Public Open Space (POPOS). There is also an off-limits private work area.

tenable. In such a context, flexibility, meeting general guidelines, and adaptability become the keys for a successful security approach (see Figure 7.2).

Scenario planning in both types of commercial public facilities is a powerful tool to identify possible assets, threats, and mitigation strategies. Scenario planning also works as a method for teaching about security and how it can be part of the project program. As Peter Schwartz in *The Art of the Long View* stated "Scenarios are . . . the most powerful vehicles I know for challenging our mental models about the world and lifting the blinders that limit our creativity and resourcefulness" (1996). Scenarios are "stories" about possible future events that address uncertainty, improve decision making, and provide tools for tracking change. They do so by contextualizing a design problem in external environments and providing possible alternatives for how a design connects with the overall program. Scenarios can be utilized during the design process as a vehicle to elicit reactions, for participatory and deeper-level programming, and as a mechanism for identifying, both for the designer, as well as the user or manager of the space, means of addressing possible incidents of security issues and problems prior to the completion of the project.

The question of scenario planning and emergency evacuation procedures has brought about innovative research and development in areas dealing with the built environment. For example, Siikonen, Bärlund, and Kontturi in their research on high-rise building evacuation, state that, "the **evacuation goals** should be established early in the planning phase of a building project, which in turn sets requirements on the buildings spatial organization and its structural and automation systems" (2003). Traditionally, the egress design of buildings has primarily been targeted in fire scenarios. Fire protection and its related egress regulations do not provide enough time for occupants to empty buildings in extraordinary situations. The distressing development of increasing terrorism and acts of violence has brought new threats and risks to buildings and the built environment. The norms on fire resistance and compartmentalization may be inadequate to protect building occupants during the

7.3 The Los Angeles International Airport uses the CPTED 3-D approach to move travelers through security.

time needed to evacuate a building in this relatively new situation. These researchers are developing ways in which the elevator system becomes a viable component and functionality of the emergency evacuation procedure.

CPTED IN PUBLIC ENVIRONMENTS

As discussed earlier, the CPTED 3-D approach can be the overarching umbrella for security consideration within any context. (See Figure 7.3.) The 3Ds as applied to public environments are as follows:

- *Designation.* What is the purpose or intention that the space is used for? For example, lobbies are the first impression and orientation space, they also are seen as the first line of "protection."
- *Definition.* How is the space defined? What are the social, cultural, legal, and psychological ways the space is defined? Especially in mixed-use facilities, how are the public areas differentiated from semipublic and private zones? How is access controlled into each of the zones?
- *Design.* Is the space defined to support prescribed or intended behaviors? For example, the reception desk/monitor is placed with unobstructed line of sight of entry as well as a clear view of main circulation elements to the remainder of the space.

Unauthorized Entry (Forced and Covert)

Protecting the facility and assets from unauthorized people is an important part of any security system. This aspect becomes even more complicated in a commercial public setting: who will define authorized users and authorized behaviors? Some items to consider include compound or facility access control, perimeter intrusion detection systems, personal identification systems, and protection of information and data.

Compound or Facility Access Control

Think of a layered approach for compound or facility access control, starting from the site and through the lobby, as follows:

- Control perimeter: fences, bollards, anti-ram barriers
- Traffic control, remote controlled gates, anti-ram hydraulic drop arms, and hydraulic barriers, parking
- Forced-entry-ballistic-resistant doors and windows

Perimeter Intrusion Detection Systems

Consider the following for securing a perimeter, using intrusion detection systems:

- **Clear zone**: an uninterrupted area with clear visibility maintained on both sides of a barrier
- Video and CCTV, enhanced visibility and detection through natural surveillance (seating outside the facility, encouraging social interaction, and possible identification of threats)
- Alarms
- Detection devices (motion, acoustic, infrared)

Personnel Identification Systems

The following personal identification systems are good options for staff and for monitoring deliveries into and out of the facility:

- Access control
- Fingerprints
- Biometrics
- ID cards

Protection of Information and Data

The following are examples of how to protect information and data:

- Acoustic shielding
- Shielding of electronic security devices from hostile electronic environment
- Secure access to equipment, networks, and hardware, e.g., satellites and telephone systems, credit card information, employee information, etc.

Insider Threats

One of the most serious threats may come from people who have authorized access to a facility. These may include disgruntled employees or people who have gained access through normal means (e.g., contractors, support personnel, etc.). To mitigate this threat some items to consider include:

- Implementing personnel reliability programs and background checks
- Limiting and controlling access to sensitive areas of the facility
- Providing a stress-relief program
- Enhancing natural surveillance

Explosive Threats

Explosive threats tend to be the criminal and terrorist weapon of choice. Devices may include large amounts of explosives that require delivery by a vehicle. However, smaller amounts may be introduced into a facility through mail, packages, or simply hand-carried in an unsecured area. Normally the best defense is to provide defended distance between the threat location and the asset to be protected. This is typically called **standoff distance**. If standoff is not available or is insufficient to reduce the blast forces reaching the protected asset, structural hardening may be required. If introduced early in the design process, this may be done in an efficient and cost-effective manner. If introduced late in a design, or if retrofitting an existing facility, such a measure may prove to be economically difficult to justify. Some items to consider include:

- Provide a defended standoff with rated or certified devices such as fencing, bollards, planters, landscaping, or other measures that will stop people, if required, and vehicle-delivered threats.
- Consider structural hardening and hazard mitigation designs such as ductile framing that is capable of withstanding abnormal loads and preventing

progressive collapse, protective glazing, strengthening of walls, roofs, and other facility components.
- Design the facility with redundant egress and other critical infrastructure, such as redundant utilities, to facilitate emergency evacuation and control during an event.

Ballistic Threats

These threats may range from random drive-by shootings to high-powered rifle attacks directed at specific targets within the facility, particularly through windows and spaces beyond. It is important to quantify the potential risk and to establish the appropriate level of protection. Materials are rated based on their ability to stop specific ammunition (e.g., projectile size and velocity). Some items to consider include:

- **Visual shielding**, such as opaque windows or screening devices
- Ballistic-resistant rated materials and products
- Locating **critical assets**—people, products, or information that if destroyed would have a debilitating impact—away from direct lines of sight

Weapons of Mass Destruction

Commonly referred to as WMD, these threats generally have a low probability of occurrence but the consequences of an attack may be extremely high. While fully protecting a facility against such threats may not be feasible with the exception of very special facilities, several common-sense and low-cost measures can improve resistance and reduce the risk from the WMD threat. Some items to consider include:

- Locate such facilities away from other functional areas, with controlled access.
- Protect pathways into the building.
- Control access to air inlets and water systems.
- Provide detection and filtration systems for HVAC systems.
- Provide for emergency HVAC shutoff and control.
- Segregate portions of building spaces (i.e., provide separate HVAC for the lobby, loading docks, and the core of the building).
- Consider providing positive pressurization to keep contaminates outside of the facility.
- Provide an emergency notification system to facilitate orderly response and evacuation.

Cyber and Information Security Threats

In today's world, business continuity and function rely heavily on the transmission, storage, and access to a wide range of electronic data and communication systems. Protecting these systems from attack is critical for most users ranging from individuals, businesses, and government agencies. Some items to consider include:

- Understanding and identifying the information assets that you are trying to protect. These may include personal information, business information such as proprietary designs or processes, national security information, or simply the ability of your organization to communicate via email and other LAN/WAN functions.
- Protecting the physical infrastructure that supports information systems. For example, if your computer system is electronically secure but is vulnerable to physical destruction you may not have achieved an adequate level of protection.
- Providing software and hardware devices to detect, monitor, and prevent unauthorized access to or the destruction of sensitive information.

DEVELOPMENT AND TRAINING ON OCCUPANT EMERGENCY PLANS

The best emergency plans can fail if they are not practiced, maintained, and managed vigilantly. Emergency plans should be developed for building operations staff and occupants to be able to respond to all forms of credible attacks and threats. Information related to emergency egress, safe zones, and elements of environmental control should be visible, logically placed, and communicated in various formats. Clearly defined lines of communication, responsibilities, and operational procedures are all important parts of emergency plans. Emergency plans are an essential element of protecting life and property from attacks and threats by preparing for and carrying out activities to prevent or minimize personal injury and physical damage. This will be accomplished by pre-emergency planning; establishing specific functions for operational staff and occupants; training organization personnel in appropriate functions; instructing occupants of appropriate responses to emergency situations and evacuation procedures; and conducting actual drills.

LOBBIES

In an era of security reassessment, building entryways and lobbies are a high priority. The "First Impressions" initiative, created by the federal General Services Administration in consultation with building managers and designers, offers tips for

7.4 Lobbies provide visible lines of security to separate outside and public spaces from private areas.

evaluating and improving security management at the building entrance. Though the advice is generally intended for high-security government environments, some may be applicable to lower-security labs as well. Evaluate the required level of security; do not set it arbitrarily high.

Why lobbies? They are the transitional spaces between what is perceived to be outside/public and inside/private or semiprivate, and offer an important line of safety and defense. (See Figure 7.4.) The lobby of any commercial, corporate, mixed-use, or other is often the first impression that customers have of that environment. As such, it is the space where a positive, secure, and open first impression, or the opposite may be set. However, this asset can be compromised by inappropriate use of security devices—mostly after the fact—and spatial articulation producing a mismatch of spatial queues.

FYI: **"The lobby space type includes** foyers, hall entries, and security screening areas at or near the entrance to a building or demarcated space, and are meant to welcome and direct tenants and visitors, control access, and provide exit ways from buildings. This space type is often designed with both secure and non-secure areas. The lobby space type does not include elevator lobbies. Building lobbies often serve as the 'public face' of building interiors."

—Cecily Channell from *Whole Building Design Guide*, 2007

The character and function of a lobby space often influence a visitor's first impression and possibly the whole spatial experience upon entering a building. Key features and subsequent design concerns for this space type include balancing design objectives—elements dealing with aesthetics, functional, environmental, social, cost, security—and operational considerations.

- Utilize appropriate finishes, furniture, signage, and art to reflect the public nature of the space and withstand frequency of use.
- A spatial compression/release experience can enhance the overall entry experience (outside approach, compression through entrance doors/vestibule, release in lobby/atrium) and simultaneously provide an integrated access control opportunity.
- Well-designed lobbies provide workers/occupants with a relief opportunity, such as breaks, from more confined spaces thus reducing stress and affording better sense of natural control and surveillance.
- Provide "just enough" number of entries.
- Design space to accommodate peak loads without overwhelming security.
- Equipment that must be installed in lobbies should be of a low-profile variety and consolidated with other equipment to minimize bulk.
- Consider air pressurization and entrance-door design to mitigate stack effect at a tall building entrance and elevator lobbies.
- Specify durable finishes to accommodate maximum pedestrian traffic.
- Lobby spaces requiring 24-hour operation should be provided with a dedicated HVAC system and afford complete controlled segregation potential from the reminder of building in case of emergency.
- For lobby spaces at the exterior of a building, a dedicated air-handling unit should be provided to maintain positive pressurization.
- In higher-risk facilities, separate secure and non-secure areas with turnstiles, metal detectors, or other devices used to control access to secure areas. A control desk and bag-checking area should be located within the secure area. Mechanical ductwork, piping and main electrical conduit runs should not extend from one area to the other. Traffic separation devices should be flexible and portable to allow for changing traffic patterns.
- Design control points such that secure areas cannot be bypassed. Ensure that security personnel can properly observe all areas of control points.
- Larger security screening areas should be located in conjunction with art installations, visitor seating, and exterior entrances. Adequate space should be set aside for queuing. If queuing will occur, the area should be enclosed in blast-resistant construction.
- Avoid installing features such as trash receptacles or mailboxes that can be used to hide devices in non-secure areas.

- Avoid using raised floor systems in non-secure areas.
- Location of a fire command center and an emergency elevator control panel requires design integration with lobby wall finish, BAS systems, fire protection systems, and building communications systems.
- Design of lobby doors to street must account for egress from higher floors if stairs exit into lobby, and not directly to the outside.
- For lobby spaces at the exterior of a building, utilize daylighting, control glare, enhance visibility, minimize risk of falls, and reduce electric lighting needs.
- Consider air lock or vestibules at entrance doors to prevent loss of heating/ cooling and minimize risks associated with falls.

MIXED-USE FACILITIES

Most commercial construction fits in the mixed-use category, affording opportunities for live-work, work-work, and recreate-work-live combinations of use as well as adaptable, tenant-improved facilities over the building's life span. The security concerns, attributes, and issues in such cases take on an added complexity: how to develop balanced approaches to security, and establish realistic priorities and expectations for implementing them both for short- and long-range processes.

Consider the complexity of security needs in a facility that combines a small pharmaceutical office, a lawyer's suite, a community organization, an exercise club, and studio apartments all in one building for example. The pharmaceutical or biotech companies and offices alone need to meet growing regulatory requirements, while protecting their intellectual property and the integrity of their product development efforts. The same can be said about the law professional office, however those needs may differ drastically from the gym space. Success in meeting security needs in such situations comes down to making innovation and flexibility an all-the-time, everywhere capability. Security needs in mixed-use facilities begin on the outside through enhancing connectivity with the context, and follow with well-communicated and perceived layers of protection, separation, and security breach mitigations. (See Figure 7.5.)

Many of the built-in security measure in new office buildings/office towers have to do with ventilation, surveillance, and communications. The goals are to dampen a blast, to get smoke out in one direction and people out in another, and to keep the building from falling. Following several crisis situations involving evacuations from facilities, new buildings will have more routes to emergency exits, which will no longer spill into lobbies but directly into the street. Rescue workers will often have their own access points. Overall, consider the following general guidelines (CPTED principles) when designing and managing mixed-use facilities:

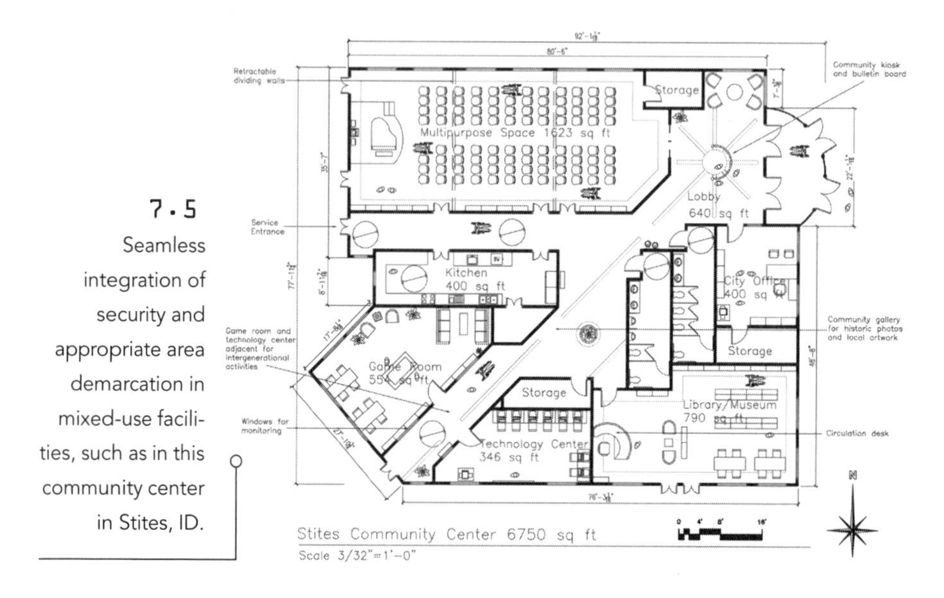

7.5 Seamless integration of security and appropriate area demarcation in mixed-use facilities, such as in this community center in Stites, ID.

- Ease of visual and physical surveillance:
  - Locate windows so that they look onto key areas.
  - Contain open spaces within the building layout.
  - Select and layout plant materials to enhance, rather than hinder, surveillance and security.
- Maximize the security:
  - Ensure there is adequate lighting.
  - Use lockable gates and doors.
  - Install video cameras with monitors.

Territorial Reinforcement

Consider the following when reinforcing and planning territories:

- Provide clear boundaries between publicly controlled spaces (streets), community controlled spaces (shared open space), and privately controlled spaces (retail, dwellings, and private open space).
- Enclose or partially enclose open spaces with project buildings to provide clear boundaries.
- Provide visual access to shared open spaces from individual units.
- Use clear and logical zoning.

RETAIL

Quite a few residents in many cities and small towns prefer to power walk in shopping malls; high-school students can enjoy a burger and soda while playing the most exciting video game and waiting for their own work schedule. Friends may find a place to socialize and enjoy the latest fashions, or simply enjoy the bustling open space that the shopping mall affords, or the opportunity to observe children play indoors while the parents are carrying on their retail and social interactions. Shopping malls, as they are designed and managed today, are very difficult to secure against random acts of crime or even planned terrorist attack. The openness of space, unrealistic mechanisms for observing behaviors within the mall, or as a mall walker stated in a personal interview, "Of course, you can think that as long as people, anyone, can come in into the mall without any search, there is a possibility that someone may bring a gun, a bomb, or anything like that and causes harm to everyone else . . . but then, searching or screening everyone entering the mall is not really the experience that we will welcome" (Personal Interview with a police officer, 2007). Actually, the clientele count may drastically drop in cases where customers are constantly profiled and screened. Successful store and general mall security hinges on developing an **organizational layout** that accommodates easy traffic flow while providing maximum store security.

The key to articulating security needs in such a large and complex space is developing an organizational layout, focusing on wayfinding, circulation patterns, and areas of visibility that accommodate easy traffic flow while providing maximum independent store security. Taking the layered Onion Philosophy, in the first layer, one can see the general overall planning or security for the whole facility, separating entries, providing an emergency plan, providing safe spaces, and communicating a sense of inclusion. The second layer relates to the individual stores, where depending on the type of experience desired, merchandise, and corporate image, a security system can be adapted that fits with the mall security. A third layer is utilizing security personnel. An issue that appears to be repeatedly questioned is the role of security personnel in shopping malls. Some consider that role to be more cosmetic rather than preventative, others define it as deterring shoplifting, vandalism, and rowdy behavior, not as a defense against random acts of gun violence. A third opinion deals with the need for armed security personnel and airport-style metal detectors at all entry points, while a fourth objects vehemently to this approach citing the need for a welcoming environment, not a visually and psychologically heightened awareness of threat This opinion also explains logical pitfalls due to numerous points of entry into the shopping mall, adding also the notion of inside crime, such as suicide by office crimes, or patron/employee violence. Whatever the philosophy and approach for employing security personnel, the advantages and disadvantages of the system must be examined and assessed,

7.6 The Apple store in New York offers a unique sense of place and comfortable retail experience, while securing products on the premises.

as each brings forward a set of new vulnerabilities. Organizational layout, demarcation of territories, visibility, and securing retail environments must be balanced with a unique sense of place, a comfortable retail experience, and security of products and premises (see Figure 7.6).

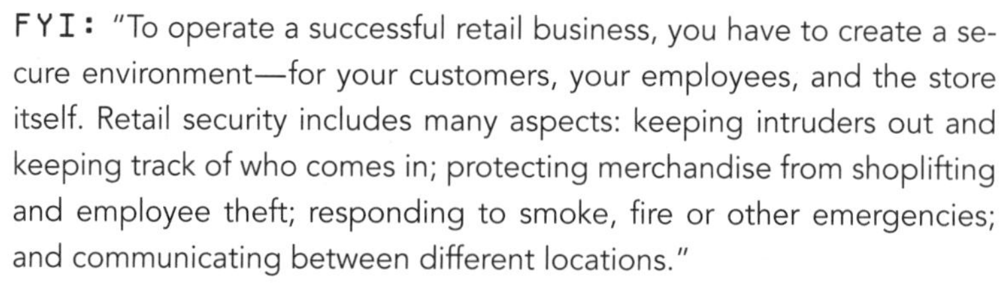

FYI: "To operate a successful retail business, you have to create a secure environment—for your customers, your employees, and the store itself. Retail security includes many aspects: keeping intruders out and keeping track of who comes in; protecting merchandise from shoplifting and employee theft; responding to smoke, fire or other emergencies; and communicating between different locations."

—Garrett's Smart Electronics Store's promotional material, 2007.

In a survey of 120 mall security directors, 60.2 percent said that training for security staff at their center has not improved since 9/11 and another 94 percent said that there has been no change in hiring requirements for security officers. At the same time, shopping centers remain among the most readily accessible targets for both terrorists and garden-variety criminals—since 1998, more than 60 attacks have taken place at shopping centers around the world, according to the RAND Homeland Security "Reducing Terrorism Risk at Shopping Centers" 2006 report.

Commercial facilities such as malls where large numbers of people are present in high concentrations are "attractive targets for terrorists" (LaTourette, et al., 2006).

Shopping malls are seen as vulnerable soft targets due to the nature of their openness to the public, operation where people often carry large parcels, and the existence of multiple entrances and exits. "With a shopping center, you open your doors for business in the morning and anyone is able to go in," says Scott Born, vice president of corporate relations with Marietta, Georgia–based Valor Security Services, a firm that works with 180 malls nationwide. "It's not like an airplane where people go through prescreening and there are bomb-sniffing dogs and x-rays." In addition, during visits to eight different malls, researchers for the Department of Justice found that none had established a chain of command for alerting first responders and most of the guards didn't have a clear idea how to coordinate an evacuation plan. "It was not encouraging that, in one mall, the security director said that he would refer to his company's manual in the event of an emergency," they wrote (Davis, et. al., 2006).

FYI: In December, 2006, the US Department of Justice released, "An Assessment of the Preparedness of Large Retail Malls to Prevent and Respond to Terrorist Attack." The report highlights new standards for industry responsibility. The report states, "Recognizing the importance of security in the retail sector," the 9/11 Commission determined that businesses have a "duty to care" about the security of their customers. The Commission endorsed the National Fire Prevention Association standard (NFPA 1600) for disaster and emergency management preparedness in the private sector. According to the Commission, "We believe that compliance with the standard should define the standard of care owed by a company to its employees and the public for legal purposes. The NFPA 1600 standard specifies that emergency management programs should address the four phases of emergency management and recovery, which include: (a) mitigation, or efforts to eliminate or reduce the risk of a disaster or emergency, (b) preparedness, or activities and programs intended to support recovery from disaster, (c) response, or activities to address immediate and short term effects of a disaster, and (d) recovery, or activities and programs designed to return conditions to normal."

—Davis, et al., 2006

Ylan Q. Mui, *Washington Post* staff writer, speaks of shopping malls' security guards and a new training program that will add to their safety and protection responsibilities. "But starting this month, malls across the country will begin training guards for another task: fighting terrorism. The 14-hour program is being developed by the International Council of Shopping Centers, a trade group, and the

Homeland Security Policy Institute at George Washington University at a cost of $2 million. It is the first standardized anti-terrorism curriculum written for the nation's estimated 20,000 mall security guards" (2007). Mui, through customers and other stakeholders' interviews, raised significant issues, "Customers expect shopping centers to be free and open, and malls are loath to introduce stringent security measures, as airports have done, that might limit shoppers' access—or scare them off altogether. Though security officers are usually uniformed, they are not intended to appear threatening. 'Their job is to be welcoming,' said Robert Rowe, director of development for the American Society for Industrial Security, an advocacy group for private security officers. 'The shopping mall doesn't survive unless people come.' 'You want to see the sales slip?' said Bill Burley IV, director of public safety and security at the mall, as he directed one of the more than 100 cameras to zoom in on a shopper looking at jewelry" (2007).

Affording opportunities for territorial control can mean community engagement in the act of policing the environment (remember "eyes on the street" concept by Jane Jacobs?). It is this blurring of boundaries that has great potential in the retail environment. Beginning with retailers' initial understanding of the rationale for appointing security personnel, and moving through the contracting process to deployment to the store, the paper identifies some of the issues that impact upon effective service delivery. These include unclear expectations within the security contract, inadequate communication of expectations to all parties involved, and lack of training of retail managers in managing security personnel.

Another area of concern is **Organized Retail Crime** (**ORC**), which has a considerable impact on profits at various types of shopping centers, including grocery stores. Many security experts say grocery stores are at a greater risk for being hit by organized shoplifting gangs because of the large number of high-ticket and easily stolen items, such as razors and over-the-counter (OTC) remedies. Store layout issues—high shelves, overnight stocking, and multiple entryways and exits—contribute to the relative ease with which organized shoplifting gangs go about their illegal business. Additionally, employee theft has long been the number one source of inventory shrinkage in retail. Increasingly, however, these inside thefts appear connected to ORC activity. Technology use in surveillance such as closed-circuit cameras and electronic article surveillance are among the security protocols used by retailers to prevent shrinkage, but they no longer appear to be enough.

THE COURTHOUSE

The courthouse signifies and symbolizes the "democratic process," a symbol of government; "the American ideals of freedom, liberty, and pursuit of happiness"; and "the accused are innocent until proven guilty" system. On the other hand, security systems in place aim to deter criminal behavior, detect crime and its perpetrators, and detain offenders. The notions of the two (security system and political culture/justice system) seem to be contradictory. As designers we plan, design, and manage environments to support an institution's highest goals for public discourse and to bring new life to the communities they inhabit; such are the goals for justice architecture.

Major questions that we ask ourselves as we design, assess, or use civic buildings include:

- How can a federal office building retain a sense of identity while integrating with a community?
- How can existing county buildings become more user-friendly?
- How does our design help government and cultural institutions serve a truly civic purpose, engaging our citizens?

FYI: Public Access and Use. "When it comes to our public buildings, we must re-inoculate ourselves with a commitment to fundamental values—to openness, to engagement; to accessibility."

—D. Woodlock, US District Judge, Massachusetts

The tragic shooting at the Fulton County Courthouse, in which a perpetrator overpowered a deputy, stole her gun, and opened fire in the Atlanta courtroom, exemplifies some of the risks associated with justice settings. A judge and court reporter were killed inside a courtroom, and two federal agents were killed trying to apprehend the perpetrator in a related carjacking. Justice facilities house a variety of occupants requiring different levels of safety and security, with the constant possibility of volatility. From small county jails to maximum security prisons, justice facilities represent a unique design challenge. Issues relating to occupant response, destruction of system components, and significant egress/life-safety issues make the typical justice facility a complex protection problem. In addition to the traditional life-safety and health concerns common to all buildings, federal courthouse facilities must adhere to guidelines for aesthetic qualities, security, adjacency and circulation, barrier-free access, mechanical/electrical systems, automation, acoustics, interior finishes, and signage. Understanding such guidelines include the following:

- Acknowledging a "protect-in-place" design approach that focuses on protecting occupants where they are located with less emphasis on occupant egress during a fire or a threat. To achieve this, the designer must have a clear understanding of the applicable codes and standards and have the experience with, and knowledge of, the systems (technology) that work in this type of environment.

7.7 The federal courthouse in Seattle, Washington, uses a hybrid security approach.

- Finding the balance between the need for security and the principles embodied in the civic environment.
- Understanding the urgency of the problem. The United States Marshals Services USMS uses Weekly Activity Reports and Incident Reports collected at Headquarters as a data source. In addition, USMS uses the National Security Survey to determine the level of security deficiencies (construction and equipment) in USMS-controlled space and provide a basis for prioritizing renovations.
- **GSA Urgency Score criteria**—evaluative criteria used to prioritize courthouse/federal building need for modifications or new construction
- CPTED criteria includes using natural access control to limit entry (in some instances egress), and to establish a perception of risk to potential offenders; natural surveillance to observe intruders; and territorial reinforcement through easily identified boundaries. (Sometimes this is beefed up to build a fortress.)

An excellent example of a seamless, integrated, and clearly hybrid security approach is the US Federal Courthouse in Seattle, Washington, designed by the internationally leading architecture firm NBBJ (See Figure 7.7). Integration of both visible and transparent security was in place. Security needs have been met with creative strategies conceived to emphasize an image of open access:

Site perimeter security has been achieved with the use of landscape buffers, courthouse steps, reinforced tree guards, and low-height bollards designed as seating elements.

Upon entry, an expansive public lobby conveys the importance of the courthouse to the public without perceived physical barriers. The security barriers include a reflecting pool, public artwork, and an invisible infrared security curtain.

Steel cables run parallel to the building's superstructure to prohibit progressive collapse in the event of a blast.

SAFETY AND SECURITY IN PUBLIC SPACE

Safety and fear factors in commercial public facilities and spaces are real, but the methods to counter them do not necessarily have to result in sterile, alienating places. Security of interior public spaces could be enhanced by inviting the public to share in their design, planning, and use, and as such take an active role in their protection. Public commercial facilities need to be designed with flexible usages in mind, providing a range of uses and activities, so it is easy to get to and connected to the surrounding community ("access"); is safe, clean, and attractive ("comfort and image"); and, perhaps, most important, is a place to meet other people ("sociability"). Security officials agree that an actively used, thriving public place is much safer and easier to protect than an empty one.

EMERGING ISSUES AND BEST PRACTICES

Creativity, resiliency, fit, and stakeholders' engagement in the outcome often characterize best practices and articulate their response to contextual or global issues. Pertaining to security in the public environment, linking security to sustainability, investigating economic connections, and posing serious questions about professional responsibility appear to be the drivers for change in this category of the security dialogue.

Balancing Security and Sustainability

Providing for sustainable designs that meet all facility requirements is often a challenge to the design community. With limited resources it is not always feasible to provide for the most secure facility, the most architecturally expressive design, or energy-efficient building envelope. From the concept stage through the development of construction documents, it is important that all project or design stakeholders work cooperatively to ensure a balanced design. Additionally, **survivability** (the ability to maintain a degree of functionality) in conditions of blackouts and energy failures must be taken into account. Successful designs must consider all competing design objectives.

Designing for Fire Protection and Physical Security

Care should be taken to implement physical security measures that allow fire protection forces access to sites and buildings and building occupants with adequate means of emergency egress. GSA has conducted a study and developed recommendations on design strategies that achieve both secure and fire-safe designs. Specifically, the issue of emergency ingress and egress through blast-resistant window systems was studied.

Integrated Systems

In recent years, there has been a general trend towards integrating various standalone security systems, integrating systems across remote locations, and integrating security systems with other systems such as communications, and fire and emergency management. For example, CCTV and fire and burglar alarm systems have been integrated to form the foundation for access control for seamless systems compatibility and better efficiency.

Research and Development

As we investigate new uses for current products and new materials and their incorporation into the interior designs of shopping malls, restaurants, hotel lobbies, and tourist attractions, we should consider:

- Shrapnel-absorbing interior materials
- Wider emergency stairwells
- Interior wallcoverings with flame-retardant composite materials (such as gypsum) to slow the spread of fire
- Strategic placement of HVAC systems to prevent tampering
- HVAC photocatalytic intake filters that turn hazardous bio chemicals into carbon dioxide and H_2O

Interdisciplinary Connections—Security and Economy

Security at the beginning of the twenty-first century is in a powerful shift. Now and for the near term, the strong engine of a robust economy has surpassed crime, or the perception of crime, as the factor that most influences the purchase of security equipment and services. For 75 percent of all dealers/installers and just as many end-users surveyed in SECURITY/SDM market research, economic conditions—including but not limited to indicators such as business capital expenditures and residential building activity—affect security purchases now more than ever before. Among corporate and government security end-users, the powerful force of today's competitive economy has become a mandate for greater accountability. Scare tactics or status quo purchasing is out. Direct, bottom-line return on security investment, lean and efficient operation or consequential cutbacks, are now standard operating procedure.

New construction and reconstruction of commercial properties, expected to sustain steady growth in keeping with the overall economy, also bodes well for

7.8 The Petronas Towers has a strict and layered security system.

near-term security sales. In general, low interest rates coupled with high employment needs to promote greater demand for commercial office facilities. Office construction that plunged in the 1980s—with urban and suburban vacancy rates hitting as high as 21 percent in some areas—has rebounded sensibly. Since 1977, vacancy rates have leveled around 10 percent, construction has returned to robust levels, and savvy developers are likely to ease up on construction to prevent the overbuilding mistakes of the 1980s.

Securing those spaces spawns the need for access control, surveillance, and garage and parking lot protection. And as developers seek to lure tenants and businesses to new or renovated facilities, security is becoming part of the sales picture—with services and features that ensure stable occupancy.

FYI: Long-term Factors that Drive Security Sales

- Economic conditions
- Crime
- Sales and marketing prowess
- Disposable consumer income
- Capital spending by businesses

Standard security practice mandates that an organization's assets cannot be adequately protected without knowing what risks will be faced. Future risk dictates every market that will then protect an organization's assets (people, information, property, or reputation). This standard security practice also urges a continued future risk-assessment process to support the deterrence, detection, denial, response to, and/or recovery from foreseeable risks. Future security must account for an integrated risk perception and assessment, and include measures of survivability.

The Petronas Towers (see Figure 7.8), designed by Cesar Pelli & Associates, are the centerpiece of the mixed-use Kuala Lumpur City Centre (KLCC) complex, set in the heart of the commercial district of the city. The design draws from strong cultural heritage and affords a strict, layered security. Limited number of free entrance tickets, airport-type security, and immense control over who enters the premises may be seen as extraordinarily cumbersome measures, however, the level of control sought over the environment and its occupancy demands this structured approach to security.

Policing/Profiling/Facility Access and Use

In her 2003 *Selling Security* study, Wakefield offers six categories of activities that guards in retail environments conducted: "housekeeping, customer care, preventing crime and anti-social behavior, rule enforcement and the use of sanctions, responding to emergencies and offenses in progress, and gathering and sharing information" (p. 165). "Housekeeping" (see Figure 7.9) entails reporting small problems before they become big problems, such as leaking water or uncollected trash, a very similar idea to the "Broken Windows" approach and theory of crime prevention (Wilson and Kelling, 1982). As Wakefield (2003) notes, in addition to preventing crime, security personnel "were required to prevent any behaviors that were seen to discourage the custom of other visitors" (p. 170). There were three categories of facility visitors who were subject to guard monitoring and surveillance: "those seen to be behaving in an 'antisocial' manner, those who fitted 'risk

7.9 Patrolling and housekeeping by officers and guards help to reduce crimes and misconduct.

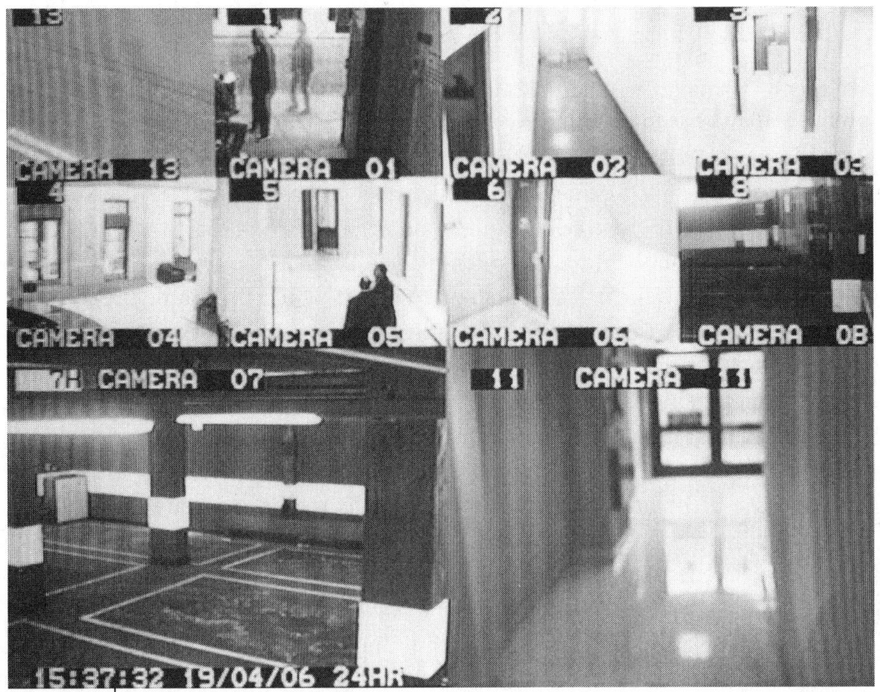

7.10 Well-managed CCTV helps security guards maintain effective management of different areas at the same time.

profiles,' and 'known offenders'" (p. 171). Security personnel had fairly broad criteria in identifying antisocial behavior, and it certainly included behaviors that were perfectly legal, such as begging.

Preventing crime and antisocial behavior gets to the heart of what most of us likely think of when we think of the role of security. This function also raises some of the hard questions about the rights of nonconformists in a public space and the danger of legitimate crime prevention and criminal profiling measures degenerating into racial and other forms of stereotyping and discrimination. (See Figure 7.10). Risk profiles refer to likely criminal traits, behaviors, and attributes. These range from youth, to blackness, to homelessness, to actual criminal behavior, such as public masturbation. Although Wakefield acknowledged that prejudices "might" be behind some of these risk profiles, she seems to understate this problem, although she offers at least three examples of racist assumptions in her quotes from guards. 'Known offenders' were the most likely of the three candidates to actually be engaged in criminal behavior—shoplifting was a key concern—but here too deviancy rather than criminality seemed to shape guards' views (pages 175–190).

CONCLUSION

We spend the majority of our lives in public spaces and places. Our sense of safety and security within those built environments is an integral part of our experiences with the place. With heightened security awareness, public environments pose critical and challenging demands on design and security. A central responsibility for the designer is to pose critical questions about the implications of any design solution to the overall nature of a public space. Witold Rybczynski, architect and critic, writing on the fear factor stated, "While it would be irresponsible not to take what measures we can against the threat of terror, there is something slightly hopeless about installing security devices aimed at foiling a terrorist plot whose precise shape remains unknown. . . . If there is one thing that events in Belfast, Beirut, and Baghdad have demonstrated, it is that while it's possible to protect some places some of the time, it's impossible to protect all places all of the time" (Rybczynski, 2005). The dialogue on security in public spaces and places is not about marginalization of threat, environment, or users, but rather it is about effectiveness, responsiveness, and sustainability.

The complexity of protecting the public environment and its assets from unauthorized people or behaviors is seen from the onset of attempting to define authorized users and authorized behaviors. An integrative approach that involves a critical reflection and context-specific risk assessment is key to addressing security needs in the various types of public environments.

Just as lobbies are the first impression indicator, the courthouse is a signifier of justice and presumption of innocence. Each of these public environments has its own unique characteristics and security needs. Mixed-use facilities perhaps afford the most diverse array of security-related needs, requiring solutions that help integrate a public environment into its context through physical and visual permeability, frequency of use, access, and interconnections. The layout or a public environment affects its safety and the perception of safety and security. Legibility—the ability of the environment to communicate a sense of place and give messages about orientation and direction—is an important quality of safe places as it strongly influences the feeling of security. Additionally, a safe and legible public environment has a well-defined and clearly understood movement framework and public spaces that support natural surveillance. Anonymity and freedom of movement and action are associated with public environments. For that reason, CCTV should not be considered as a form of surveillance and detection unless accepted by the stakeholders in the setting.

Regardless of the businesses "duty to care" about what happens to their customers, the design solutions in public areas should pass public scrutiny. The circumstances in which specific security physical features are built and operated in commercial and public spaces are sometimes unclear. Overall however, they bring forward serious ethical questions about the responsibility of the designer regarding making exemptions of use or occupancy in the public domain. Such questions include: Are the arguments of "exemption" and "unique circumstances" enough to justify actions that can affect civil liberties, and effectively change a direction of the social and spatial ethics of a space? How can public and commercial facilities communicate an ethic of social cohesion and urbanity while simultaneously protecting safety and welfare?

KEY CONCEPTS

- The design professional should pay special attention to balancing the security and experience of public environments, by employing context-based risk assessment, User-Centered Design perspective, and fostering an integrative security paradigm in the built environment.
- Designing for security in public settings demands an increased level of due diligence in relation to ethical dimensions of design and planning decisions.
- Although public environments imply freedom of access and movement, diversity of public environments (such as lobbies versus courtrooms) present the designer with diversity of challenges and situations.
- To each action there is a reaction; the designer should anticipate a reciprocal relationship between the public environment, security solutions, experience, and behavior.
- Emerging issues and best practices in securing public environments illustrate a dynamic system of challenges, interdisciplinary connections, ethical implications, innovative strategies, and systematic integration.
- Balancing security and sustainability, policing and profiling, protection and experience, and understanding factors that may create a culture change related to security in the built environment.

ASSIGNMENTS

1. Describe ways to integrate security needs in a variety of public settings from program to schematic design.
2. Discuss security concerns of the twenty-first century and their impact on the built environment.
3. Provide examples of public and mixed-use facilities and describe why each of them need systematic integration.

ACTIVITIES

1. Journaling activity: cognitive mapping in public areas, in an open mall, retail, or hospital, discern elements of the environment that render a sense of orientation, safety, and security.
2. Reflect about juxtaposing security features with experience in the public realm and follow that with statements of presumed design goals.
3. Investigate tenants' improvements related to security: what are the needs?
4. Create a project that requires, as a component of the programming and design process, the integration of security needs/theories in identifying and articulating design problems.
5. Visit a site that has implemented obvious security control measures with a required exercise analyzing whether the type of implantation, appearance, function, and location, are in concert with the facility's function, spatial attributes, users, and image.
6. Develop conceptual product designs for the smallest component of a security "chain" in a commercial environment.
7. Develop a strategic plan for how design can facilitate communication in emergency situations: when the emergency occurs, and when the all-clear signal is given.
8. Investigate the possibilities of using an everyday product in the interior space to deter and mitigate crime without impeding the quality of the experience: such as, benches in a shopping mall to be used as a means of protection, etc.

5 8 3 4 1 0 7 2 9

8 SECURITY-RELATED NEEDS IN EDUCATIONAL AND DAY-CARE FACILITIES

Our nation's schools should be safe havens for teaching and learning, free of crime and violence. Any instance of crime or violence at school not only affects the individuals involved but also may disrupt the educational process and affect by-standers, the school itself and the surrounding community.

—Henry 2000

OBJECTIVES

- Review the principles of balancing security needs within the context of educational settings.
- Develop an awareness of safety and security codes and regulations and their application within educational environments.
- Identity aspects of security risk assessments as related to educational settings.
- Review the principals of Crime Prevention through Environmental Design (CPTED) and their relationship to the security of educational facilities.
- Increase awareness of the roles of the interior designer, architect, landscape architect, and administrators as they relate to the design of safe and secure educational environments.

EDUCATIONAL SECURITY SCENARIOS

Cafeterias are predictable gathering spots. As a result, they can serve as easy destination points for intruders bent on destruction. This was the case with Springfield, Oregon's Thurston High School shootings in 1998. Combined weaknesses in that campus layout included "dead" walls blocking surveillance to the north, an unsupervised parking lot, access to a dark breezeway, and an insecure cafeteria entry. Images seen on videotape captured Kip Kinkel, (a suspended Thurston High student), walking across the parking lot, wearing a bulky trench coat, failed to convey any critical information, such as the student's identity or the weapon hidden under his coat. Victims were shot in the breezeway as well as in the cafeteria. A locked or supervised breezeway might have deterred this troubled young man from his chosen route.

The tragic events at Columbine High School, Columbine, Colorado, in April 1999, in which two students, Eric Harris and Dylan Klebold, embarked on a shooting rampage, killing 12 students and a teacher, as well as wounding 23 others, before committing suicide. It is the fourth-deadliest school killing in United States history, after the 1927 Bath School disaster, 2007 Virginia Tech massacre, and the 1966 University of Texas massacre. The incidents at Columbine began at approximately 11:15 a.m., with both young men parked in adjacent parking lots in spaces not assigned to them. From these spots, both of them had excellent views of the cafeteria's side entrance and each one was covering a main exit of the school. After the two bombs that Harris and Klebold had planted earlier in the school cafeteria failed, they met near Harris's car, armed themselves with their weapons, and walked toward the cafeteria. They went to the top of the west entrance steps, which was the highest point on campus. From this vantage point, the cafeteria's side entrance was at the bottom of the staircase, the school's main west entrance was to their left, and the athletic fields to their right. After entering the school undetected, the two went on a shooting rampage, eventually walking out of the school library at 11:42 a.m., ending the brutal massacre, and taking their own lives (CNN, 2000). (See Figure 8.1.)

It was shortly before 9:30 a.m., in the middle of the first break of the day when the assailant, later identified as an 18-year-old former student of the school, strode into the schoolyard dressed in a long black coat and wearing a black gas mask. "At first we all laughed at him, the way he was standing there. He looked totally ridiculous," said Dennis, a pupil in the seventh grade of the Geschwister Scholl secondary school in Emsdetten, a small town of 36,000 in northwestern Germany. "Then he suddenly started firing and it scared us." Dennis ran to safety with his schoolmate, Jannick, age 12. The bullets fired wounded a pregnant teacher, the janitor, and seven pupils. Other people were injured through smoke inhalation from the smoke canisters set off in his rampage around the school on typical Monday morning (MSNBC 2006).

In 2006, a 10-month-old child was abducted from a day-care center in Ohio. An **AMBER Alert**—notification to the public by various media outlets of a confirmed child abduction—was not issued because the abductors were his aunt, uncle, and a cousin. In many instances, in this post-September 11 era, high-tech

8.1 CCTV security video from the Columbine school shooting and students escaping to find security.

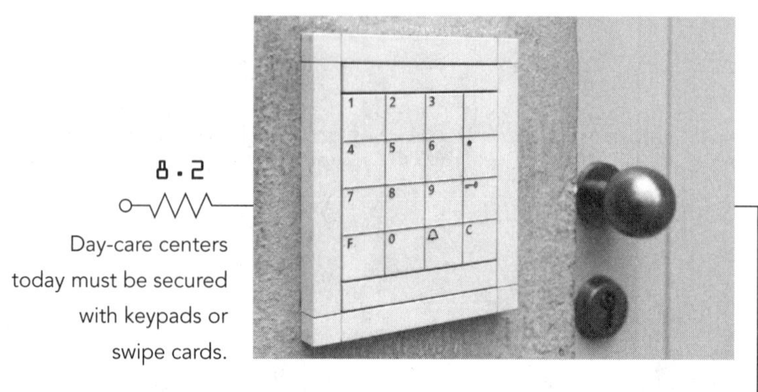

8.2

Day-care centers today must be secured with keypads or swipe cards.

biometric devices and keypads are being used to control access to society's children as security concerns increase and day-care centers are confronted with issues ranging from custody disputes to the threat of child abductions and terrorism. Today, many day-care centers monitor or restrict access to their buildings by using digital keypads or swipe cards, door buzzers, and surveillance cameras, features rarely seen a decade ago. (See Figure 8.2.)

A review of most child care center's policy and procedures guidelines illustrates that security is of utmost concern to parents when leaving their children in the trusted hands of any one of the thousands of child care facilities available across the United States, Canada, and Europe. "Security at a day-care center is paramount," says Geoff Still, director of finance and operations at the Mailman Segal Institute for Early Childhood Studies, which operates two preschools and an infant-toddler program at Nova Southeastern University in Florida. "Ten years ago, parents might have looked at which day care had the best playground equipment or the friendliest teachers. That . . . has changed. The trend is to focus on a more personalized security system" (Kernicky, 2007).

FYI: Child Care Security and Parental Concerns. "I am concerned that security procedures at my son's day-care center are insufficient. There are two child-accessible doors exiting to ungated areas outside, you can just turn the doorknob and go! This has never happened, but there has been a near miss. Of equal concern is that anybody off the street can walk into the building. I have actually witnessed this happening twice in the last two years . . . men came in asking for directions. When I spoke to the owner about my concerns, she claimed nothing could be done because of fire codes. I have since learned from the fire marshal that this is not quite true."

—Concerned Parent—www.childcarelounge.com/Parents/questions

CONTEXT AND EXPERIENCE—BALANCING SECURE AND WELCOMING ENVIRONMENTS

It is a terrible truism today that children in fear cannot learn, and teachers who are on guard against violence in their classrooms cannot impart a love for learning at the same time (see Figure 8.3). However, how do we ensure safety without turning schools into virtual prisons in the name of security?

8.3

Children have an easier time learning in a secure environment.

While the use of behavioral science and methods of reporting suspicious behavior has been instituted in most educational settings, architects and designers are now being asked to consider their design decisions in light of providing built-in security that does not suggest a prison-like atmosphere. Educational places should provide an inviting environment in which children can be protected from threats and learning can take place. The physical environment of schools plays a critical role in keeping students safe (Lawry, 1995). Researchers are continuing to study the role that a facility's physical environment plays in school safety. Notably the high-profile school shootings that have taken place in recent years—Columbine, Colorado, and Thurston, Oregon, and the Virginal Tech shootings within the United States, the 2006 Dawson College shooting in Montreal, Canada, and the 2000 shooting in Brandenburg, Germany, have all increased public, educator, and parental awareness of the importance of providing a safe school environment. It only makes sense that children who feel safe are receptive to learning. How do schools ensure a safe physical environment? What is the important role that designers and architects play in this most important design scenario?

FYI: **Schools of the Twenty-first Century.** Each day more than 59 million students, teachers, and education employees spend considerable time in our nation's schools. With school enrollment projected to increase at record levels through 2013, and spending on school construction, renovation and maintenance expected to total nearly $30 billion annually, the need to transform our schools has never been more urgent. "What we are suggesting is nothing less than a fundamental redefinition of the American schoolhouse. You cannot expect children to learn twenty-first century skills in schools built for the 1950s. We need schools designed for twenty-first century success."

—American Architectural Foundation

DESIGNER'S ROLE

The interior designer's, architect's, and landscape architect's responsibility is to provide school administrators with the principles and techniques to design a school that is safe from attacks and acts of violence, while at the same time creating an environment that is functional, aesthetically pleasing, and meets the needs of the students, staff, and administration. Protecting a school building and grounds from physical attack is a significant challenge because the ability to design, construct, renovate, operate, and maintain the facility is spread across numerous building users, infrastructure systems, and a variety of building design codes (Gaustad, 1999).

FYI: Students Reactions to Safety and Security. A 2002 study completed by CBS News found that 96 percent of students said they felt safe in school. However, 22 percent of those same students said that they knew students who regularly carried weapons to school. This does not mean that students did not fear a school violence incident like Columbine, as 53 percent said that a school shooting could happen in their own school at anytime.

—CBS News, October 2006

CONDUCTING A SECURITY ASSESSMENT

Although overall crime in schools has not increased within the United States and abroad in the past few years, there has been a series of high-profile shootings with multiple victims. The media attention given to these shootings has generated substantial fear and concern in the general public, traumatized victims, and terrified parents. Around the world, we have had waves of bomb threats, angry youth have drawn up hit lists, and in some cases, groups of youth who have conspired to obtain weapons and commit similar atrocities. The Architectural and Design (A & D) community must take note that these shootings deserve our attention, and though as designers we cannot change some of the pervasive problems in our youth culture, we can make the school environment a safer place through the implementation of thoughtful and effective safety and security design solutions (Nadel, 2006).

Preventing school violence through environmental design and technology involves assessment of the physical school environment, whether it is a remodeling or new construction plan, with the intention of increasing the safety and security within the educational setting. As school safety concerns intensify internationally, architects, designers, and school administrators are concluding that although schools should not operate as secure *fortresses*, school building design must integrate security functions into design solutions that control access to school property, as well as maintain control on the premises (see Figure 8.4). Preventing school violence through environmental design enables school officials to provide a safe and secure learning environment that stimulates learning and development. As discussed in Chapter 2, literature dealing with **place-based crime prevention** demonstrates that the design *and* management of places go hand-in-hand.

Therefore, designers cannot view these as separate concerns, but rather, understand they are intimately connected in "real world" scenarios, where day-to-day uses of places can easily affect the original design intent. For example, the design intent of windows facing building entryways to facilitate surveillance fulfills a fundamental crime prevention principle (see Figure 8.5). Within educational settings, if administrators allow staff or students to obstruct the windows (by closing blinds or covering them with posters), their effectiveness as a natural surveillance solution is severely compromised. Management policies and practices must therefore be linked to design to complement crime prevention and deterrence on a continuing basis. It is important to think through the connections between design and management so that local administrators can better appreciate the implications that their decisions may have on facility design and use, and ultimately on crime prevention.

EDUCATIONAL SECURITY RISK ASSESSMENT

When involved in the design of educational facilities, the design professional must understand the basic four questions to be analyzed in any Educational Security Risk Assessment. The four basic questions are:

1. What are the educational assets (people, places, information, and property) that require security protection?
2. What are the criminal or other threats (Street crimes, acts of violence, terrorism, or sabotage) against which the assets must be protected?
3. What are the vulnerabilities of the assets to the threats? (For example, if violence is a threat, can uncontrolled people enter an educational setting unchallenged?)
4. What are the countermeasures within the educational setting to mitigate threats? (For example, does the space planning and design solution channel visitors through a controlled access entry area.) (See Figure 8.6.)

CPTED PRINCIPLES AND EDUCATIONAL SETTINGS

With safety such a high priority in schools, Crime Prevention through Environmental Design (CPTED) offers designers, school planners, and administrators, principles that guide them in creating a safe school environment using enhanced security measures.

As discussed in Chapter 3, the growing awareness about ways in which the physical environment affects human behavior is integrated into a knowledge base known as CPTED. Although CPTED's crime-prevention principles have been successfully applied throughout the world in various community settings, most existing educational facilities were not designed with this knowledge in mind. Most schools in the United States, for example, were built 30 to 60 years ago, with many constructed in the early 1900s. Security issues were almost nonexistent at the time, and technology was dramatically different. As a result, many educational buildings are generally dysfunctional in today's more

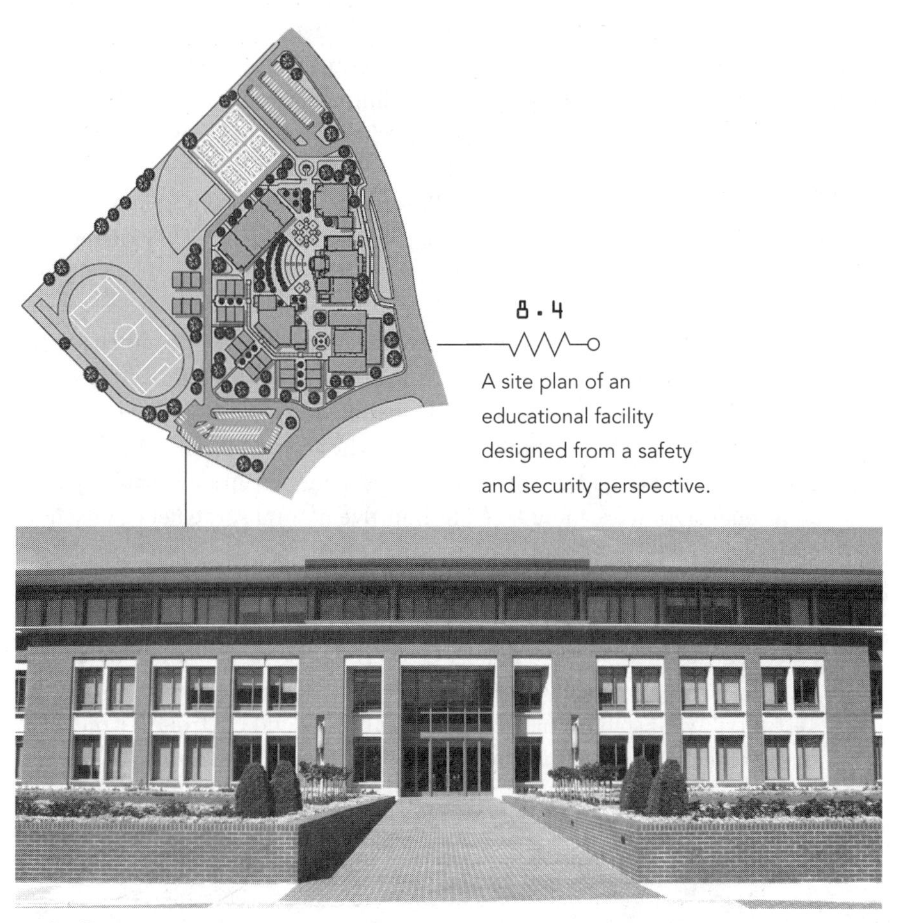

8 • 4

A site plan of an educational facility designed from a safety and security perspective.

8 • 5 An exterior view of an educational facility with visual access control.

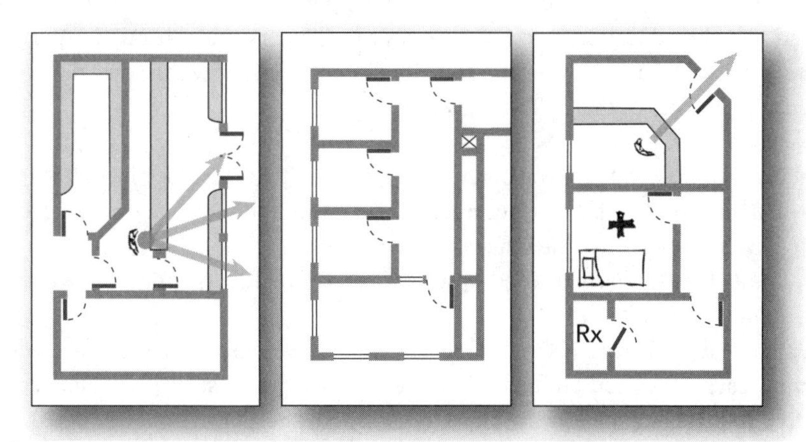

8 • 6 Floor plans of administrative areas and visual surveillance.

security-conscious environment. Current best practices require applying the basic principles of CPTED from the onset of a design project. Not only does the application of the CPTED principles have a minimal impact on a project's costs, but the end result is a safer and more secure school that can focus on its mission of teaching and learning.

How can the key elements of Crime Prevention through Environmental Design be applied to educational environments? Recall that the three key elements of CPTED include:

1. Natural surveillance—Keeping an eye on the whole environment without taking extraordinary measures to do so. *Educational Consideration:* Typical obstacles to natural surveillance include solid walls and a lack of windows that provide visibility to areas of the school building that have experienced a high incidence of problem behaviors. Pruning shrubbery is an additional step that can be taken to improve natural surveillance of school grounds.
2. Natural access control—Determining who can or cannot enter a facility. *Educational Consideration:* Obstacles to access control include unsupervised, unlocked entrances to the building. Converting several secondary doors into locked, alarmed, emergency exits is one way to improve access control.
3. Territoriality—Establishing recognized authority and control over the environment, along with cultivating a sense of belonging. *Educational Consideration:* Poor border definition can impede territoriality, such as uncontrolled park land adjacent to a school's grounds. School uniforms offer one approach to both establishing a sense of belonging, thus creating territoriality, making it easier to distinguish between students and non-students.

CPTED principles and guidelines provide us with a framework that can be integrated into the educational design process, as designers learn through experience and begin to develop case-specific security design solutions within the educational setting. The basics of the CPTED 3-D approach is:

- *Designation.* What is the purpose or intention that the space is used for?
- *Definition.* How is the space defined? What are the social, cultural, legal, and psychological ways the space is defined?
- *Design.* Is the space defined to support prescribed or intended behaviors?

From a CPTED perspective, any arrangement that makes it easier for students to know each other and build bonds while enhancing staff surveillance and access control abilities is a step in the right direction. A site that is well protected with natural surveillance, access control, and territoriality will require less staff time and energy to maintain as a safe environment. This leaves teachers more time to focus on teaching, and students more time to focus on learning, while promoting the overall safety and security of the educational environment.

The use of CPTED principles while planning and programming educational environments assists designers in identifying central problems and providing solutions for change in both the physical and social environment that address safety and security concerns. The CPTED principles of surveillance, access, and territoriality are easily integrated through identification and discussion throughout the design process, into the design, budget, and building of educational facilities. Selected examples of CPTED questions as related to educational settings are covered in the next section.

Design Programming—CPTED Principles

- What risks and opportunities do students encounter between home and school?
- What risks and opportunities are posed in areas directly adjoining school property?
- Can office staff observe approaching visitors before they reach the school entry?
- Do staff members have the physical ability to stop visitors from entering?
- How well can people see what is going on inside the school?
- Do staff members have immediate lockdown capability in classrooms and other locations?
- Is the overall school climate prosocial?
- Are there any identifiable or predictable trouble spots or high-risk locations?

For each of the problems or locations identified above, the design team should determine the following three things:

1. How can we improve natural surveillance?
2. How can we improve access control?
3. How can we improve territoriality?

For example, schools can include visible signage within their community area that formally posts the school's "rules," an exhibit space displaying artwork reinforces a prosocial curriculum, and a greater use of windows to enhance visibility and reduce isolation. These solutions all deal with the CPTED principles of access control, territoriality, and natural surveillance, and are all measures that can be addressed by the interior designer. A problem such as bullying might

8.7 The use of convex mirrors in educational settings provides added security for students, staff, and administration.

require the design response to alter the environment or eliminate isolated locations where bullying incidents occur. This might involve installing convex mirrors, or moving the staff lunch area to improve natural surveillance (see Figure 8.7).

ASSESSING SCHOOL DESIGN

In the design of security programs for K–12 schools, Russell Riddell, of the Thomas Group, a Security Management firm, regularly uses CPTED principles as a steppingstone to guide the design process within educational settings. For example, Riddell's security design team looks at areas within a school where people are not necessarily welcome. To deter would-be thieves from breaking into the building after hours, a design plan would have planting areas three to four feet wide featuring "ornamental-yet-hostile" vegetation underneath accessible windows. The plants might be nice to look at, but the three-inch spines on them would likely have possible intruders thinking twice about breaking and entering.

At one high school, administrators reported between 50 to 60 vandalism incidents in the student parking lot. They turned to the Thomas Group for a budget-minded (but effective) solution. "We looked at the site and asked, 'What's the best way to get natural surveillance?" Riddell recalls, adding that the firm decided to make use of the school's large student body as a means of built-in surveillance. "We moved the student lot to the front of the cafeteria, which is used six or seven periods of the day for lunch and study halls, and created an adjacent outdoor patio," Riddell says. "We oriented the parking layout so that students sitting on the patio could see down the rows of cars" (Suhell, 2006).

It worked. After the change, school administrators noted that vandalism incidents plummeted. They now deal with only two or three occurrences each year. "That's an example of designing a facility to create a natural security environment without putting cameras [around] the perimeter of the building," Riddell says. "There's no doubt that there are areas where technology applications need to be the first and foremost thought, but it doesn't mean that's the case in every facility when you take a comprehensive approach. They may only need a few cameras and an access control system that maintains a secure perimeter. That's why CPTED is getting a closer look" (Suhell, 2006).

FYI: Administrative Areas and CPTED. CPTED principles apply to the administrative areas within an educational setting as well the design security intent of many of these concepts can be applied to other areas within the school environment, such as faculty offices, libraries, and classrooms, as follows:

Natural Access Control
- Locate administration areas adjacent to the main entry and lobby.
- Provide the reception/visitor information area with adequate protection by utilizing a counter and, when necessary, a protective shield.
- Secure faculty offices, student records, and clinic supplies.

Natural Surveillance
- Incorporate extensive interior glazing in administration areas to provide unobstructed views and natural surveillance. (Refer to Figure 8.6.)

Territorial Integrity
- Design and locate the administration area to reinforce its role as the guardian of school facility.
- Provide seating at reception/visitor information areas, and student meeting areas to increase a sense of belonging and community.

Although the fine details of safe school planning can become overwhelmingly complex and every school must consider its different strengths and weaknesses, the CPTED principles are excellent frameworks for the development of an educational safety and security plan. As in most security solutions, integrating security requirements into educational environments, whether a large high school or smaller day-care facility, requires achieving a balance among many objectives. The balance includes reducing risk, facilitating proper building function, meeting required building codes and standards, and aesthetic considerations, all while creating a school environment conducive to learning and social interaction.

Planners, architects, interior designers, and landscape designers play an important role in identifying and implementing these crucial security measures. Throughout the risk-assessment process, the design team must coordinate closely with school districts and school administrators to make certain that the optimal balance of risk, function, life safety, and aesthetics is achieved. Communication and collaboration is critical among members of the design team, as most school safety and security objectives can be achieved during the early stages of the design process when mitigation measures are the least costly and most easily implemented.

CPTED PRINCIPLES IN SCHOOLS—FROM THEORY TO APPLICATION

As discussed throughout this text, safety and security in the built environment is based on several premises: detection, deterrence, and response. Using these premises, Crime Prevention through Environmental Design (CPTED) developed the concepts of Natural Surveillance, Natural Access, and Territoriality to reduce crime through proper facility and site design to create safer built environments.

In addition, the CPTED principles of the 3-Ds, designation, definition, and design, reduce the fortress-like look often associated with highly secure facilities, using a site's natural security defenses to provide some (or all) of the facility-hardening design criteria. This approach considers three aspects of space to gather functional security-design information: understanding the proposed use of the space, how the space is defined, and whether safety and security design recommendations made support issues raised in the areas of designation and definition.

Selected examples of CPTED principles that most relate to the interior environment, and can be addressed through interior design and architectural related design solutions, are highlighted here to further illustrate the application of CPTED principles, security-assessment processes, and considerations specific to educational settings that are integral to the design of safe and secure educational environments:

Observing approaching visitors—Can office staff observe approaching visitors before they reach the school entry? An attentively designed educational facility should provide the opportunity for the main office to serve as a security-screening tool. Its placement should allow staff and administrators, (key players within any educational facility), to evaluate and direct visitors, prohibit undesirables from entering, placate the disgruntled, and help to alleviate general security problems.

By establishing one main entrance and placing appropriate signage identifying it as the main entrance, all visitors will be directed to the main office, assuring natural surveillance and alleviating unauthorized access. A reduction in the number of doors that can be opened from the outside also increases overall safety and security. This does not mean chaining doors or creating a fire hazard. It does mean using doors that cannot be opened from the outside, but can be used from the inside in the event of a fire or other emergency.

Conversely, main offices hidden deep within schools are poorly positioned to guard against unwelcome visitors. Even if offices are located near exterior doorways, the school may have many alternative access points in which intruders may be able to gain entry through secondary doors or even through windows. In addition, a poorly designed signage system can further exacerbate the problem. If signage lacks maps, arrows, or specific directions, and the main office location is unclear, it can be an invitation for a visitor to prowl the halls while presumably looking for a destination. Even if the office is located near the main entry, it may lack appropriately positioned windows, eliminating the important CPTED principal of natural surveillance.

Stopping Visitor Access—Do staff members have the physical ability to stop visitors from entering? Even if staff members can see intruders approaching, can they do anything in response? Are doors locked as a matter of course, once school starts? How quickly and easily can staff lock all entries? Once an intruder is inside the building and approaching or entering the main office, is the situation better or worse? Can staff members protect themselves as well as the student body? The architectural design solution should offer security equipment and technology that allows the school staff to react quickly if presented with a security risk.

Lockdown Capabilities—Do staff members have immediate **lockdown capability** in classrooms and other locations? If ever a crisis were to arise within a school involving staff and students, immediate and important questions occur: how do we call for help, make ourselves safe, protect students, and resolve the situation? It is important to remember that every location within the facility may have to also serve as a safe haven during a crisis.

Interior Visibility—How well can people see what is going on inside the school? Blind corners, "dead walls," alcoves, and stairwells provide "cover," or hidden areas, for unsuitable behavior. Typically, these areas are predictable locations for misbehavior because they are out from under the eyes of authorities. If 90 percent of the school design incorporates natural surveillance, the remaining 10 percent will be prime territory for drug use, bullying, harassment, and other illicit activities. Some areas are easily observed when empty, but become difficult to watch during times of peak use—the "transitional" times before and after classes when most conflicts occur. The use of strategically placed convex mirrors is a cost-effective solution to this common problem. (Refer to Figure 8.7.)

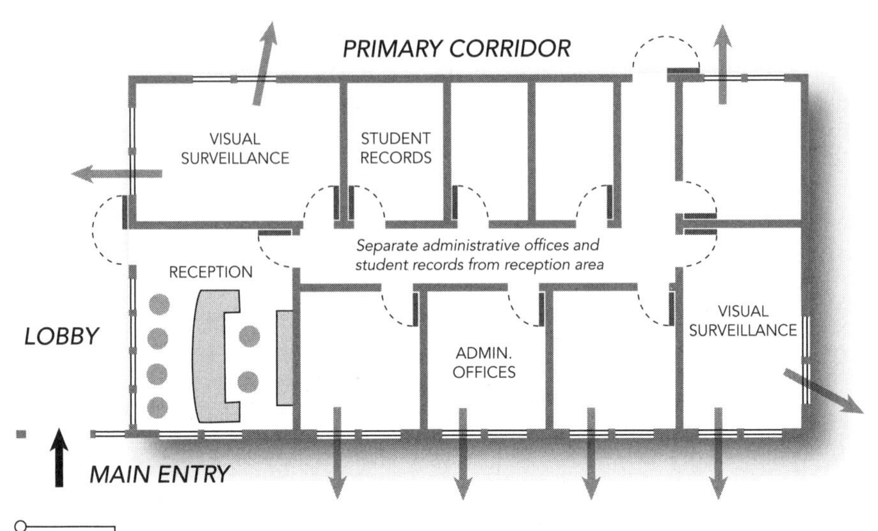

8.8 Corridors that are designed using the CPTED principles are open for easy evacuation and have visual surveillance.

High-Risk Locations—Are there identifiable or predictable trouble spots or high-risk locations? Hallways suffer from a population explosion every 45 minutes. Within a small window of time, most of the student body is competing for space. Hallway locker doors and locker owners create obstacles for the pedestrian traffic flow, as does social interaction. Staff generally avoids hallways during these brief rush hours, and when they are present, lack natural surveillance beyond the students closest at hand. An obscured commotion at the far end of the hall may be completely camouflaged by the chaos blocking the view. (See Figure 8.8.)

FYI: **A Frightening Educational Scenario.** Consider this frightening scenario; classrooms and many other areas have outward-opening doors, designed to meet fire and/or building code egress requirements. If the door is standing open during an emergency, a teacher will have to reach into the hallway—which could be the scene of the crime—to pull the door closed. Even worse, the teacher may have to insert a key on the outside in order to lock the door. That means they will have to step into the hallway, extract a key ring, find the correct key, and insert it into the lock. If the teacher is in distress, their physiology will go through changes as blood rushes to their major muscle groups for fight-or-flight preparation. As a result, the teacher will lose some or all of their fine motor skills, which are required to manipulate a key and insert it into a lock. If this is the only means of securing the door, there is a risk of failure.

Best Practices—Interior Design Recommendations

The following guidelines are selected examples that represent best practices and strategies for school safety and security as considered by the interior designer when evaluating an existing educational facility or planning a new one.

Entries and Lobbies

- School entrances and doorways must create a positive and welcoming first impression, while at the same time incorporating appropriate and necessary security devices, such as locking mechanisms, intercoms, and access-card readers, if appropriate.
- To control access and limit intrusion, visitors should be guided to a single control point and required to pass directly through to administration reception areas when entering or leaving the building.
- Lobbies should be designed to be easily secured after hours and during emergencies.
- The combination of a main entry with a carefully located and constantly staffed administration area can enhance supervision of school entries, stairs, and hallways.
- The entry area should be positioned to allow for unobstructed surveillance of lobby doors, stairwells, and perpendicular hallways.
- When planning a school design, doors should be secured with hardware that is unobtrusive and does not affect the aesthetics of the environment.
- Electronic controls governing the front door would provide a significant opportunity for access control. Staff would be empowered to enact a lockdown with the touch of a button.
- Reconsider any security measures that create vulnerable gathering spots. If tight security at the entry point is required, consider alternate points of access, or staggering attendance times per school grade.
- Maintain natural lines of sight—do not build walls that eliminate natural surveillance. (see Figure 8.9)

Main Office, Visitor Information, and Administration Areas

- Placing the administrative area on an exterior wall provides the additional benefit of increased surveillance and a distant view of outside areas, especially visitor parking, drop-off areas, and exterior routes leading up to the main entrance.
- If appropriate, the office should protrude into a main hallway, allowing natural surveillance up and down at least the main hallway, and perhaps secondary hallways as well. This also establishes access control over visitors.

8.9

Classrooms and offices with windows instead of walls enhance natural surveillance.

- The visitors' information counter, faculty offices, student records, and clinics need to have a high degree of security while maintaining a "sense of accessibility" to students, parents, and visitors.
- Faculty offices and student records should be separated from reception areas and accessible through lockable corridor doors.
- Administration areas should be adjacent to main entry areas and designed to allow a visual connection through windows between administrators and students or visitors.
- The reception/visitor information area should be provided with the minimum protection of a counter. In certain circumstances, a protective shield of Plexiglas may be required.
- When appropriate, consider providing a safe room in the administration area. This room should consist of a lockable door and a working telephone.
- Two remote exits should be provided from the principal's office, one of which could be a window to the exterior.

Classrooms

- Design classrooms to be locked down quickly by faculty inside during an emergency.

- Provide extensive exterior windows from classrooms to enhance surveillance of school campus.
- Design classrooms for easy monitoring and unobstructed visual supervision. Designs should include windows and glazing between hallways and classrooms to help increase surveillance.
- When applicable, lockers, built-in furniture, and storage units in classrooms should be designed so as not to obscure surveillance of the room or provide hiding places.
- Design doors with view panels or sidelights to increase visibility.
- Whenever possible, provide special classroom security locksets, which give teachers the ability to secure a door from inside the classroom without having to enter the corridor. This lockset function should allow egress from the room at all times.

Windows

- Design classroom windows to allow for quick surveillance of the campus by staff and students during the course of their normal activities.
- Windows should not be placed lower than three feet from the floor unless they are protected in some manner from active feet.
- Windows should not be located in exterior play or gathering areas.
- Where constant window breakage is experienced, wire mesh security screens or grillwork can be used. Grillwork, if thoughtfully designed, can be attractive and not convey a prison-like atmosphere. As many fire codes limit the use of wire mesh, check building codes prior to design and installation.

Visibility, Safe Havens, and Communication

- Provide open (cubicle) or screened lockers, specifying lockers that are approximately 42 inches high.
- Design spaces that eliminate the ability for students to gather in large groups to hide inappropriate activities.
- Integrate mirrors, cameras, or observation posts that provide a view over the heads of students and increase visibility.
- Libraries can serve as **safe havens** if securable, and offer thick furniture and piles of books as protection.
- Most importantly, escape routes within safe haven areas must be considered. An emergency exit door, or in some cases windows, should offer alternative means of escape in a crisis.
- Every schoolroom should be designed as a potential safe haven. It should be possible to lock the door during a crisis without entering a danger zone.

- Building and fire codes require an outward opening door if room capacity is beyond a specified number of occupants (check local building codes).
- Each room should have reliable communication device installed. The administration should have the ability to tell everyone, immediately, to lock down, relocate, or evacuate.
- Each room should be examined to determine where best to take cover. Generally, the thicker and denser the material, the better a shield it provides. When planning new construction, thicker materials up to six-feet high (180 centimeters) should be used to provide shielding in walls.

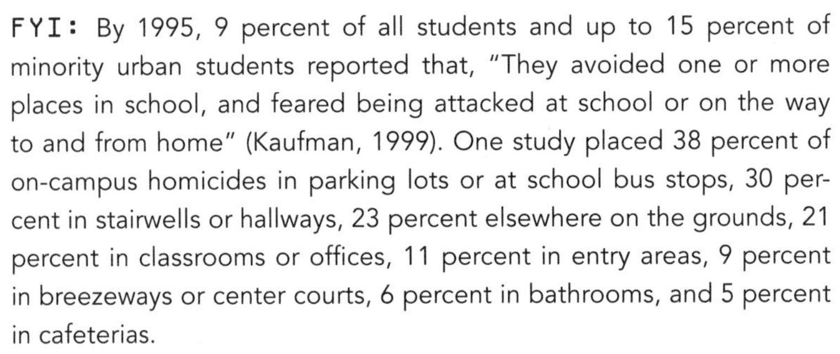

FYI: By 1995, 9 percent of all students and up to 15 percent of minority urban students reported that, "They avoided one or more places in school, and feared being attacked at school or on the way to and from home" (Kaufman, 1999). One study placed 38 percent of on-campus homicides in parking lots or at school bus stops, 30 percent in stairwells or hallways, 23 percent elsewhere on the grounds, 21 percent in classrooms or offices, 11 percent in entry areas, 9 percent in breezeways or center courts, 6 percent in bathrooms, and 5 percent in cafeterias.

—Kachur, 1996

Hallways, Corridors, and Stairwells

- It is recommended that corridors be designed beyond the minimum required width whenever feasible.
- Corridors should be carefully designed to accommodate large numbers of students during peak-use hours.
- Corridor designs that lead to sudden 90-degree turns should be avoided, as they eliminate natural surveillance.
- Convex mirrors mounted high can improve surveillance over crowds and around corners.
- To reduce hiding places and possible injury, water coolers, vending machines, trash containers, and lockers should be either low profile or recessed to be flush with the wall.
- Stairs, like corridors, are susceptible to congestion and consideration should be given to designing stairs and landings beyond the minimum code requirements.
- Open handrails allow visual access to areas on both sides of the stairwells.
- The entire area under all stairs should be enclosed and made inaccessible to students.

- Place staff break rooms at appropriate locations to give the impression of surveillance—mirrored windows can leave students guessing as to whether they can be seen.
- Incorporate interior glazing where possible to avoid long corridors with dead walls that block off natural surveillance.

Bathrooms

Bathrooms have a reputation as unsafe locations within educational settings, in which illicit activity and bullying are common. Many students avoid using school bathrooms altogether for this reason. Even though bathrooms should respect the needs for people's privacy, in this post-9/11 era, one solution has been to provide bathrooms in each classroom. If that is not feasible, the following design considerations are of value for schools with group bathroom facilities:

- Design group toilet rooms that open to the building interior with maze entries (with walls for privacy but no closing doors) utilizing screen partitions rather than double-door entries.
- Utilize vandal-resistant materials, fixtures, and hardware.
- Toilet rooms' entrances should be located in places where natural surveillance can occur such as primary corridors and administration areas.
- Using magnetic latches on stall doors can help prevent students from hiding in stalls to avoid detection, flush away any evidence or illegal contraband, and act as predators.
- Toilet partitions and their doors will be more vandal resistant if they are constructed of laminated plastic that is a mixed dark color.

Cafeterias

- Escape routes are critical, as are communication devices to call for help.
- Locate a well-defined control point near the main entrance of cafeteria that has an unobstructed surveillance of entire cafeteria.
- Design kitchens and serving areas so that they can be secured both during and after school hours.
- Design well-defined one-way entry and exit doors to control circulation patterns and increase visual surveillance.

Lockers and Locker Rooms

- Lockers should be either recessed into the wall or sloped on top to minimize opportunities to gain access to ceiling areas.

- Locate gym instructors' and coaches' offices near the main entrance to the locker room.
- Provide windows in gym instructors' and coaches' offices with unobstructed views into locker area.
- Place lockers along the perimeter walls of locker rooms or limit locker height to enhance surveillance.
- Acoustical ceiling tiles, which allow access to ceiling areas, should not be used in any area of the locker room.
- Place hallway lockers in open areas to provide natural surveillance.
- Recess lockers to eliminate hiding places and limit access to ceiling areas.
- Utilize vandal resistant materials, fixtures, and hardware.

Libraries and Media Centers

- A control point, the circulation desk or reception area, at the main entrance should have unobstructed surveillance of entire library/media center.
- Install detection devices and alarm systems when possible to minimize opportunities for theft of materials and equipment as well as minimize possible hiding places.
- Low stacks that are well spaced and placed parallel to the circulation librarian's line of sight will aid in visual control, as well as reduce hiding places for storing stolen goods, controlled substances, or people.

SECURITY TECHNOLOGY

Recent tragedies involving guns and bombs have prompted many school districts to consider adding high-tech hardware to their traditional lock-and-alarm systems. Metal detectors are an expensive and controversial option. Their potential usefulness for a given school depends on many factors, including the severity of current weapons problems, the availability of funds for staff and training, the physical design of buildings, and possible negative effects on the overall atmosphere of the school.

Metal detectors may help calm public and parental concerns, but a few pieces of security equipment alone will solve the problem. This type of equipment is most effective as one element of a broad-based safety and security plan, which might include CCTV, for example, to observe all public corridors, stairwells, and exterior doors, as well as the cafeteria and gymnasium, during school hours and when in public use on evenings or weekends.

Access control to school campuses and buildings is a top concern for most school officials (see Figure 8.10). School administrators struggle with maintaining a balance between having a user-friendly, welcoming school climate and a facility that is secure from unwanted intruders. Although even the best of schools access

8.10

Entry access security equipment is used by many educational facilities in the twenty-first century.

control efforts will not guarantee that a determined outsider will not be able to gain access to the school, designers and school administrators must take reasonable steps to reduce the risks of unauthorized access. The use of metal detectors, and other types of security hardware, may involve potential civil liberties or liability concerns. Designers and school administrators, together with parents and the community, must undergo a detailed risk assessment to determine their individual level of need for use of security technologies.

FYI: Security cameras and other technologies are not a substitute for human beings. As Hill Walker (1999) of the University of Oregon's Institute on Violence and Destructive Behavior points out, Columbine High School's video cameras were not in use at that school. "If they had been monitored," he says, "perhaps the bombs brought into the school prior to the shootings would have been detected and the plot uncovered."

CHILD CARE FACILITIES

Security design considerations and risk assessment analysis for child care facility are similar to other types of educational settings in that they apply CPTED principles, and have the far-reaching goal of creating a safe and secure environment in which children can learn, play, and grow. In today's post-9/11 era, parents are asking specific security-related questions when selecting a child care center, such as:

- Is there restricted access to the classrooms and play areas?
- Is there a security fence around the playground and outside perimeter?
- Are there surveillance cameras monitoring indoor and outside activity?
- What are the center's policies when signing out a child?
- Do employees ask for identification or a password?
- What is the policy and lockdown procedure in the event of emergencies?

These important parental questions of concern are all areas that can be addressed through the design of the physical environment by the design professional. A thorough risk assessment of the facility that includes designers, administrators, and parents, will clarify the important safety and security concerns that must be implemented to best protect young children while not under parental care. In the next section are selected examples of safety and security design considerations and recommendations that are critical components in the design of a safe and secure child care facility.

Assessing Child-care Environments

- Ideally, classrooms should have direct access to the play yard.
- Entry should be restricted through one secured main entrance and perhaps an additional secured service entry for kitchen and other bulk supply deliveries.
- Provide maximum visibility of entry points from inside the center.
- The play yard should be directly accessible from the building or as close to it as practical.
- At least one interior viewing panel at children's height should be located both adjacent to corridors and between classrooms, where possible.
- The entry approach should be visible by center staff located inside.
- Position the reception area adjacent to the entry and director's office.
- Ensure that a child is unable to leave the center without the knowledge of the staff.
- Avoid placing operable windows near a public sidewalk and be mindful of the ability of children to open exit doors.
- Have a keypad at the entry door for authorized entry to the center without relying on other staff for assistance or monitoring and it should be suitable for use by the disabled.
- Alarms at all entry points and delayed alarm locks at exit doors.

- Natural light into the interior, visual access from the interior to the outside, and visual access within the center are important in environments for children.
- Windows should be provided from classrooms to the outside, between classrooms, and from classrooms to circulation paths. Visibility and standing heights of both children and adults should be considered.

ALLIED PROFESSIONS

As a member of the design team, the interior design professional must appreciate many of the basic safety and security solutions undertaken by allied design professionals, such as architects (AIA) and landscape architects (ASLA), when planning safe learning environments. Several architectural and landscape architectural considerations can be implemented to mitigate the effects of a bombing, shooting, and/or an act of violence on a school facility. Detailed information about security solutions and considerations for these allied professions can be found at www.aia.org and www.asla.org. The next two sections list selected examples of security design considerations as practiced by the architectural and landscape architecture professions:

Best Practices—Architecture

- Avoid eaves and overhangs, because they can be points of high local pressure and suction during blasts. When these elements are used, they should be designed to withstand blast effects.
- Design walls and architectural features that do not allow footholds or handholds to prevent roof access.
- Use smooth exterior building materials and finishes on columns and other supports to discourage climbing.
- Avoid having exposed structural elements (e.g., columns) on the exterior of the school to maintain structural integrity in event of a blast.
- Avoid putting unnecessary niches in exterior walls that can create hiding places.
- Provide exterior vandal-proof lighting at building entrances and along glassed areas of the building.
- Provide foyers with reinforced concrete walls, and interior and exterior doors offset from each other in the foyer.
- Use wire mesh in plaster to reduce the incidents of flying fragments.
- If possible, ground-floor windows should be eliminated.
- Increase leves of illumination at potential points of access into the building, such as the main entrance, side entrances, and delivery entrances.

Best Practices—Landscape Architecture

- Design landscaping and tree placement to eliminate roof access.
- Do not let shrubs, trees, and landscape features impede visual surveillance on the school site.
- Use fencing to limit the number of entry/exit points onto school grounds.
- Utilize fencing that does not permit footholds.
- Locate site entry points in high-visibility areas where they can be easily observed and monitored by school personnel.
- Locate visitor parking adjacent to main entry and administration.
- Use gates and removable bollards to restrict unwanted traffic from walks and driveways.
- Keep bushes against buildings low and shrubs limited to low ground cover.
- Keep trees at least ten feet from buildings to prevent window and roof access.
- Place prickly plantings next to walks and buildings to channel pedestrian traffic (some nursery associations can provide recommendations for plants that are suitable for crime prevention purposes).

CONCLUSION

Recent research, and the many tragic events that have occurred in schools and child care facilities around the world in the twenty-first century, makes a strong case for the importance of safety and security design solutions within educational settings. Some believe that, if possible, future educational environments should be designed as smaller schools. The belief is that in order to promote more personal learning communities, boost academic performance, improve the likelihood of personal connections and attention, reduce isolation and achievement gaps, build group cohesion, and make staff coordination easier, as well as to improve school safety, the overall scale of future designed educational settings should be smaller in scale. The research suggests a size limit of 300 to 400 students in elementary schools, no more than 600 in junior high or middle schools, and between 600 and 900 students in high schools (Lackney, 2001).

Realistically, many social, political, and economic factors make it impossible for most communities to design smaller educational facilities. Typically, schools are designed to accommodate hundreds, and oftentimes, thousands of students. One example of large scale educational setting, the AE Stevenson High School, Lincolnshire, IL, designed by the architect OWP/P, provides an excellent paradigm of a school designed for the twenty-first century. The use of CPTED principles throughout provides an open and inviting educational setting that creates a sense of community, while allowing administrators and staff to monitor students' activities—all without feeling like a prison, but rather an

8.11

This contemporary educational facility creates a sense of community, while still providing a secure environment.

open, attractive, and inspirational learning environment in which to learn and grow. (See Figure 8.11.)

Regardless of the size of the educational environment, it is the responsibility of the design professional to provide school administrators with the basic principles and techniques to design a school that is safe from attacks, and acts of violence, while at the same time creating an environment that is functional, aesthetically pleasing, and meets the needs of the students, staff, and administration.

KEY CONCEPTS

- Within the context and experience of educational settings it is important to find the balance between secure and welcoming environments. It is a terrible truism today that children in fear cannot learn, and teachers who are on guard against violence in their classrooms cannot impart a love for learning at the same time. How do we ensure safety without turning schools into virtual prisons in the name of security?
- While the use of behavioral science and methods of reporting suspicious behavior have been instituted in most educational settings, architects and designers are now being asked to consider their design decisions in light of providing built-in security that does not suggest a prison-like atmosphere.
- The interior designer's, architect's, and landscape architect's responsibility is to provide school administrators with the principles and techniques to design a school that is safe from attacks, and acts of violence, while at the same time creating an environment that is functional, aesthetically pleasing, and meets the needs of the students, staff, and administration.
- Protecting a school building and grounds from physical attack is a significant challenge because the ability to design, construct, renovate, operate, and maintain the facility is spread across numerous building users, infrastructure systems, and a variety of building design codes.
- Preventing school violence through environmental design and technology involves assessment of the physical school environment, whether it is a remodeling or new construction plan, with the intention of increasing the safety and security within the educational setting.
- As school safety concerns intensify internationally, architects, designers, and school administrators are concluding that although schools should not operate as secure fortresses, school building design must integrate security functions into design solutions that control access to school property, as well as maintain control on the premises.
- With safety such a high priority in schools, Crime Prevention through Environmental Design (CPTED) offers designers, school planners, and administrators principles that guide them in creating a safe school environment using enhanced security measures.
- The use of security technology within educational settings depends on many factors, including the severity of current weapons problems, the availability of funds for staff and training, the physical design of buildings, and possible negative effects on the overall atmosphere of the school.
- Security design considerations and risk-assessment analysis for child care facilities are similar to other types of educational settings in that they apply CPTED principles, and have the far-reaching goal of creating a safe and secure environment in which children can learn, play, and grow.

ASSIGNMENTS

1. Discuss the important role of security in the design of educational environments.
2. Discuss how the changing standards of care in design and construction are integrated into educational settings as security solutions.
3. Provide examples of how programming issues, design criteria, and risk-assessment issues are involved in educational settings.

ACTIVITIES

1. Journaling activity: respond in written and graphic format. Probes may include visiting educational environments that have obvious and obtrusive security measures versus sites that provide more transparent security design solutions. Orally share your experiences while generating a list about the physical and psychological differences between theses varied educational settings.
2. Conduct interviews with peers, friends, and family to identify a variety of educational security scenarios. Research examples of types of security measure and/or equipment stated in interviews. Discuss how these products might be integrated into the built environment.
3. Research security equipment–related Web sites and compile a list of five products. Note the dimensions, installation methods, maintenance requirements, finish selections, and so forth to become familiar with security technology products.
4. Create a project that requires, as a component of the programming and design process, the integration of security needs/theories in identifying and articulating design problems within educational settings.
5. Visit a site that has implemented obvious security control measures with a required exercise in behavioral mapping.
6. Interview members of the allied professions, i.e., architects, landscape architects, school administrators, and so on for an overview of how professional practice and design challenges have changed with the added security measures of the twenty-first century. Follow up with a systematic discussion.

7 2 9 6 5 8 3 4 1 0

9 DESIGNING FOR SAFETY AND SECURITY—AN INTEGRATIVE PARADIGM

To whom does design address itself: to the greatest number, to the specialist of an enlightened matter, to a privileged social class? Design addresses itself to the need.

—Charles Eames

OBJECTIVES

- Look in the rearview mirror and discover the designers' role in creating safe and secure environments.
- Develop an appreciation for building security and the need for involvement and participation by the design team members.
- Develop an understanding of crime prevention and environmental design principles and how they compare to transparent versus hardened security approaches.
- Realize the designer's critical role in and relationship to security perspectievs and emerging issues.
- Articulate a system's model for design and security in the built environment.
- Provide an integrative framework to the investigation of design and security in the built environment.
- Explore interdisciplinary lessons and paradigms on security, design, and context.
- Make connections and investigate parallels between security in the built environment and other fields.

Exciting partnerships and innovative approaches are developing to effectively and proactively address design and security in the built environment. The goals of many of these partnerships move beyond the immediate response to threat, and focus on investing environments with people. One such partnership is between the New York City Art Commission and the Design Trust for Public Space, and the emergence of interdisciplinary design fellowships dealing with security in the built environment. This partnership is aimed at identifying the means by which art and design can play an important role in making facilities safe directly and indirectly. By enhancing facility users' interaction with their environment, a sense of satisfaction and ownership develops. "The Commission believes that a positive aesthetic experience (for example, enjoyment of a mural in a school or hospital) gives the public a personal stake in assuring the security of a public space." (Russell et al, 2002).

Fossil Ridge High School in Fort Collins, Colorado, demonstrates another example of participatory, proactive, integrative, and collaborative spirit. The school is designed to house 1800 students, while simultaneously affording them the environment and attention common in smaller schools. In a true approach of User-Centered Design, RB+B Architects, Inc., and a committee of educators developed the idea of one 300,000-square-foot, $38.5 million, building containing three separate learning communities, and affording great opportunities for direct environmental involvement with the building as teaching tool. Each of three wings in the north half of the school operates as a semi-autonomous institution for 600 students, with its own core curriculum, student work areas, and administration. This configuration provides an intimate and flexible learning environment within a larger footprint, encouraging creativity and collaboration among both teachers and students. Specialty courses, such as music, are taught outside the smaller communities. South of the three wings are a large, daylight-filled media center; physical education facilities; and spaces for the visual and performing arts. Teachers are delighted with how the unusual configuration is working and report a strong sense of community among the students. Territorial reinforcement and active participation in the learning communities translates into investment in and protection of place.

LOOKING IN THE REARVIEW MIRROR

Although the realities of increased threats of terrorism, crime, and workplace violence are not disputed, liability concerns over the security of interior spaces and places has also become of greater importance. The design professional's commitment to protect the health, safety, and welfare of the public can be merged with proactive safety and security perspectives to provide opportunities for fresh and innovative design solutions to the built environments of the twenty-first century.

Chapter 1 considered the questions: are safety and security tangible and measurable concepts? Are they physical? Are they psychological? How do we assess

9.1 A social commentary on security.

the degree of the human need for safety and security? How can we design environments that satisfy a diversity of basic, as well as situational safety and security, needs? What are the characteristics of safe environments? When is it that we feel and are secure? Chapters 2 and 3 outlined theoretical perspectives and applications in the built environment related to security. Chapters 4 through 8 addressed security pertaining to specific types of environments. Throughout the book, the premises of interdisciplinary integration, systems thinking, and centrality of a design and security dialogue have been stressed. Researchers and stakeholders are investigating the various aspects related to safety and security from a wide range of disciplines and paradigms, such as; psychology, sociology, physiology, ethics, and forms of social commentary. (See Figure 9.1.) It is important that the interior designer, in partnership with related design disciplines, investigate the relationship between these varied perspectives and their potential for integration and innovation as they relate to the built environment.

FYI: **Interior Design as a profession** deals with the health, safety, and welfare of the public through its understanding of accessibility, ergonomics, and building codes, to improve quality of life. The security component has gained more significance and is recognized as an additional layer of professional responsibility to minimize risk and therefore increase safety in the planning and integration of security features into the design solutions of the interior environment.

The interior designer's commitment to protect the health, safety, and welfare of the public through his or her professional work requires that we become effective leaders and contributors in the creation and implementation of the new security guidelines and measures as they relate to the built environment in general, and the interior domain in particular. As designers grapple with the impetus of the demands of the new heightened risk awareness and the importance of considering new and safer design alternatives, our responsibility is to our clients. We must assure them that security has become an integral part of the programming process, and is as important as the issues of accessibility, fire safety, and other life safety codes.

As designers, we are involved in this web of intricate dialogue between environment, people, and security. Our built environment is an important canvas for our hopes, dreams, fears, and everyday lives. An intimate relationship exists between the physicality and the perception of the environment; between our experience with the environment and the memories we carry with us about those environments. The personal and universal iconography of our spaces and places can be affected with the solutions we create, and as we face new security threats, the sense of place and place attachment can become victims of such solutions (see Figure 9.2).

BUILDING SECURITY OVERVIEW

General building security involves technical, physical, and operational solutions. Design strategies that have been proposed by security professionals, architects, landscape architects, and facility managers revolve around several themes or strategies. Some of these strategies are applicable in interior design settings; however, it is in the collaborative interdisciplinary approach from the inception of the idea until its conclusion—and beyond—that the full potential of these strategies is realized. Interior designers, facility managers, fire, security and code officials, other design professionals, and building occupants should be involved at the onset of the planning and design process. This allows the project team to look at issues holistically and remain flexible to the challenges of potential risks and security concerns. Security in this sense is similar to accessibility, if a designer approached the problem from only a "meet the code" perspective or as an afterthought, the resulting solution is often costly, lacks cohesion and flexibility, and does not meet the spirit of universal access (see Figure 9.3).

The tendency to **harden targets**, to modify building elements, such as walls, doors, and windows, as a strategy to meet security needs become ineffective, and most likely obtrusive to the experience of public space. The demand to balance the need for life-safety, openness, and enhanced security while maintaining high levels of preparedness requires project-specific **transparent design solutions**. Transparent design solutions integrate security and design in ways that most people do not

9 • 2

When barriers are placed in familiar environments, our perception and relationship with these areas are often affected as well.

9 • 3

Designers need to consider what kind of space they are designing—a solution for one environment may not necessarily work in another.

even notice. They are the creative solutions that provide security that is unobtrusive to the public eye, minimizes obvious barriers, and maximizes design excellence.

CRIME PREVENTION THROUGH ENVIRONMENTAL DESIGN

As reviewed in Chapter 2, *Crime Prevention through Environmental Design,* or CPTED, advocates various venues for integrating security within the design and management of the built environment. CPTED's mission is defined as "the proper design and effective use of the built environment that can lead to a reduction in the fear and incidence of crime and an improvement in the quality of life." The goal of CPTED is to reduce opportunities for crime that may be inherent in the design of structures, and to that goal, they propose several guidelines that have been adopted by law enforcement, planners, architects, and policy makers internationally. An overriding design principle of CPTED when integrating security into the built environment is the principle goal of maintaining a setting that is welcoming to the visitors and users of the facility.

Opportunities to create security amenities that are transparent and seamlessly integrated with the character of the space not only enhances the experience of the users, but also provides the necessary security layering needed. The significance of many of the acts of violence as previously discussed throughout this textbook is the characterization of those targets as **soft targets**, which essentially describes the majority of the everyday built environments in which we live, work, and play.

FYI: **A CPTED Review.** Conceptually, the four CPTED principles are applied through the 3-D approach, or the three functions or dimensions of human space: designation, definition and design. The 3-D approach is a simple space assessment guide that helps the user to determine the appropriateness of how a space is designed and used.

In addition, CPTED emphasizes the connection between the functional objectives of space utilization and behavior management. As reviewed in Chapter 2, *Natural Surveillance* is the capacity to see what's occurring without having to take special measures to do so; *Natural Access* control is the capacity to limit who can gain entry to a facility; and *Territoriality* is the capacity to establish authority over an environment, making a statement about who is in charge, who belongs, and who is an outsider. From the onset of the design problem, security considerations should become an integrated and transparent component of the problem definition and criteria used to solve the design problem (see Figure 9.4). The outcome of such an integrated approach is a more sustainable and effective design solution, where a seamless connection between security and other functional, social, aesthetic, and economic considerations is achieved.

DESIGNERS' ROLES AND RELATIONSHIPS TO SECURITY ISSUES

The universal need for security and safety is not the issue at question, rather, it is how one can define and conceptualize parameters of the idea, and go about addressing it in the built environment. Theorists and researchers have addressed both physical and psychological dimensions of security, and attempted to define the conditions necessary to increase safety and minimize crime and violence. Some of the methods advocated raise serious questions regarding issues of inclusiveness, displacement, psychological and social impact, design fit, and intrusion, as well as sustainability of solutions.

A transformational approach to security consideration in the built environment has been in the making for many decades, and provides a prime window of opportunity for designers to become actively involved in the formation and emergence of a new era of security consciousness. Designers understand that vital, active places are critical to the health and long-term sustainability of communities. Designers are also cognizant of the role they can play in facilitating and advancing a security plan that is seamless and integrated in the design, construction, and management of the environment. The concern here is for proactive and responsible security considerations that add to, not take away from, the civic vision of a place, that highlight, not hinder, the identity of an environment, and ones that empower, not stifle a community's health and participation.

Architecture and design are not only about major civic and iconic buildings and structures; they are also truly about the everyday places and spaces for

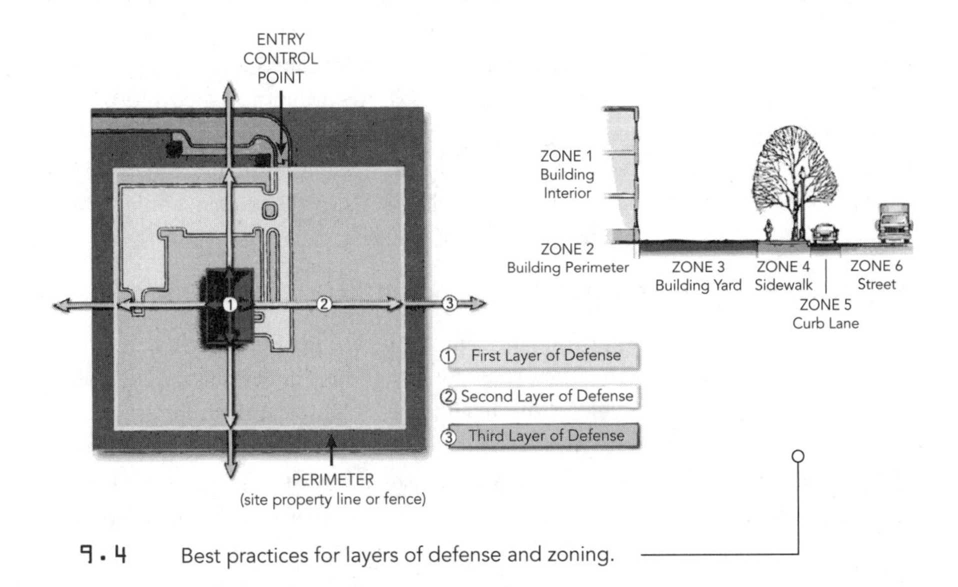

9.4 Best practices for layers of defense and zoning.

people, with their dreams and aspirations. Design and construction professionals are entrusted to design, build, and operate these environments in a way that assures public health and safety, preserves the environment, and promotes security. This role is perhaps one of the most significant as it directly affects the physical, mental, psychological, social, and economic aspects of life.

The interior design profession can fulfill its specialized role in protecting the health, safety, and welfare of users of public spaces by partnering with clients, end-users, and allied professionals to provide design solutions that increase the safety and security within the built environment. Designers have an active and participatory role in looking at design solutions from risk-perception as well as safety-management perspectives from the onset of the preprogramming process of any design project. Proactive security design solutions offer psychological comfort to inhabitants knowing that these spaces have been "secured" the best they can through thoughtful risk assessment, with measures added that may decrease the likelihood of harm, damage, and physical and/or psychological injury.

Whether in reaction to crime, natural disaster, terrorist attack, or in the course of everyday life, security, together with global warming, is now the world's number one concern, and those with professional expertise in this area have never been more needed. Interviews with security experts, designers, and users of spaces and places articulate the need for normalcy and contextual grounding in security solutions. Dr. Rand Lewis, who is a veteran of more than 30 years of military and security experience, and the founder of Transnational Strategic Solutions, Inc. (TS2 Corp), gives firsthand testimony on behalf of security in the built environment and directs security breach scenarios to building professionals, the military, and security organizations. Lewis (personal interview, 2007) believes that the largest impact of the September 11, 2001, terrorist acts in the United States is that people, at the outset, are demanding to know how to mitigate threats realistically and proactively without negatively impacting their everyday lives. According to Lewis (2007), the main points for successful security solutions are often common sense approaches, multifaceted and interrelated, ranging from locating facilities in areas that are not as susceptible to attacks, to increasing activity levels in those environments and populating them with stakeholders instead of vacating them.

Standards of Care in Design and Construction

Fundamentally, owners, designers, and contractors are held to a high standard of care in performing their work. The professional standard of care has been applied most frequently in cases alleging the negligence of physicians, architects, engineers, and attorneys, but any professional may be held to the acceptable degree of knowledge, training, and skill ordinarily possessed by others in the profession, including interior designers. Negligence in relation to planning for safety and security within the built environment has become evidence for not meeting the *reasonable standard* of care for the architectural and design community. Generally, reasonableness is determined by foreseeability—what a reasonably prudent person could be expected to foresee as a possible consequence of his or her acts or omissions. Security dialogues and emerging security solutions in the twenty-first century are considered the reasonable standard of care within the profession.

User-Centered Design

User Centered-Design (UCD) is a philosophy and a process. It is a philosophy that places the person (as opposed to the "thing") at the center; it is a process that focuses on cognitive factors (such as perception, memory, learning, problem-solving, etc.) as they come into play during peoples' interactions with things. This approach is significant in design and particularly while addressing transactional scenarios involving people and environment, such as when one design decision leads to unanticipated behaviors within the setting. UCD seeks to answer questions about users and their tasks and goals, and then uses the findings to drive development and design. UCD seeks to answer questions such as: Who are the users of this space/product/service? What are the users' tasks and goals? What functions do the users need from this space/product/service? UCD and participatory design strategies can improve the usability, acceptance, integration, and usefulness of design solutions from the outset. Designers must think of and employ security design solutions from a user-centered perspective.

Security Layering—the Onion Philosophy

Thinking that a single security countermeasure will address all security issues within a building or a space is misleading. The layering of security, or the "**Onion Philosophy**," is a more appropriate and realistic perspective in how effective design and security can be implemented. For example, one may see the first layer as being the outside skin of the onion, which translates to the site perimeter of the property. Subsequently, the building skin of the architecture is the next layer. Sensitive areas within a building are deeper layers requiring protection, and finally special people, information, or property may require point protection or the center of the onion. The site perimeter is the first, the building skin is the next layer of protection, and the next layer is the interior space planning and security. The same principle, seen at a microscale can be applied within the interior environment, moving from general to more specialized areas and zones of security. The process of risk assessment and security design is especially relevant in the architecture of schools, hospitals, airports, office buildings, multifamily apartment buildings, or other types of environments that may be exhibiting signs of architectural or social vulnerability to attack.

The result of the preliminary security assessment should be integrated as a seamless countermeasure in the design solution. In addition, in the case of required government standards, such as any federal building, the assessment results are assigned a defined Level of Protection (LOP) with specified countermeasures. When the LOP is defined, the specified countermeasures are priced and again the owner may select appropriate measures depending on a prudent level of protection and the cost effectiveness of the measure.

Systems Approach

The nature of security in the built environment is complex and multifaceted, with environmental, psychological, physical, economic, social, cultural, aesthetic, functional, and political variables and dimensions. The complexity presented by addressing security in the built environment demands an integrated systems-based approach. Systems theory provides an internally consistent framework for classifying and evaluating the world.

A system is any set of patterns, entities, or components that interact together to form a whole. Any particular built environments can be characterized as a system, or as a subsystem within a larger ecosystem (see Chapter 1). For the particulars of security in the built environment, the systems approach is helpful because it can be addressed at conceptual, schematic, and design development stages, as well as the post-occupancy level in an action-oriented framework.

A systems approach provides a common method for the study of societal and organizational patterns. It offers a well-defined vocabulary to maximize communication across disciplines. Rather than being an end in itself, systems theory is a way of looking at things. It is an internally consistent method of scholarly inquiry that can be applied to all areas of social science. In a sense, those same characteristics become evident in our dialogue on security, related to the degree of freedom of access and control for various stakeholders in an environment. In this instance, designing for security should not take a "one size fits all" approach.

A SYSTEM'S MODEL FOR DESIGN AND SECURITY

The approach advocated here is based upon several suppositions that make up the model illustrated in Figure 9.5. The model begins with the belief that security is a basic human right and need (see Chapters 1 and 2). The link between security and the cultural context (which is used here to mean the overall context of a person or an environment) is embedded in concepts of cultural understanding of risk perception and management (see Chapter 2). This relationship is reflected in our built environment design, use, and management (see Chapters 3 through 8). Risk perception and management affects decisions made about the design, use, occupancy, and articulation of interior spaces, as well as site and building design and construction.

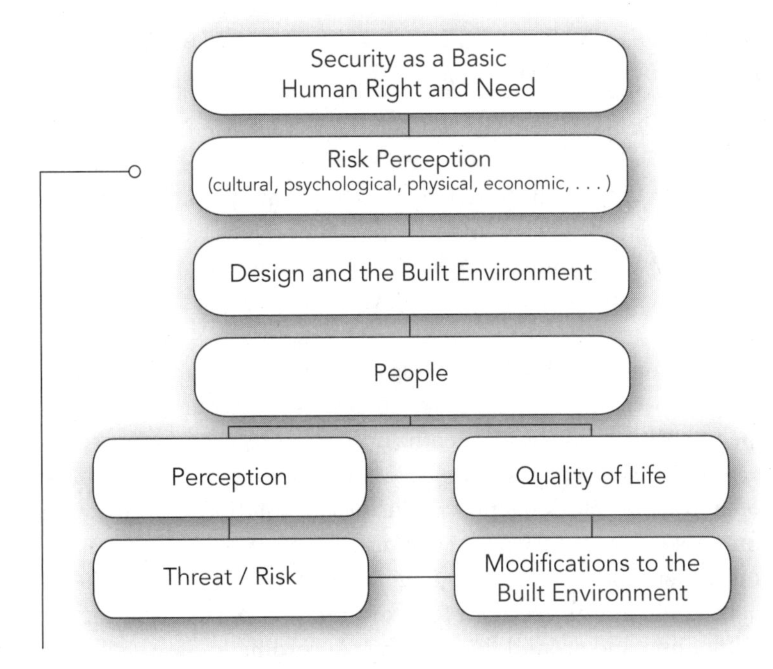

9.5 An integrative system's model for design and security in the built environment.

People's perception of how the environment fits their image of the good life, as well as the actual congruence between the environment and an occupant's needs and desires, manifest quality-of-life indicators in the built environment. The degree to which occupants can modify, alter, or control their environment conversely affects their sense of control in the face of threats and risks, which in turn, affects the quality of life. Overall, for the cycle of the perception and management of issues of security and safety to be sustainable and complete and to create a sense of security and control, the discussion must include all design professionals, end-users, and mangers of the built environment.

As we aspire to represent people's needs and wants in our designs, we continually strive to affect their quality of life and their experience of the spaces and places that we create. Threat to either the quality of life or to the environment is filtered through the cultural risk perception first and mediated by the modifications or changes to the built environment. In this sense, we are all involved in this web of intricate dialogue between environment, people, and security. While preparing a project brief, it behooves us to reflect on the details of the context, program, users, and overall design goals, and to situate safety and security solutions as seamlessly as possible within an eye for the everyday life of the project and its stakeholders.

INTERDISCIPLINARY LESSONS AND PARADIGMS ON SECURITY, DESIGN, AND CONTEXT

Brandon Lorenz, Senior Editor of *Building Operating Management* magazine, states that "While construction in the U.S. may have slid since 9/11, high-rise innovation has not. As the industry rebounds, unique approaches are being found to solve both familiar challenges and new post-9/11 difficulties that have slowed the market" (2007). This innovation is taking place with greater focus on direct lessons from sustainability, security, business, engineering, sciences, and human resources.

Realizing that one size doesn't fit all is a significant lesson in the recent security dialogue. A customized approach to design and security that was based on site-specific threat assessment led to utilization of transparent security in innovative strategies in Chicago's 111 S. Wacker Drive building commissioned by developer, the John Buck Company. The design solution elegantly embodies innovation, lessons learned from the World Trade towers' collapse, sustainability, and recognition of the demanding needs of tenants. The building sports an open lobby, which was designed to afford security personnel clear views of what is going on in and around the building. According to Steve Nilles, a partner at Goettsch Partners, Inc., who designed the building, "Security doesn't mean enclosure. Sometimes it means transparency, especially when it comes to desk monitoring locations. From that desk you can see the whole neighborhood, which is better than walling yourself off, in my opinion" (Brandon Lorenz, 2007 and AEC, 2005). Hardened stairwells are also used in the building. While some buildings go beyond code on stair width, the decision is still controversial according to Nilles, as it will translate into added costs for the building and tenants as well.

ACCESS CONTROL, LAYERS OF SECURITY, AND SENSE OF PLACE—LESSONS FROM INFORMATION TECHNOLOGY

Access control is a significant aspect of any design and security approach. Perhaps a most intriguing parallel is how *role-based access* is defined in information technology and its possible implications in the built environment. Role-based security is built on the premise that users are authenticated, which is the process of identifying the user. A *role* is a category of users who share the same security privileges. When granting a given role access to an environment, access is granted to all members of that role, rather than to specific individuals. Questions about who are the legitimate users of the space, the authorized or anticipated degree of interaction with the space and its users, how identity is verified, how access may be both open and controlled at the same time are all necessary questions to be investigated

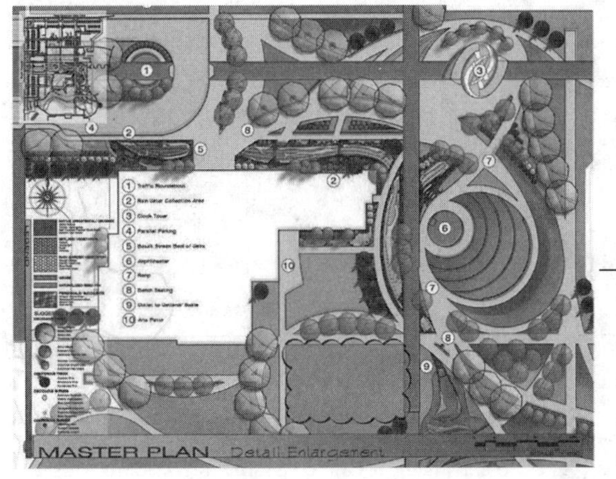

9.6

This example provides an intergrated approach of systems thinking and crime prevention through environmental design.

when addressing access control. On many campuses and particularly in design studios for example, access to the studio is role based; the after-hours access is given to individuals who are teachers or students, once those individuals are out of this role, access is no longer provided after hours.

Once identified, the user can be authorized or assigned roles and permissions. Becoming aware of myriad available equipment and related technologies and how identity is verified and access authorization is made, designers are able to make educated design decisions about achieving secure access to controlled environments. Role-based security allows security administrators to assign access permissions to users based on the roles they play rather than on their individual identities. In health-care facilities for example, visitor's and vendor's badges are issued and screened at controlled access points, and visitors and vendors are assigned authorized access for a specified duration and movement within specific area within the setting. Discovering the roles users play in any environment requires analysis of possible user groups, the general public, and authorized activities within the identified context and its parameters. An innovative approach that creatively solves design challenges and seamlessly integrates evolving levels of security in a new University of Idaho branch campus in Sandpoint, Idaho, is provided by Jordan Wu, senior University of Idaho Landscape Architecture student and his supervising professor Stephen Drown (see Figure 9.6). The solution exemplifies systems approach as it capitalizes on the natural setting, connects to city protection services, affords flexibility of controlled access, and embraces values of openness, beauty, and levels of transparency. By engaging stakeholders in the setting it tends to become a less-appealing crime target, people who use it or live near it also have less to fear. This is consistent with the theories that come out of the "Broken Windows" research, other research in the crime-prevention community, and the personal interviews conducted for this textbook.

9.7

By integrating streamlined cameras and technology and sensitively locating security checkpoints, designers can protect historic sites. Designers can also use features and forms that are contextually based, such as this verandah and decorative barriers.

Interdisciplinary Lessons, Information Technology, and Segregation

An analogy between information technology, biological systems, and the built environment can be made related to behavior when a threat is made. This analogy is primarily that of segregating components, and affecting hierarchical levels of protection. The realization of how information technology deals on a continuous basis with various forms of threats and ameliorates risks can be of great benefit to the dialogue of the evolving nature of threats in the built environment, specifically as it relates to crime displacement, scale of risk, and significance of situation. Hierarchical ordering of levels of security is necessary to be able to deal with the myriad of risks. In some instances for example, some lapses may be unavoidable, and threats are manageable, however, in others, such lapses can be disastrous. The hardening of specific targets within a security dialogue and providing other forms of protection for others is, on a particular level, a hierarchical ordering of risks and valuing of targets. They can be synonymous to multimodal ITS components that are put in place to protect the central infrastructure and the most significant information that is central to the sustainable life of the system after a security breach.

The threat to our sense of safety and security is not only about the breach in security at hand; but often it is about the significance of the breach in context as well as the risks associated with particular security solutions. The central point is the impact on our life as we choose to live it. Respect for context and minimizing the degree of security-solution intrusion on significant aspects of the built environment is key to mitigating the effects of the risks perceived. (See Figure 9.7.)

Lessons from Vulnerability Sciences—Vulnerability–Human Security Relationships

The current and heightened sense of and attention to security evokes discussions related to vulnerability and social change. As designers, it is imperative to understand the degree to which stakeholders are attuned to the whole of their environment, and to what degree certain measures related to security may be embraced or rejected; hence our attention to vulnerability studies and social change. The various practitioners and scientists engaged in global-change research come from different disciplines, bringing with them the nuances and approaches associated with their respective fields. Consequently, much debate has been aimed at clarifying what users mean by "vulnerability" and, more importantly, "resilience" and/or adaptive capacity, defined as the general ability to adjust to potential damage, to take advantage of opportunities, or to cope with the consequences. Within human dimensions research, vulnerability has been discussed in relation to poverty, risk, coping capacity, adaptability, assets and entitlements, and other features or characteristics of human society. These differences in perspectives have different policy implications. For example, some assessments that use a vulnerability perspective focus on exposure to a stress or event and emphasize the element of risk—vulnerable areas or groups are predisposed to *risk*, broadly defined as the chance of a defined hazard occurring. In the simplest terms, vulnerability is thus considered equal to the risk (potential loss) in relation to the hazard (e.g., drought or flood).

Abilities to cope and adapt are, moreover, influenced by various institutional dimensions or "institutional architecture" that in turn will determine how a group or ecosystem can respond to change. From this perspective, a vulnerability assessment would not only focus on the exposure and sensitivity to a risk or hazard, but it would also integrate approaches from various social science disciplines to explain other factors determining adaptive capacity. We have witnessed, for example, the fallout in safety and security preparedness from the built and social environment perspective following Hurricane Katrina in 2005, although a disaster management strategy was said to be in place. Due in some part to lack of careful thought around the institutional coordination between departments and implementation, the disaster management strategy is generally thought to have failed.

Vulnerability approaches can be used to assess the seven categories of threats that fall under human security needs. Within the context of each category, any assessment must consider the question, "vulnerable to what?"

- Economic security (assured basic income)—vulnerability to global economic changes
- Food security (physical, economic, and social access to food)—vulnerability to extreme events, agricultural changes, etc.

- Health security (relative freedom from disease and infection)—vulnerability to disease
- Environmental security (access to sanitary water supply, clean air, and a non-degraded land system)—vulnerability to pollution and land degradation
- Personal security (security from physical violence and threats)—vulnerability to conflicts, natural hazards, or creeping disasters (e.g., HIV/AIDS)
- Community security (security of cultural integrity)—vulnerability to cultural globalization
- Political security (protection of basic human rights and freedoms)—vulnerability to conflicts and warfare

With all the renewed activity and interest surrounding vulnerability science, one would expect vulnerabilities to decrease, while appropriate interventions to build adaptive capacity would be expected to increase. This, however, does not seem to be the case in many regions. In fact, the incongruity between theory and action elicits the following questions for scientists, researchers, policy makers, and designers to consider:

- How can vulnerability science contribute to a better understanding of complex daily realities?
- Do vulnerability assessments need to pay greater attention to the institutional context within which decisions are made (e.g., issues of social justice) to provide policy makers with a more realistic range of options for reducing vulnerability?
- Do current conceptualizations of vulnerability contribute to "meaningful" enhanced human security, or are they merely a way of categorizing and differentiating the winners and losers under global change?

At the same time as the scientific community moves towards more dynamic, contextual, and complex analyses, the design community also requires quick and effective actions that can reduce vulnerability. For example, campuses across the nation are conducting "An Active Shooter on Campus" scenarios. However in some instances, it has been observed that because of this heightened awareness of possible threat attention, other design- and built-environment strategies and issues are being ignored, or worse misappropriated (such as permanently blackening windows in classrooms, thus restricting access to daylight). While general prescriptions related to mitigating security may serve as a way to reduce vulnerability, concrete actions should also be identified. Given the growing interest and attention to the concept of vulnerability, it is perhaps timely to address the gap between theory and action while designing for security.

One such concrete action approach is the Australian Institute of Criminology report on "Crime Reduction through Product Design" (Lester, 2001). A number of ways in which technology and protective features are integrated into products to reduce their potential of becoming targets of criminal activity, as well as preventing their use as instruments of crime, are highlighted (see Figure 9.8). The term "product" encompasses any physical property and forms of currency, as well as electronic information and computer software, which opens the door to consider built environments in the same category. The product-design innovations in the context of crimes such as theft, fraud, tampering, and graffiti, considers implications of their use, such as user acceptance and crime displacement.

Parallels Related to Sustainability and Security

What is our "**resilience**"? What is our "**adaptive capacity**"? Those two key terms are necessary in the dialogue about any human type of adaptation or adjustment to stress/threat/risk. They are as applicable to the discussion about sustainability, as they are to survival, hunger, safety, or security. Take for example lessons learned from the UK Foresight Sustainable Energy Management and the Built Environment Project as announced in *The Energy Challenge* (DTI, July 2006). The Energy Challenge participants were teamed to suggest possible central questions that the project should address. Some examples of questions that offered the greatest breadth of scope and integrative strategic thinking that have a direct parallel with that of security dialogue were:

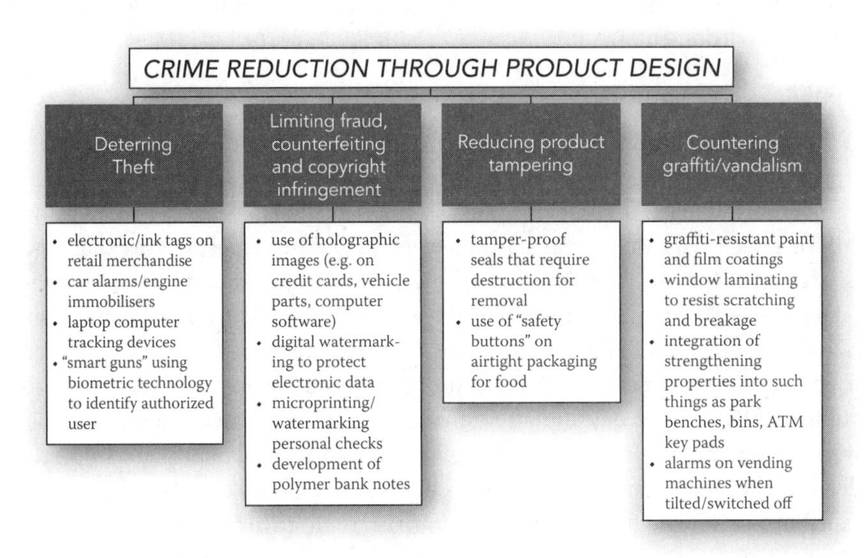

9.8 The key to successful protection is to provide an integrated approach that will not impinge on the stakeholder's experience of the environment.

- How can we deliver a sustainable built environment which sources, manages, and delivers energy, minimizing carbon emissions and maximizing resource efficiency, while delivering the level of service (quality, comfort, reliability, security) required to maintain economic growth and quality of life?
- How do we develop the UK built environment over the next five decades to meet people's energy needs and expectations via sustainable and cost-effective energy services (within the EU and wider international context)?
- In the context of behavioral change caused by technological advances, communication, and limited resources, what are the socioeconomic technological, regulatory, and infrastructure requirements on Sustainable Energy and the Built Environment to meet societal needs 10, 20, or 50 years in the future? (DIUS, 2007)

It is interesting to note from these questions the relationship between energy, the built environment, the economy, and people and how they are viewed as highly interdependent. These suggested questions have helped define the central project question: "To explore how the UK built environment could evolve to help manage the transition over the next five decades to secure sustainable, low-carbon energy systems that meet the needs of society, the requirements of the economy, and the expectation of individuals" (DIUS, 2007). It is important to note that the same issues that impact how sustainability is integrated for future practices are also impacting the dialogue about security. Factors driving change and trends also illustrate more similarities and possibilities for both sustainability and security in the built environment.

What Factors Might Drive Change—Similarities and Differences?

In the UK Foresight Sustainable Energy Management and the Built Environment Project, we were asked to understand how current and future developments in science, technology, and society might impact sustainable energy management and the built environment. Participants were invited to suggest factors that would drive change in these areas. These factors were then grouped under relevant generic headings or clusters. Nearly half of these clusters related to social factors, such as attitudes toward energy management and consumption and shifting patterns of population. Approximately one-fifth of the clusters were political and related mainly to the need to develop an international response to the challenges posed by global warming and energy, and the need for strong political leadership in the UK to ensure that behaviors change. Technological clusters mainly referred to the availability and deployment of technology fixes to improve sustainable energy use. Economic clusters focused on the increase in fuel prices, the cost of global warming, and new business models. Environmental clusters focused on the urban form and existing built environment.

Once again it is important to note that these themes reflect the linkages between people, energy, the built environment, and the economy. In essence, it is hypothesized that society's willingness to invest in the future, public education, and engagement, and creating a sustainable/safe/secure built environment are significant drivers for change in designers' and stakeholders' attitudes about approaching and addressing design security in the built environment. Another example of the connection between sustainability and security is the Genesis Project in the UK. It addresses parallels between sustainability and security in an integrative approach, whereas others may highlight a bunker mentality. Specifically, lessons and best practices can be seen in relation to context, in particular in affording connections between people, place, and other systems that impact the interrelation of the two.

ARCHITECTS AND DESIGNERS SEEK SECURITY GUIDANCE

The experience of Grosvenor Square, UK, with the use of CCTV cameras in a public area and subsequent public reaction to them is only one manifestation of the architectural and urban aspects of the current security climate in London. It demonstrates that decisions taken in the name of security render many of the city's physical, social, economic, and statutory mechanisms unsustainable; that, once taken, they are difficult to reverse; and that they no longer have an affinity with classic architectural practice. A similar scenario occurred when two security cameras had suddenly appeared November 2006 atop Jaume Plensa's brightly lit glass-block towers at Millennium Park in Chicago. The park anchoring the downtown area to Grant Park and the lakefront "became an unlikely battleground in a culture clash over security in post-9/11 America" (Janega, *Chicago Tribune,* 2006). The cameras were part of a $52 million Department of Homeland Security grant given to the Chicago area, and the two cameras in question were two of several installed in Millennium Park. However, while the others were tucked away in the park, the two in question leaned from the tops of the towers on curving arms, where they hung over the JumboTron-sized faces of the art below. In many ways, they were seen as degrading to the spectators' experience, the civic life in the park, and to the artwork upon which they perched.

Designing for people, creating places that are safe and secure must be inspired by empathy and an ethic of social cohesion, and aim to benefit the urban public by contributing to the sustainability and safety of their city and everyday spaces and places. In this light, it is essential to register how changes in our public buildings and spaces are implanting models of control and infringement that may undermine the free civic life, movement, and communication that together compose one of the cornerstones of democracy, and how we as designers have the responsibility and ability to address such complexity.

The practice of design has been affected in other ways as well. A 2003 *Best Practices Bulletin* issued as a joint advisory by the American Institute of Architects, the National Society of Professional Engineers, and the U.S. General Services Administration targeted information management and requests for buildings' floor plans in particular; which is an activity that has been considered routine for design professionals. Design professionals are now specifically asked to exercise reasonable caution and good judgment in reviewing requests for building plans that appear unusual due to characterization of the structures identified in those requests as significant, or if the request is made by people or organizations unknown to them, and to immediately report such requests to the Federal Bureau of Investigations (FBI) (AIA, 2003). This request is significant because it points to yet another layer of engagement in the security dialogue that design professionals need to address.

FYI: **Design and Security.** "Ninety percent of an estimated 3,000 architects who gathered on the Web Nov. 5 [2001] for an interactive seminar on 'anticipating and responding to security threats through building design,' said in a live poll that security planning needs to start at the programming stage, although several questioners expressed frustration at the lack of risk-assessment guidelines available to them for advising their clients."

—Tom Sawyer, McGraw Hill Construction, 2001

CONCLUSION

The universal need for security and safety is not the issue in question, rather, it is how designers can define and conceptualize parameters of the idea, and go about addressing it in the built environment. Theorists and researchers have addressed both the physical and psychological dimensions of security, and attempted to define the conditions necessary to increase safety and minimize crime and violence. Some of the methods advocated raise serious questions regarding issues of inclusiveness, displacement, psychological and social impact, design fit, and intrusion, as well as the sustainability of design solutions.

An integrated, systemic, dynamic, and transformational approach to security in the built environment is central to promoting safe, healthy, and sustainable communities, and living environments. The design community has a compelling window of opportunity for effective and responsive leadership in addressing security in the built environment.

Achieving a positive relationship and integrated solutions for security concerns will greatly depend on our ability to find ways of bringing together those who design spaces, those who secure them, and those who use them. Active participation in the security dialogue, learning from past experiences dealing with security design issues, and a willingness to educate others about the value of the built environment need to be partnered with an understanding of the security measures that can make a significant impact on the health, safety, and welfare of the public. This will assist the design profession in defining, articulating, and designing appropriate solutions for the twenty-first century that create a seamless connection between security and other functional, social, aesthetic, and economic considerations.

Members of the design community can encourage clients to make ethically responsible decisions concerning safety and security, by themselves staying informed about emerging security technology and by devising ways in which that technology can be creatively and unobtrusively incorporated into the built environment. Interior design educators and practitioners serve a valuable role in the integration of design security in the built environment in the twenty-first century. Our ability to influence a solid commitment and multifaceted fundamental understanding of the value of health, safety, and welfare issues as they relate to security in the built environment is unparalleled in the profession. It is imperative that we continue investigating and learning these crucial issues and impart that knowledge to future designers, our clients, and our colleagues.

The significance of assessing not only what security measures in the built environment need to be taken into consideration, but also the impact of these measures on the functionality, meaning, and user perception of those environments must be addressed. An integrative dialogue among design professionals including landscape architects, architects, and interior designers must take place at a level that promotes future-oriented design thinking from all those involved in the creation of the built environment.

KEY CONCEPTS

- The design professional's commitment to protect the health, safety, and welfare of the public can be merged with proactive safety and security perspectives to provide opportunities for fresh and innovative design solutions to the built environments of the twenty-first century.
- The personal and universal iconography of our spaces and places can be affected with the solutions we create as we face new security threats, and the sense of place and place attachment can become victims of ill-conceived or reactive security solutions.
- Designers understand that vital, active places are critical to the health and long-term sustainability of communities. Designers are also cognizant of the role they can play in facilitating and advancing a security plan that is seamless and integrated in the design, construction, and management of the environment.

- Significant lessons from historical precedent and interdisciplinary connections reveal that one size does not fit all in security solutions, and underscores the need for customized and integrated approaches to design and security that are based on site-specific threat assessment and contextual parameters.
- User-Centered Design, security layering, and a systems approach together provide design professionals with ample conceptual tools to investigate and address security and design.
- Situate design solutions in an integrative framework to visualize impact on systematic complements of the problem at hand.
- Parallels and convergence points related to sustainability and security; information technology, biology, and security; and business, human behavior, and security reveal the centrality of interdisciplinary lessons and paradigms on security, design, and the built environment.
- Society's willingness to invest in the future, public education and engagement, and creating a sustainable/safe/secure built environment are significant drivers for change in designers' and stakeholders' attitudes about approaching and addressing design security in the built environment.

ASSIGNMENTS

Following a security-related event (guest lecture, scenario, reading), respond to the following questions reflecting on the time following your reading/guest lecture/visit:

1. Please answer *Always, Sometimes,* or *Never* to the following questions:
   a. Wore a seatbelt in a car.
   b. Wore a helmet when you rode a bicycle, roller blades, skateboard, or scooter.
   c. Helped or reminded your parents/friends/others to replace the batteries in smoke detector.
   d. Planned a fire-escape route for your home?
   e. Decided on a "safe meeting place" with your family?
   f. Obeyed pedestrian safety laws?
   g. Obeyed bicycle safety laws?
2. What did you do immediately following the event?
3. What was the best part of the fire-safety evacuation scenario?
4. Name two things you learned in relation to visibility and natural surveillance.
5. How have your design thinking changed?
6. Please provide any additional comments about your design and security training.

ACTIVITIES

1. Application of the layering/onion metaphor during the design process for a component of a contract project: provide a diagrammatic explanation that illustrates the following: project design goals, security goals, functional goals, sustainability goals, etc., finding points of convergence or divergence among goals and demonstrating the designer's role in making an educated responsive design decision.
2. Discuss ways of encouraging varying degrees of involvement by stakeholders in the project. During the programming phase, model a User-Centered Design process or a participatory design approach; solicit input and identify possible threats and security-related possibilities from diverse perspectives and their impact on the built environment design, use, and management.
3. Envision and document conceptually security within a particular built environment from a system's perspective, identifying the system's components, their overlays, and interrelationships. Engage a scenario-planning exercise to demonstrate how the system attempts to reach its state of equilibrium after the security breach. Discuss parallels in designed environments.

GLOSSARY

ACCESS CONTROL · The use of design, including spatial definition and designation strategies, to deny or increase the effort and risk of entry and detection to offenders.

ADAPTIVE CAPACITY · The general ability to adjust to potential damage, to take advantage of opportunities, or to cope with the consequences; also coined "resiliency."

AFFORDANCES · Term coined by theorist J.J. Gibson in 1979, connecting perception and action in the environment. Affordance translates into possibilities for action as perceived by users of an environment.

ALL-HAZARDS APPROACH · Encompasses natural hazards and man-made threats (criminal, workplace violence, technological accident, terrorism) while dealing with hazards in a more comprehensive manner.

AMBER ALERT · In the United States and Canada, an AMBER Alert is a notification to the public, by various media outlets, of a confirmed child abduction.

ASSET ANALYSIS · Identifies and prioritizes the assets to be protected, including people, operations, information, trade secrets, and property. This analysis should prioritize the assets in order of importance by the ability of an organization to survive should an asset be destroyed or stolen.

BEST PRACTICES · A term that refers to those practices that have produced outstanding results in one situation and that could be adapted to another situation, including formulas and procedures that have proven successful in architectural practice.

BIOTERRORISM · Terrorism by intentional release or dissemination of biological agents (bacteria, viruses, or toxins); these may be in a naturally occurring or in a human-modified form.

BIOMETRICS · The process of making a positive identification through the scanning of a unique body characteristic, such as a fingerprint or the iris of the eye.

CIVIC ARCHITECTURE · Refers to buildings that are necessary for exercising the tasks of the government in a town, city, or country and communicate to the public socially as symbols of civic pride and identity, such as city halls, places of city assemblies, parliament buildings, or court buildings and prisons. The term also refers to buildings financed by the government like schools, libraries, or hospitals.

CLEAR ZONE · Uninterrupted, fan-shaped, or linear distance/area with clear visibility and free from obstacles maintained on both sides of barriers and spatial designations (inside and outside) in order to observe any movement toward protected area.

CLOSED-CIRCUIT TELEVISION (CCTV) · The use of video cameras to transmit a signal to a specific, limited set of monitors. CCTV is often used for surveillance in areas that need monitoring, such as banks, casinos, airports, military installations, and convenience stores.

CPTED 3-D APPROACH ·

Definition—How is the space defined? What are the social, cultural, legal, psychological ways the space is defined?

Designation—What is the purpose or intention that the space is used for?

Design—Is the space defined to support prescribed or intended behaviors?

CRIME PREVENTION THROUGH ENVIRONMENTAL DESIGN (CPTED) · Design concepts based on the theory that criminal and illegal behavior can be influenced by how physical environments are designed and managed. CPTED applies natural, mechanical, and organizational concepts for access control, surveillance, and territorial definition.

CRIME TRIANGLE · The core of environmental criminology theory that brings together victim or target, offender, and place or environment. This analytic tool/concept suggests that those who commit crimes or other undesirable activities with a rational mindset do so on the basis of judging the available opportunity to take advantage of a victim without being caught and/or identified as the perpetrator of the act.

CRITICAL ASSETS · Recognizing certain parts of a nation's infrastructure as critical to its national and economic security and the well-being of its citizenry. Within the built environment it can be viewed as people, products, and/or information that if destroyed would have a debilitating impact.

DEFENSIBLE SPACE · Theory developed in the 1970s by architect and city planner Oscar Newman encompassing ideas about crime prevention and neighborhood safety. Newman's theories focused on ideas on social control, crime prevention, and public health in relation to community design.

DISPLACEMENT · The movement or change of a crime event as a result of some preventive action.

DUTY TO CARE · The legal obligation imposed on an individual or a business requiring adherence to a reasonable standard of care in that business or other operations that could foreseeably harm others, and is enforceable in cases of negligence of liabilities.

EGRESS LOCKDOWN · A system designed to lock and alarm for 15 seconds before allowing an individual to exit. Often used in facilities requiring specialized security measures for occupants with clinical needs, the egress lockdown system is overridden by the fire protection system in the event of fire.

ENVIRONMENTAL/ARCHITECTURAL DETERMINISM • A theoretical approach that sees behaviors as predetermined by the environmental features and whole environment where they occur.

EVACUATION GOALS • Systematic procedures, plans, and targets for occupants' evacuation in cases of risky situations. Seeks to optimize evacuation with the capability of tracing the occupants in every compartment of the facility at every step, and include time for evacuation efforts, crowd movements through the buildings' exits, and speed, crowd-flow patterns under emergency conditions, travel distance and egress routes, and overall performance and safety factors.

EYES ON THE STREET • Term coined by Jane Jacobs, author of *The Death and Life of Great American Cities* (1961). Jacobs believed that the way cities were being designed and built meant that the public would be unable to develop the social framework needed for effective self-policing. She suggested that the lack of "natural guardianship" in the environment promoted crime.

FORCE MAJEURE CLAUSES • *Force majeure* (French for "greater force") is a common clause in contracts which essentially frees one or both parties from liability or obligation when an extraordinary event or circumstance beyond the control of the parties, such as war, strike, riot, crime, an act of God (e.g., flooding, earthquake, volcano), prevents one or both parties from fulfilling their obligations under the contract.

FORCE-PROTECTION • Plans and programs to protect assets within an area of responsibility. Force-Protection conditions are a set of specific security measures promulgated by the commander after considering a variety of factors including the threat level, current events that might increase the risk, observed suspicious activities, etc.

FORTRESS DESIGN • An approach to creating self-contained environments surrounded by strong barriers or walls, and focusing on making the environment or the structure impenetrable, such as a prison, for example.

GSA URGENCY SCORE CRITERIA • Rubric/evaluative criteria including the year a courthouse runs out of space, the number of judges without courtrooms, security concerns, and operational inefficiencies, used to prioritize courthouse/federal building need for modifications or new construction.

HAZMAT • A *hazardous material* (hazmat) that is solid, liquid, or gas that can harm people, other living organisms, property, or the environment. Dangerous goods may be radioactive, flammable, explosive, toxic, corrosive, biohazardous, an oxidizer, an asphyxiant, a pathogen, an allergen, or may have other characteristics that render it hazardous in specific circumstances.

HIERARCHY OF NEEDS • The term coined by psychologist Abraham Maslow that articulated a hierarchy of human needs based on deficiency needs, growth needs, and self-actualization needs.

HISTORICAL PRESERVATION • The act of maintaining and repairing existing historical materials and the retention of a property's form as it has evolved over time.

HISTORICAL RESTORATION • The process of the renewal and refurbishment of the interior and/or exterior fabric of a building.

ICONOGRAPHY • Critical reading and reflection on identification, description, and interpretation of "imagery" in an attempt to explore social, cultural, and political values within a community or society.

INTERAGENCY SECURITY COMMITTEE (ISC) • Created by Executive Order # 12977 in 1995 following the domestic terrorist bombing of the Alfred P. Murrah Federal Building in Oklahoma City, Oklahoma, to address the quality and effectiveness of physical security requirements for federal facilities (3.4 billion square feet of space in 491,465 buildings) that may be vulnerable to acts of terrorism and other forms of violence. Chaired by the GSA Administrator, the ISC was composed of representatives from each of the executive branch agencies, the Office of Management and Budget, the Environmental Protection Agency, and the Central Intelligence Agency. Other members included the Director of United States Marshal Service (USMS); the Assistant Commissioner of the Federal Protective Service (FPS); the Assistant to the President for National Security Affairs; the Director of the Security Policy Board; and other federal officials appointed by the President; and is also authorized to consult with other parties, including the Administrative Office of the US Courts.

INVISIBLE SECURITY • Security measures that are deliberately hidden from view and the public eye.

LOCKDOWN CAPABILITIES • The ability to "lockdown" a room or facilities when under threat.

MAINTENANCE AND BROKEN WINDOW THEORY • Neglected and poorly maintained properties are breeding grounds for criminal activity.

MITIGATE • To make the impact or intensity of a security breach less intense; to intervene in the consequences of an event.

NATURAL ACCESS CONTROL • The capacity to limit who can gain entry to a facility, and how.

NATURAL SURVEILLANCE • The capacity to see what is occurring without having to take special measures to do so.

ONION PHILOSOPHY • A term referring to the "layering" of security design solutions from the exterior to the interior of a building.

ORGANIZATIONAL LAYOUT • The overall underlying structure of organization and planning of a space, an environment, or a strategy, for example; overall zoning schemes, zoned circulation diagrams, or recognized spatial hierarchies could be seen as examples of organizational layout.

ORGANIZED RETAIL CRIME (ORC) · Professional theft rings that move quickly from community to community and across state lines to pilfer large amounts of merchandise that is fenced and sold back into the marketplace. ORC is a growing problem for retailers in the United States.

PARADOX OF SECURITY · Term used by many theoreticians, policy analytics, and writers including Robert Ivy, editor of *Architectural Record* magazine, to signify the seemingly inconsistent and contradictory security-related situations that exist largely because of the dualities and complexities involved in decisions about openness and security, physical and psychological dimensions of security and fear, and addressing threats and perceptions of threats that are continuously evolving and changing.

PLACE-BASED CRIME PREVENTION · Based on CPTED strategies that rely upon the ability to influence offender decisions that precede criminal acts through design and manipulation of a particular contextual parameter or a specific attribute in the environment.

POST-TRAUMATIC STRESS DISORDER (PTSD) · Post-Traumatic Stress Disorder (PTSD) is the term for a severe and ongoing emotional reaction to an extreme psychological trauma. The latter may involve someone's actual death or a threat to a person's or someone else's life, serious physical injury, or threat to physical and/or psychological integrity, to a degree that usual psychological defenses are incapable of coping.

PREMISE LIABILITY · Victims of crime seek compensation from owners and/or managers of properties based on the allegations that the building owner failed to provide adequate security and thereby contributed to the occurrence of the crime. Claims of inadequate security include systemic, organizational, human, and environmental design flaws. Alleges that the crime that occurred was foreseeable and the owner/manager had the legal duty to provide adequate security.

PRESCRIPTIVE SOLUTIONS · Concerned with identifying and linking specific perceived needs with design and management directions, guidelines, injunctions, and solutions that have been tried in similar situations.

PROSPECT-REFUGE MODEL · Jack Nasar and Thomas Fisher's 1993 research/framework related to geography of crime. This approach delineates the relationship between crime triangle components (victim, offender, and place) and the impact on crime occurrence from a perspective of opportunity/prospect (victim—open or closed), offender's concealment (or refuge), and boundedness (mental map and connection to the place where a crime occurs).

PROTECT-IN-PLACE · Protection of occupants in where they are located with less emphasis on occupant egress during a fire or a threat.

PROTECTIVE SECURITY ZONES · An integrated system that incorporates high levels of security while responding to central architectural needs such as human activity, climatic concerns, and structural integrity.

REASONABLE STANDARD • Reasonableness is determined by foreseeability—i.e., what a reasonably prudent person could be expected to foresee as a possible consequence of his or her acts or omissions.

REDUNDANT EMERGENCY UTILITIES • Emergency power systems, which may include lighting, generators, and other apparatuses, to provide backup resources in a crisis or when regular systems fail.

REMOTE SCREENING • Software developed to authenticate clients, as well as restrict the clients' and/or employees' level of access within a built environment.

RESILIENCY • The general ability to adjust to potential damage, to take advantage of opportunities, or to cope with the consequences, also coined "adaptive capacity."

RISK ANALYSIS/RISK ASSESSMENT • Examines the security measures to be taken against identified threats, along with the extent of costs of each measure (monetary and operational). Ultimately, a plan is developed that identifies which level of security will be provided against each threat.

RISK • Broadly defined as the chance of a defined hazard occurring.

SAFE HAVEN/SAFE ROOM • A place guaranteed safe from danger or attack. Used in health-care settings the term describes a designated room that can be locked from the inside, as a place for staff, patients, and even visitors to hide due to an immediate threat of danger.

SAFE/SAFETY • The condition of being safe from undergoing or causing hurt, injury, or loss; free from harm or risk; secure from perceived threat of danger, harm, or loss, affording safety or security from danger, risk, or difficulty.

SCENARIO PLANNING OR SCENARIO THINKING • A strategic systemic thinking and planning method that combines known facts about the future in various systems, elements, or components, with plausible alternative outcomes and drivers of change; to make flexible and dynamic long-term plans. Scenario planning as used in business, design, and organizational change paradigms is an adaptation of a classic technique/method used by military intelligence—the degree of its plausibility and effectiveness is dependent on the information used to build the scenarios and their fit with contextual and systemic definitions.

SECURITY MANAGEMENT PLAN (SPM) • A plan that identifies security threats, possible adverse impacts on stakeholders and property, and proactive approach for protection.

SECURITY POST • Any structure or identified location that houses trained individuals/guards/monitors who provide a first line of observation, access control, and defense.

SECURITY SENSITIVE AREAS • Locations within the built environment that may require unique security protection. Sensitive locations require special training, additional physical protection, and policies or procedures specific to the location identified.

SECURITY • The quality or state of being secure and affording safety; free from risk of loss, danger, fear, or anxiety.

SIGNAGE • A kind of graphics created to display information to a particular audience, typically wayfinding information on streets and outside and inside of buildings.

SITUATIONAL CRIME PREVENTION • Approach that focuses on reducing the opportunity to commit a crime by improving the design (i.e., reducing concealment areas, affording better lighting, employing access controls, etc.) and management of the environment (maintenance, visibility, frequency of use, etc.), simultaneously addressing architectural/environmental and social factors.

SOFT TARGETS • Military term denoting assets (environments, properties, and people) that are not armored, in the built environment the term describes structures and environments that are publically accessible, not guarded or armored.

STANDOFF DISTANCE • The distance/separation between an identified vulnerability/area/structure/asset and a potential source of threat; defended distance between the threat location and the asset to be protected.

STIMULUS-RESPONSE • Environmental psychology theoretical foundation that attributes behaviors in the environment as a reaction to external sensory information.

SURVEILLANCE • The general crime prevention strategy that seeks to decrease crime opportunity by keeping access points, critical environments, and intruders under observation and/or by increasing the perception of the risk of being observed.

SURVIVABILITY • The ability of a system/environment to function and maintain integrity with adaptation following a catastrophic condition, the ability to maintain a degree of functionality, such as in conditions of blackouts and energy failures.

SUSTAINABLE COMMUNITIES INITIATIVE • A UK initiative that utilizes a systems thinking integrated approach; Inspired by CPTED principles and emerged as an alternative vision for governmental policies in countering crime and terrorism. Sustainable communities focus on how a community may succeed economically, socially, and environmentally, and respect the needs of future generations, and are designed places where people feel safe and secure; where crime and disorder, or the fear of crime, does not undermine quality of life or community cohesion.

SUSTAINABLE SECURITY • Any approach to security that is enduring over time and does not affect a person or community's future use of an environment; management of enduring solutions that address and represent adaptability, compatibility, and expandability to crime prevention.

SYSTEMS THINKING OR SYSTEMS APPROACH • A scientific, philosophical, management, and technological approach, which identifies and links common themes and manages complex interrelated entities and elements. A system is a dynamic network of interconnecting elements, as all systems tend toward equilibrium, a change in only one of the elements produces a change in all the others.

TARGET HARDENING · The process of increasing the resistance of a building to the effects of forced entry, attacks, and bombings.

TERRITORIALITY/TERRITORIAL REINFORCEMENT · An environmental-behavior construct, epitomized in studies by Edward T. Hall, of both animal and human behavior; expresses a degree of control exerted over a space, a sense of ownership that triggers mechanisms of defense. Oscar Newman "Defensible Space" theory (1973) utilizes this construct and focuses on the physical environment's capacity, through the design and marking of space, to create in users and residents the sense of *responsibility* for and *control* of that space such that they will protect and defend it, if necessary. In CPTED, territoriality means the capacity to establish authority over an environment, making a statement about who is in charge, who belongs, and who is an outsider.

TERRORISM · The unlawful use of force or violence against people or property to intimidate or coerce a government, a civilian population, or any segment thereof in furtherance of political or social objectives.

THREAT ANALYSIS · Assesses the types of threats that can occur against the organization. These threats can cause harm or death to employees, destruction to property, disclosure of sensitive material, interruption of operations, or denial of services. This analysis also identifies the potential individuals or groups who represent a threat and the level of motivation they might have.

TRANSPARENT DESIGN SOLUTIONS · Solutions that provide security while not visible to the public eye. Transparent design solutions minimize obvious barriers and maximize design excellence.

USER-CENTERED DESIGN (UCD) · Both a philosophy and a process. As a philosophy, it places the person (as opposed to the "thing") at the center; as a process, it focuses on cognitive factors (such as perception, memory, learning, problem solving, etc.)

VISUAL SHIELDING · A form of ballistic threat mitigation strategy and enhancement of protection by providing opaque windows or screening devices to limit visual access of intruders into protected environments.

VULNERABILITY ANALYSIS · Identifies weaknesses that can be exploited or taken advantage of to carry out a threat. This analysis—which includes site topography and facility location on-site, as well as facility security operations and facility hardening—is conducted on either existing site or facility conditions or proposed projects in development.

WAYFINDING · Encompasses all of the ways in which people orient themselves in physical space and navigate from place to place.

WORKPLACE VIOLENCE · Considered any threatening type of behavior that happens in a work environment. This includes shaking fists, throwing objects, or other overt physical acts, as well as any verbal or written threats to cause harm to anyone or anything.

10729658 3

REFERENCES

CHAPTER 1

Alderfer, C. (1972). *Existence, relatedness, & growth*. New York: Free Press.

American Institute of Architects AIA. (2001). Building security through design: A primer for architects, design professionals and their clients. (Booklet).

CPTED—Crime Prevention through Environmental Design. Accessed regularly since 2004 from http://www.cpted-watch.com/.

International CPTED Association ICA. Accessed regularly since 2003 from http://www.CPTED.net.

Karr, K. (Ed.). (2002). *CSO Magazine*. Retrieved December 2006 from http://www.csoonline.com/read/110802/briefing_design.html.

Maslow, A., & Lowery, R. (Ed.). (1998). *Toward a psychology of being (3rd ed)*. New York: Wiley & Sons.

Meyer, M. (2002). *World Workplace*. Emergency preparedness—World workplace proceeding: *corporate workplace planning saves lives—Ten steps to better prepare companies for life safety, evacuation, & disaster recovery*. Retrieved July 2004 from http://www.ifma.org/tools/ep/wwp/saveslives_meyer.cfm.

Nadel, B. (2004). *Building security. Handbook for architectural planning and design*. New York: McGraw Hill.

National Safety Council. Accessed on July 2008 from http://www.nsc.org/news/nr111703.htm.

Smith, L.E. (October 2003). Interior design and the public's welfare. *Interiors & Sources*.

The National Capital Planning Commission (NCPC). Accessed May 2005 from http://www.ncpc.gov/planning_init/security/security.html. (Site accessed February 12, 2008, http://www.ncpc.gov/.)

United Nations. Universal Declaration of Human Rights. Accessed regularly since 2000 from http://www.un.org/Overview/rights.html.

U.S. General Services Administration. Accessed regularly since 2004 from http://www.gsa.gov/Portal/gsa/ep/home.do?tabId=0.

CHAPTER 2

21st Century Libraries: Changing Forms, Changing Futures. A joint initiative between CABE and RIBA. The 2004 Buildingfutures, a joint initiative between CABE and RIBA 21st Century. Retrieved January 2, 2006 from http://www.buildingfutures.org.uk/pdfs/pdffile_31.pdf.

A police executive research forum publication—reporting on innovative approaches to policing. Summer 1993. *Problem solving quarterly*, 6(3). Retrieved July 10, 2007 from http://www.popcenter.org/Library/PSQ/1993/Summer%201993%20Vol%206_No.%203.pdf.

Alexander, C. (1977). *A pattern language: towns, buildings, construction*. New York: Oxford University Press.

American Institute of Architects (AIA). (2001). Building security through design. A primer for architects, design professionals and their clients. (Booklet).

Angel. S. (1968). *Discouraging crime through city planning.* (Unpublished doctoral dissertation. University of California at Berkeley: Institute of Urban and Regional Development).

Bain, W., McConnell, S., & Tully, J. (2004). Rethinking the courthouse from inside out: Designers seek to shine light on the judicial process—with windows. Retrieved January 10, 2006 from http://www.djc.com/news/co/11161363.html.

Bartholomew, R., Richards, L., Jin, B., & Chun, J. (2004). Security solutions: It's time to consider safety alternatives for open-access commercial environments. *Interiors & Sources.*

Bernasco, W. & Luykx, F. (2003). Effects of attractiveness, opportunity, and accessibility to burglars on residential burglary rates of urban neighborhoods. *Criminology,* 41 (3), 981–1002.

Briggs, R. (2002). Corporate security after September 11th. *Global Thinking, The FPC Newsletter.* Retrieved January 10, 2006 from http://fpc.org.uk/articles/165.

Briggs, R. (2005). Invisible security: The impact of counter-terrorism on the built environment. Retrieved January 10, 2006 from http://www.cabe.org.uk/data/pdfs/policy/counter_terrorism.pdf.

Brower, S., Dockett, K., & Taylor, R. (1983). Residents' perceptions of territorial features and perceived local threat. *Environment and Behavior, 15,* 419–437.

Brown, B.B., & Altman, I. (1983). Territoriality, defensible space, and residential burglary: An environmental analysis. *Journal of Environmental Psychology, 3,* 203–220.

Clay, R. (Spring 2005). Integrating security and design. *ASID ICON,* 36–41.

Coaffee, J. (2003). Terrorism, risk and the city: The making of a contemporary urban landscape.

Coaffee, J. (2004). Rings of steel, rings of concrete, and rings of confidence: Designing out terrorism in central London pre- and post-September 11th. *International Journal of Urban and Regional Research, Vol 28.1.*

CPTED—Crime Prevention through Environmental Design. Retrieved from http://www.cpted-watch.com/.

Design Center for CPTED. Vancouver, BC. Retrieved from http://www.designcentreforcpted.org/Pages/Principles.html. Accessed regularly since 2005.

Horne, T. (2001). Indystar (*The Indianapolis Star*); Library Facts, April 15, 2001; Retrieved January 21, 2006 from http://www2.indystar.com/library/factfiles/crime/national/1995/oklahoma_city_bombing/stories/2001_0415.html.

Interagency Security Committee Action Plan — Calendar Years 2007–2008. Office of Security. Department of Homeland Security. Retrieved May 15, 2008 from http://www.dhs.gov/xlibrary/assets/isc_action_plan_2007-2008.pdf.

Jacobs, J. (1961). *The death and life of great American cities.* New York: Random House.

Jeffery, C.R. (1977). *Crime prevention through environmental design.* Beverly Hills, CA: Sage Publications.

Jeffery, C.R. (1990). *Criminology: An interdisciplinary approach.* Englewood Cliffs, NJ: Prentice-Hall.

Jeffrey, C.R. and Zahm, D.L. (1993). Crime prevention through environmental design, opportunity theory and rational choice models. *Routine activity and rational choice: Advances in criminological theory.* Clarke, R.V. & Felson, M. (Eds.) New Brunswick: Transaction Publishers.

Keib, R.E. (Spring 2000). Creating a safe and secure workplace: An achievable goal or wishful thinking? *Property Management Magazine.* Retrieved July 7, 2007 from http://www.greggservices.com/prot_article.shtml.

LaGrange, R., Ferraro, K., and Supancic, M (1992). Perceived risk and fear of crime: Role of social and physical incivilities. *Journal of Research in Crime and Delinquency,* 29, (3), 311–334.

Luedtke, Gerald, and Associates. (1970). Crime and the physical city: Neighborhood design techniques for crime reduction. Washington D.C.: U.S. Department of Justice.

Mautner, M.F. (Ed.). (April 2005). Conference to commemorate the 30th anniversary of the Helsinki Final Act: Democracy and security in the 21st century and the evolving role of regional organizations.. *Proceedings of the Austrian Center for International Studies* in cooperation with the Organization for Security and Cooperation in Europe.

Monroe, L.K. (Ed.). (2006). Transparent security: Security doesn't need to be obtrusive, obvious, or restrictive to be effective. *Buildings*. Retrieved August 17, 2007 *from* http://www.buildings.com/functions/print_article.aspx?contentID=2982.

Murray, C. (1994). The physical environment. *Crime*, 349. Wilson, J.Q. & Petersilia. J., (Eds.) San Francisco, CA: Institute for Contemporary Studies.

Murray, D. (2005). Anger at airport-style security for rail stations. *The Evening Standard*, 2.

Nadel, B. (2006). Security and Religious Facilities: Providing Safety and Sanctuary. *Security News-Buidlings.com* (newsletter), 1, (6).

Nasar, J.L., & Fisher, B.S. (1993). "Hot spots" of fear and crime: A multi-method investigation. *Journal of Environmental Psychology, 13*, 187–206.

National Center for Victims of Crime—Workplace Violence: Employee Information. (1997). Retrieved May 15, 2008 from http://www.ncvc.org/ncvc/main.aspx?dbName=DocumentViewer&DocumentID=32374.

Newman, O. (1972). *Defensible space; Crime prevention through urban design*. New York: Macmillan.

Obey, C. (2007). Perilous parkland: Homeland security and the national parks. (Media Center Fact Sheet). Retrieved July 10, 2007 from http://www.npca.org/media_center/fact_sheets/security.html.

O'Connor, S.D. (2001, October 10). Cited in US Supreme Court Justice O'Connor says "personal freedom" will be curbed. Andrews, J. *World Socialist Web Site—News and Analysis*. Retrieved May 10, 2008 from http://www.wsws.org/articles/2001/oct2001/ocon-o10.shtml.

Office of the Deputy Prime Minister. (2004). Safer places: The planning system and crime prevention. Retrieved January 5, 2006 from http://www.odpm.gov.uk/index.asp?id=1144466.

Peck, Robert (former GSA Commissioner). (2000). *How to turn a place around—A handbook for creating successful public spaces*. Project for Public Spaces.

Phifer, J. *Implications, Vol. 3, Issue 12*. Retrieved September 2008 from http://www.informeddesign.umn.edu.

Queensland Police Service. The state of Queensland government. *Crime triangle*. Retrieved December 20, 2007 from http://www.police.qld.gov.au/Regional+Policing/metroNorth/robbery/triangle.htm.

Robinson, M. (1996). The theoretical development of "CPTED": 25 years of responses to C. Ray Jeffery. Appears in: *Advances in Criminological Theory*, Vol. 8. Retrieved January 3, 2006 from http://www.acs.appstate.edu/dept/ps-cj/vitacpted2.html.

Saville, G. (1998). *New tools to eradicate crime places and crime niches*. Paper presented at the Conference for Safer Communities: Strategic Directions In Urban Planning, Convened Jointly By The Australian Institute Of Criminology And The Victorian Community Council Against Violence, Held in Melbourne, September 10–11, 1998. Retrieved February 2006 from http://www.aic.gov.au/conferences/urban/saville.pdf.

Saville, G. & Cleveland, G. *Second generation CPTED: An antidote to the social Y2K virus of urban design*. Retrieved January 23, 2007 http://www.pac2durham.com/resources/schools.pdf.

Saville, G. & Cleveland, G. (1997). *Second-generation CPTED in schools*. Paper presented at the Second Annual International CPTED Association Conference, Orlando, Florida.

Schieffer, T. (J. Thomas Schieffer, U.S. Ambassador to Australia, 2003). The Menzies Research Center: Security in the 21st century seminar series: Security issues in an emerging world

Schumer, C. (February 14, 2005). On heels of yesterday's mall shooting Schumer renews call on president to re-enact assault weapons ban. (Press release). Retrieved January 20, 2006 from http://schumer.senate.gov/SchumerWebsite/pressroom/press_releases/2005/PR4126.AWB.021405.html.

Secured By Design. UK Police flagship initiative for designing out crime. Retrieved February 2004 from http://www.securedbydesign.com/.

Simons, J., Irwin, D., & Drinnien, B., (1987). *Psychology—The search for understanding*. New York: West Publishing Company.

The National Capital Planning Commission. Retrieved July 2005 from http://www.ncpc.gov/planning_init/security/security.html.

Townsend, M. & Harris, P. (2003). Security role for traffic cameras. *The Observer*. February 9, 2003.

US General Services Administration. Accessed regularly since 2004 from http://www.gsa.gov/Portal/gsa/ep/home.do?tabId=0.

Veness, D. (2005). Lecture highlights for Demos, the unlikely counter-terrorists. February 22, 2005. Retrieved March 2006 from http://www.demos.co.uk.

Viollis, P. Sr. (2002). A wake-up call for not only terrorist threats. *Journal of Organizational Excellence*, 21(3), 25–29. Wiley Periodicals, Inc.

Warr, M. (2000). Fear of crime in the United States: Avenues for research and policy. Retrieved July 7, 2007 from http://www.ncjrs.gov/criminal_justice2000/vol_4/04i.pdf.

Zelinka, A. & Brennan, D. (2001). *Creating Safer, More Livable Communities Through Planning and Design*. APA Planners Press.

CHAPTER 3

American Psychiatric Association. APA help center: Facts and statistics: Stress/APA survey 2004 and 2005. Retrieved on July 10, 2007 from http://www.apahelpcenter.org/articles/topic.

APA Help Center. (2004). Warning signs of youth violence. Retrieved on July 10, 2007 from http://www.apahelpcenter.org/featuredtopics/feature.php/id=38.

APA Help Center. (April 2005). Managing traumatic stress: Tips for recovering from disasters and other traumatic events. Retrieved on July 10, 2007 from http://www.apahelpcenter.org/articles/article.php id 161.

Carney, P. (Summer 1999). School violence: The school setting is only part of the picture. Synopsis.

Cooper, C. (2007). The evolving concept of "court security." *Justice*. National Center for State Courts.

Devan, W. The impact of homeland security on the construction industry. Retrieved on July 8, 2007 from http://www.constructionweblinks.com/Resources/Industry_ReportsNewsletters/June_23_2003/homeland_security.htm.

Federal Aviation Administration. (2001). *Recommended security guidelines for airport planning, design and construction*. Washington DC: Associate Administration for Civil Aviation Security, Office of Civil Aviation Security Policy and Planning, Federal Aviation Administration.

Hockenberry, J. (2006). Fear factor: Designing in a post 9/11 world has forced architects and planners to revisit some basic tenets and belief. Retrieved May 7, 2007 from http://www.businessweek.com/innovate/content/may2006/id20060502_628628.htm.

Horonjeff, R. (1994). *Planning and design of airports*. New York: McGraw-Hill, Inc.

Hyman, S. (January–February 2002). National Institute of Health. The NIH catalyst. Retrieved May 5, 2007 from http://www.nih.gov/catalyst/2002/02.01.01/page4.html.

Jull, S. (2006). Youth violence, schools, and the management question: A discussion of zero tolerance and equity in public schooling. (Doctoral dissertation, Mount Saint Vincent University, 2006.)

Larson, E., Schaffer, M., & Newsome, B. (2004). *Infrastructure, safety, and environment*. Santa Monica, CA: RAND.

McArthur Research Network on Socioeconomic Status and Health (2007).

Mellins, T. (2005–2006). Airport program. Retrieved May 6, 2007 from https://www.acsa-arch.org/images/competitions/airport/2005-06_Airport_Program.pdf.

Moran, L.J., Skeggs, B., Tyrer, P., & Corteen, K. (Summer 2003). The formation of fear in gay space: The "straights" story. Retrieved on July 9, 2007 from http://findarticles.com/p/articles/mi_qa3780/is_200307/ai_n9279519/pg_1.

NIOSH, Occupational violence. CDC/NIOSH. Retrieved on May 4, 2007 from http://www.cdc.gov/niosh/topics/violence.

Norman, D. (2006). Logic verus usage: The case for activity-centered design. Interaction@CACM, 2006.

Schell, T., Chow. B., & Grammich, C. (2003). Designing airports for security: An Analysis of Proposed Changes at LAC. *RAND Issue Paper.* (IP–251). Santa Monica, CA: RAND.

Skeggs, B. Queer as Folk: Producing the Real of Urban Space Urban Studies. *Urban Studies Journal Limited*, 41, (9), 1839–1856.

Stout, C.E. (Ed.). (2004). *Psychology of terrorism.* New York: Praeger Publishers.

Szenasy, S. (April 2006). Fear and loathing at airports: Why not challenge design firms to evaluate our current airport security systems? *Metropolis Magazine*, 22–24.

Talarico, W. (October 2002). Survival Skills. *The Metropolis Observed.*

Talarico, W. (October 2002). Survival skills: A year after her escape from the WTC. *Metropolis Magazine*, 18–20.

Thompson, L. (2000). Saskatchewan School Trustees Association Research Centre. Saskatchewan: Canada, *Canadian Journal of Educational Administration and Policy*, 17.

Watts, M. (February 2007). Be prepared: Successful disaster recovery depends on preventing or limiting the impact of disasters before they occur. *School Planning and Management*, 32–35.

Wein, H. (December 2001). Coping with terrorism. *NIH News on Health.*

World Trade Center Building Code Task Force (WTCBCTF). (2003). Retrieved on May 5, 2007 from http://home2.nyc.gov/html/dob/downloads/pdf/wtcbctf.pdf.

CHAPTER 4

Barker, T. (1994). How to prevent violence in the workplace. *Safety and Health, 15*, 41–45.

Baron, A. & Wheeler, E. (1994). *Violence in our schools, hospitals & public places.* Ventura, CA: Pathfinder.

Bowie, V., Fisher, B., & Cooper, C. (Eds.). (2005). *Workplace violence: Issues, trends, strategies.* Portland, OR: William Publishing.

Bureau of Justice Statistics. (1994). Violence and theft in the workplace. (NCJ Pub. No. 148199). Washington, DC: Department of Justice.

Bureau of Labor Statistics. (1993). *Occupational safety and health reporter,* October 27, 1993.

Cal/OSHA Guidelines for workplace security. Retrieved on July 8, 2007 from http://www.dir.ca.gov/dosh/dosh_publications/worksecurity.html.

Centers for Disease Control and Prevention, Department of Health and Human Services. (October 27, 2006). (BLS press release.) 12/01 NCJ 190076. Retrieved from http://www.ojp.gov/bjs/abstract/vw99.htm.

Centers for Disease Control/NIOSH. (September 1992). Homicide in U. S. workplaces: A strategy for prevention and research.

Craighead, G. (2003). *High-rise security & fire life safety*, Second edition. Woburn, MA: Elsevier Science.

Davidson, M.A. (May 2007). When ex-workers won't stay away. *Security Management*, 16–18.

Di Martino, V. & Chappell, D. (1998). Violence at work, Geneva, Switzerland: International Labour Organization. Retrieved on May 5, 2007 from http://www.occuphealth.fi/NR/rdonlyres/03B804BA-3AE0-451B-9C29-42D005973E61/0/apn.

Fickles, M. (May 2004). Downtown security, uptown technologies. *Security Solutions.* Retrieved on May 5, 2007 from http://securitysolutions.com/mag/security_downtown_security_uptown.

Fireman's Fund Insurance Company. (2007). Novato, CA. Retrieved on February 3. 2007 from http://www.firemansfund.com.

Kinney, J.A. & Johnson, D.L. (1993). Breaking point, the workplace violence epidemic and what to do about it. Chicago, IL: NSWI. National Safety Workplace Institute.

Longmore-Etheridge, A. (February 2007). Nurses on guard. *Security Management,* 12.

National Institute for Occupational Safety and Health (NIOSH). (1992). Homicide in U.S. workplaces: A strategy for prevention and research. Morgantown, WV: NIOSH Division of Safety Research. National Safety Council, Workplace violence, 1993.

National Institute for Occupational Safety and Health. Retrieved on July 9, 2007 from http://www.cdc.gov/niosh/topics/violence/.

NIOSH. (1993). Alert: Request for assistance in preventing homicide in the workplace. (Pub. No. 93-109). Cincinnati, OH: NIOSH. Retrieved July 8, 2007 from http://www.cdc.gov/niosh/violrisk.html.

NIOSH. Violence in the workplace. Retrieved July 8, 2007 from http://www.cdc.gov/niosh/violrisk.html.

Norris, C., & Armstrong, G. (1999). *The maximum surveillance society: The rise of CCTV.* New York, NY: Berg.

Oliver, B.B. (2004). *Managing facility risk, 10 steps to safety,* Washington, DC: Nonprofit Risk Management Centers.

Richardson, S., & Windau, J. (2003). Fatal and nonfatal assaults in the workplace, 1992 to 2001. *Clinics in Occupational and Environmental Medicine,* (No. 3), 673–689. London: Elsevier.

Survey of workplace violence prevention (2005). 2005 Bureau of Labor Statistics, Department of Labor for the National Institute for Occupational Safety and Health.

Suttell, R. (February 2006). Security: A Blueprint for Reducing Risk. *Buildings.* Retrieved on February 3, 2007 from http://www.buildings.com/articles/details.aspx?contentID=2945.

Suttell, R. (February 2006). Security: A Blueprint for Reducing Risk. *Buildings.* Retrieved on May 5, 2007 from http://findarticles.com/p/articles/mi_hb5063/is200602

Thomas, J.L. (1992). CPTED: A response to occupational violent crime. *Professional Safety Journal,* June 1992, 37(b).

U.S. Department of Labor: Occupational Safety & Health Administration. Retrieved on September 2, 2007 from http://www.osha.gov/workplace_violence/wrkplaceViolence.PartIII.html.

Walker, H.M. (1999). Testimony for Oregon Senate Bill 555. Retrieved July 20, 2007 from http://eric.uoregon.edu/trends_issues/safety/testimony.html.

Walton, J.B. (September 1993). Dealing with dangerous employees. *Security Management,* 81–84.

Workplace violence: A prevention program. (December 1994). *Security Management,* Report No. 96-20.

Workplace violence: Protecting employees from customers. (1994). *Security Management,* April 1994 Report No. 96-10.

CHAPTER 5

Advisory Council on Historic Preservation. (1996). National Historic Preservation Act. Retrieved on October 15, 2006 from http://www.achp.gov/NHPA.pdf.

Advisory Council on Historic Preservation: Preserving America's Heritage. (2001). *Designing for security in the nation's capital.* (NCPC report). Retrieved July 12, 2007 from http://www.achp.gov/index.html.

Central Electronic Security, Inc. News. Retrieved on July 10, 2007 from http://www.cesecurity.com/news.cfm.

Conserving Architectural Heritage in a Changing World Monument Fund 2006 Annual Report. Retrieved on July 12, 2007 from http://www.wmf.org/pdf/WMF_2006_Annual_Report.pdf.

Diamonstein-Spielvogel, B. L. (2005). *The landmarks of New York.* New York: The Monacelli Press.

Dickenson, R. (September 26, 1983). *National Preservation Society.* Retrieved on January 15, 2007 from http://www.nps.gov/history/local-law/arch_stnds_10.htm.

Federal Preservation Institute National Park Service. Washington, D.C. (2006). Accessed on October 11, 2006 from http://fpi.historicpreservation.gov/.

Federal Preservation Institute. (2002). Risk preparedness principles. Retrieved October 10, 2006 from http://fpi.historicpreservation.gov/TechnicalInfo/RiskPreparedness/Principles.aspx.

Gwathmey, C. (2005). Architect of the U.S. Mission to the United Nations, New York City, from *Vision + Voice - Design Excellence in Federal Architecture: Building a Legacy.*

Historic Resources Group. (April 5, 2005). *Historic Preservation Element.* City of San Fernando, CA. Retrieved on July 10, 2006 from http://www.ci.sanfernando.ca.us/city_government/departments/comdev/forms_docs/hist_pres_elem_final.pdf.

Nadel, B. (November, 2006). Security and schools: Creating safe educational environments. *Building Design Magazine.* Retrieved on July 2, 2007 from http://www.buildings.com.

National Capital Planning Commission (NCPC). (2002). National capital urban design and security plan. (Released October 2002 and reprinted with Addendum November 2004). Retrieved July 20, 2007 from http://www.ncpc.gov/UserFiles/File/NCUDSPAddendum050505.pdf.

National Trust for Historic Preservation. Accessed on October 16, 2007 at http://www.nationaltrust.org.

NCPC. (2005). National capital urban design and security plan objectives and policies—Adopted May 5, 2005 (PDF). Retrieved July 20, 2007 from http://www.ncpc.gov/UserFiles/File/NCUDSPAddendum050505.pdf.

Park, S.C. & Alderson, C.R. (2004).Historic preservation guidance for security design. In B.A. Nadel (Ed.). *Building security: Handbook for architectural planning and design.* New York: McGraw-Hill.

Sandow, S., Brierton, J. (March, 2000). *Technical Preservation Guideline. Guide 2.1 First Impressions of Historic Buildings.* General Services Administration.

Sentry Security. (2007). *Old buildings shouldn't have antiquated security system.* Retrieved July 15, 2007 from http://www.sentrysecurity.com/news.cfm.

Swett Associates. Accessed on July 8, 2007 at http://www.swettassociates.com.

Swett, R. (2005). *Leadership by Design: Creating an Architectural of Trust,* 284–285. Greenway Communications.

The Secretary of the Interior's Standards and Guidelines for Federal Agency Historic Preservation Programs. (1998). Jointly published by: National Park Service, U.S. Department of the Interior & Advisory Council on Historic Preservation. Retrieved on January 3, 2007 from http://fpi.historicpreservation.gov.

The Statue of Liberty reopens with biometric locker technology that uses fingerprints to ensure safety. Retrieved July 15, 2007 from http://www.findbiometrics.com/Pages/featurearticles/statue-of-liberty.html.

CHAPTER 6

AIA Academy of Architecture for Health. (2006). *Guidelines for design and construction of hospitals and health care facilities.* Washington, DC: The American Institute of Architects.

Aldridge, J. Hospital security: The past, the present, and the future, part 2 of 2. (Healthcare security consultant Jeff Aldridge examines the need of risk assessments and the hospital security management plan.) Retrieved June 10, 2007 from http://www.securityinfowatch.com/article/article.jsp?siteSection=358&id=8928.

Aldridge, J. (September, 2004). Is violence over taking your ED? Hospital security news, 2 (3). Retrieved September, 2006 from http://www.saione.com/Newsletters/HSN/HSN03.pdf.

Aldridge, J., Phillips, J., & LaRoche, G. (2007). *Securing America's hospitals.* (webinar, *August 8, 2007 at 1 P.M. EDT*). Attended August 8, 2007. Archived at https://event.on24.com/eventRegistration/EventLobbyServlet?target=registration.jsp&eventid=65205&sessionid=1&key=802D52D4E18AD20C9B5DBE65E244262A&partnerref=archive&sourcepage=register.

Aldridge, J. & Wells, P. (2005). Infant abduction prevention, part 3: What hospitals should be thinking about as they seek to prevent these crimes. Retrieved August 12, 2007 from http://www.securityinfowatch.com/article/article.jsp?siteSection=357&id=11712.

Architectural Showcases. Morris Hospital, Morris, IL. Design Group Columbus, OH. (September 2006). *Healthcare Design Magazine.* Retrieved September 1, 2006 from http://www.healthcaredesignmagazine.com/ME2/dirmod.asp?sid=9B6FFC446FF7486981EA3C0C3CCE4943&nm=Articles&type=Publishing&mod=Publications%3A%3AArticle&mid=8F3A7027421841978F18BE895F87F791&tier=4&id=ED017537B5114C4A874718BE627AC770.

Carpman, J., Grant, M., & Simmons, D. (2001). *Design that cares: Planning health facilities for patients and visitors*, 2nd ed. New York: John Wiley & Sons, Inc.

Carr, R. (2007). Health care facilities. Retrieved June 20, 2007 from http://www.wbdg.org/design/health_care.php.

Carr, R. (2007). Outpatient clinic. (Last updated March 14, 2007). Retrieved April 25, 2007 from http://www.wbdg.org/design/outpatient.php.

Carter, P.G. (Updated November 28th, 2005). Securing forensic patients in the public hospital setting: Part 1: Creating workable security policies to deal with this 'invisible population'. *SecurityInfoWatch.com.* Retrieved July, 2007 from http://www.securityinfowatch.com/article/article.jsp?siteSection=357&id=6348.

Carter, P.G. (Updated January 31st, 2006). Securing forensic patients in the public hospital setting: Part 2. A look at the guidelines and patient's rights issues when working with this "invisible population." Retrieved July 2008 from http://www.securityinfowatch.com/article/article.jsp?siteSection=357&id=7095.

Erickson, L. & Williams-Evans, S.A. (2000). Attitudes of emergency nurses regarding patient assaults. *Journal of Emergency Nursing* 26, 282–288.

Green guide for health care—A best practices guide for healthy and sustainable building design, construction, and operations for the healthcare industry. Accessed May, 2007 from http://www.gghc.org/.

Facility Guidelines Institute and the AIA Academy of Architecture for Health, with assistance from the U.S. Department of Health and Human Services. (2006). 2006 guidelines for design and construction of health care facilities. Washington, DC.: American Institute of Architects/Facility Guidelines Institute.

Hansen, B. (February 11, 2005). New health care design guidelines emphasize infection control measures. *Austin Business Journal* . Retrieved June 10, 2007 from http://www.bizjournals.com/austin/stories/2005/02/14/focus5.html.

Hardy, O.B. & Lammers, L.P. (1996). *Hospitals, the planning and design process*, 2nd ed. Rockville, Md.: Aspen Publishers.

Hayward, C.(2005). *Healthcare facility planning: Thinking strategically.* Chicago, IL: Health Administration Press and the American College of Healthcare Executives.

Hospitals for a healthy environment. Accessed June 2007 from http://www.h2e-online.org/.

Huddy, J. & Rapp, M.T. (2000). *Emergency department design: A practical guide to planning for the future.* Irving, Texas: ACEP (American College of Emergency Physicians).

JCR launches health and safety design service to develop patient-safe environments. (2008). *HealthCare Design eNews.*

Retrieved February 12, 2008 from http://www.healthcaredesignmagazine.com/ME2/dirmod.asp?sid=&nm=&type=news&mod=News&mid=9A02E3B96F2A415ABC72CB5F516B4C10&tier=3&nid=EBDEF118641E4610A469A6A1C368AF3C.

Joint Commission on Accreditation of Healthcare Organizations resources. (2008). 2008 National patient safety goals. Retrieved January 30, 2008 from http://www.jcrinc.com/fpdf/IT/08%20NPSG%20Brochure-Final.pdf.

John D. and Catherine T. MacArthur Foundation. (2007). Research Network on Socioeconomic Status and Health. Retrieved July, 2007 from http://www.macses.ucsf.edu/Publications/Pubmenu.html.

Kilment, S. (Ed.). (2000). *Building type basics for healthcare facilities.* New York: John Wiley & Sons, Inc.

Leibrock, C. (1999). *Design details for health: Making the most of interior design's healing potential.* New York: John Wiley & Sons, Inc.

Malkin., J. (2002). *Medical and dental space planning,* 3rd ed. New York: John Wiley & Sons, Inc.

Pyrek, K. (April 1, 2003). *Healthcare facilities step up security to combat workplace violence, safety breaches.* Retrieved May, 2008 from http://www.surgicenteronline.com/articles/341feat6.html.

Security Management Online. (2003). *Security Management Magazine.* Accessed July 2008 from http://www.securitymanagement.com/library/Hospital_colling0901.html.

SourceSecurity. (2000–2007). Latest in healthcare: Wesley Medical Centre. (Copyright © Notting Hill Media Limited). Retrieved July, 9, 2007 from http://www.sourcesecurity.com/markets/healthcare/profile/1/wesley-medical-centre.html.

Stephens, J. (2006). *Healthcare Design.* (Magazine). Accessed November 2007 from http://www.healthcaredesignmagazine.com/ME2/Default.asp.

Stephens, J. (June 1, 2006). The Architecture of Healing. The Sambhavna Clinic in Bhopal, India, provides medical care to survivors of the world's worst industrial chemical accident. *Healthcare Design.* Clean Design Supplement. Retrieved July 10, 2007 from http://www.healthcaredesignmagazine.com/ME2/dirmod.asp?sid=&nm=&type=Publishing&mod=Publications%3A%3AArticle&mid=8F3A7027421841978F18BE895F87F791&tier=4&id=A21B2923FC9E44B4BCF3967E58403B3A.

The Joint Commission. Accessed July 20, 2007 and May 2008 from http://www.jointcommission.org/.

US Department of Justice. Bureau of Justice Statistics. (1997). Violence-related injuries treated in hospital emergency departments. (1997 Special report). Retrieved January 10, 2006 from http://www.ojp.usdoj.gov/bjs/pub/pdf/vrithed.pdf.

Watkins, N. & Anthony, K. (November 1, 2007). The design of psychologists' offices: A qualitative evaluation of environment-function fit. *AIA Academy Journal.* Retrieved January 20, 2008 from http://www.aia.org/journal_aah.cfm?pagename=aah_jrnl_20071101_watkins&dspl=1&article=article.

OTHER BENEFICIAL ONLINE RESOURCES ACCESSED FREQUENTLY:

AIA Academy of Architecture for Health (AAH)—Contains AAH newsletters, reports, and other documents related to health care design. Accessed from http://www.aia.org/aah_default.

Health Facilities Management—A monthly journal of the American Hospital Association's Health Forum. It serves the health facility operations, maintenance, construction, and environmental services community. Accessed from http://www.hfmmagazine.com.

Hospitals and Health networks H&HN HospitalConnect.Com.—A monthly journal of the American Hospital Association covering general health care news, with occasional articles on design and construction. Accessed from http://www.hhnmag.com/hhnmag_app/index.jsp

Modern Healthcare—A weekly journal for healthcare executives with frequent articles on design and construction and an annual design awards program. Online archives of articles back to 1994. Accessed from http://www.modernhealthcare.com.

Planetree (2006). Patient Centered Care. Retrieved July, 2007 from http://www.planetree.org/.

Stopford, B.M. RN, Jevitt, L., Ledgerwood, M., Singleton, C., MD, MPH, & Stolmack, M. EMT-P. (2005, August). *Bioterrorism and other public health emergencies tools and models for planning and preparedness. Development of models for emergency preparedness: Personal protective equipment, decontamination, isolation/quarantine, and laboratory capacity.* Prepared for Agency for Healthcare Research and Quality AHRC-USDHHS. Prepared by Science Applications International Corporation—Homeland Security Support Division. (05-0099). Retrieved July, 2007 from http://www.ahrq.gov/research/devmodels/devmodels.pdf.

SecurityInfoWatch.Com. (September 29, 2006). *Arteco finds intelligent video demand within healthcare and senior citizen environments.* Retrieved July, 2007 from http://www.artecous.com/default.asp?V_DOC_ID=969.

SpaceMedGuide—A Space Planning Guide for Healthcare Facilities—a popular planning tool providing state-of-the-art planning methodologies, industry benchmarks, and planning tips. Accessed July 2008 from http://www.spacemedguide.com/.

Smith, R. AIA, ACHA, Hellmuth, O. & Kassabaum, L.P., (Facilitator). (2007, April 3). *Therapeutic Environments.* The Therapeutic Environments Forum, AIA Academy of Architecture for Health. Retrieved July, 2007 from http://www.wbdg.org/resources/therapeutic.php?r=hospital.

United States Department of Health and Human Services. *Centers for Medicaid and Medicare Services.* Accessed regularly since 2006 from http://www.cms.hhs.gov/CFCsAndCOPs/.

CHAPTER 7

A sense of security. *RetailWire.* Accessed February 2007 from http://www.retailwire.com/Discussions/Sngl_Discussion.cfm?doc_ID=12000.

At the frontline: Woodruff Arts Center. (2006). Hospitality & Entertainment. *SecurityInfoWatch.com.* Retrieved March 2007 from http://www.securityinfowatch.com/online/Hospitality—and—Entertainment/At-the-Frontline—Woodruff-Arts-Center-Security-Director-Tim-Giles/9103SIW487.

Balula, L.D. (Fall 2004). Formal and ethical aspects of security in public spaces. (Paper that appears in *Technology and Society* 23(3), pp. 15–16.) Retrieved February 2005 from http://www.pps.org/civic_centers/info/civic_centers_articles/security/.

Block, R. (February 2002). America's malls prepare for the unthinkable. *The Wall Street Journal Online.*

Case studies from the Osborne Design. Retrieved March, 2007 from http://www.osburndesign.com/start_case2.html.

Davis, R., Ortiz, C., Rowe, R., Broz, J., Rigakos, G., & Collins, P. (December 2006). An assessment of the preparedness of large retail malls to prevent and respond to terrorist attack. Document No.: 216641 Washington, DC: Department of Justice.

Electronic Research Collection Department of State Archives (2007). Kidnapping survival guidelines. Retrieved July 15, 2007 from http://dosfan.lib.uic.edu/ERC/travel/security/security_kidnapping.html.

Ellison, J., Frey, C., & Chansanchai, A. (November 21, 2005). Shooting at Tacoma Mall leaves 7 injured: Man fires on shoppers, takes hostages, then gives up. Retrieved December 12, 2005 from *SeatlPI.Com* from http://seattlepi.nwsource.com/local/249155_shooting21.html.

General Services Administration First Impressions Program. Accessed regularly since 2004 from http://www.gsa.gov/Portal/gsa/

ep/channelView.do?pageTypeId=8195&channelPage=%252Fep%252Fchannel%252FgsaOverview.jsp&channelId=-14001.

Hajer, M. (October 2002). The new urban landscapes (2) *OpenDemocracy*. Retrieved from http://www.opendemocracy.net.

LaTourrette, T., Howell, D.R., Mosher, D.E., & MacDonald, J. (2006). Reducing terrorism risk at shopping centers: An analysis of potential security options. (Homeland Security program within RAND Infrastructure, Safety, and Environment (ISE)).

Liddy, T. & Luckner, C. (August 31, 2007). Body in hotel stirs fear. *NY Post.*. Retrieved September 5, 2007 from http://www.nypost.com/seven/08312007/news/regional news/body_in_hotel_stirs_fear.htm.

Lindbergh & Associates. (2001). National Symposium of Comprehensive Force Protection, Society of American Military Engineers (SAME), Charleston, SC, October 2001. Accessed from http://www.lindbergh-assoc.com/documents/2006/9/12/Lind_antiterr2.pdf.

Misonzhnik, E. (August 9, 2005). Safe and sound. Retrieved March 7, 2007 from http://www.realestatejournal.com/propertyreport/retail/20050809-block.html.

Mui Y.Q. (January 3, 2007). From monitoring teens to minding terrorists. Mall security guards to receive new training, but feasibility is questioned. *The Washington Pos*, p. D01. Retrieved July 2008 from http://www.washingtonpost.com/wp-dyn/content/article/2007/01/02/AR2007010201094.html.

Misonzhnik, E. (March 1, 2007). Safe and Sound. Retail Traffic. Penton Media Publication: Retail Traffic. Retrieved July, 2007 from http://retailtrafficmag.com/management/retail_safe_sound/.

Nemeth, J. (Fall 2004). Redefining security in public space: The case of LOVE Park. *IEEE Technology and Society Magazine*, 23(3). Retrieved August, 2006 from http://www.ushistory.org/lovepark/news/ieee2004.htm.

Newman, O. (April, 1996). *Creating defensible space*. Washington, DC: US Department of Housing and Urban Development.

Overseas Security Advisory Council (OSAC). In *Personal security guidelines for the American business traveler overseas*. Hostage survival, Hijacking survival guidelines, Kidnapping survival guidelines, 37–43 (Material originally found prior to being archived at OSAC).

Palgrave Macmillan Security Journal. Retrieved July 2008 from http://palgrave-journals.com/sj/journal/v20/n1/full/8350037a.html.

Petersen, J.W. (2006). London's security architecture: the end of the sustainable city? Retrieved September 9, 2007 from http://www.opendemocracy.net/conflict-terrorism/security_architecture_3714.jsp.

Project for Public Spaces. (2007). Retrieved July 2007 from *RetailWire*. (December 6, 2007). Massacre puts focus on mall security measures. Retrieved from http://www.retailwire.com/Discussions/Sngl_Discussion.cfm/11591.

Rybczynski, W. (June 1, 2005). The Fear Factor: The fallacies of making Ground Zero more "secure". Slate architecture: What we build. Retrieved November, 2005 from http://www.slate.com/id/2119857/.

Schwartz, P. (2006). The art of the long view: Planning for the future in an uncertain world. *Doubleday Business*. Reprint edition. (April 15, 1996).

Security Design: Achieving Transparency in Civic Architecture. (2003). Panelists: Nadel, B., Feiner, E., Mayne, T., Predock, A. & Safdie, M. *The 2003 AIA National Convention*. Retrieved May, 2007 from https://www.aia.org/caj_art_securitydesign.

Security Magazine & The Security Group. (1999). Security @ the millennium. (A white paper presentation). Retrieved January 2005 from http://www.securitymagazine.com/CDA/HTML/ec8ea5af49ab8010VgnVCM100000f932a8c0.

Securityinforwatch.com. (2007). Securing the Hard Rock Cafe. Retrieved March 2007 from http://www.securityinfowatch.com/online/Hospitality-and-Entertainment/Securing-The-Hard-Rock-Cafe/11047SIW487.

Simpson, M. (2005). Anthrax-contaminated facilities: Preparations and a standard for remediation. Congressional Research Service. Washington DC.: Library of Congress.

Siikonen, M., Bärlund, K., & Kontturi, R. (2003). *Transportation Design for Building Evacuation.* (1) KONE Corporation.

Smith, S. (Analyst in American National Government—Government and Finance Division). (April 22, 2005). *The Interagency Security Committee and Security Standards for Federal Buildings.* (RS22121). Retrieved November, 2005 from http://www.fas.org/sgp/crs/homesec/RS22121.pdf.

Till, J., (June 2006). The architect and the other (2). *OpenDemocracy.* Retrieved Sept 9, 2007 from http://www.opendemocracy.net.

U.S. Department of Justice, U.S. Marshals Service. (June 28, 1995). *Vulnerability Assessment of Federal Facilities*, 1, 1.

Wakefield, A. (2003). *Selling security: The private policing of public space.* Cullompton: Willan Publishing.

Wakefield, A. (2006). The security officer. In Gill, M. (Ed.) *The handbook of security.* Basingstoke: Palgrave Macmillan.

Wakefield, A. (2007). The study and practice of security: Today and tomorrow. *Security Journal* (2007) 20, 13–14. Doi:10.1057/palgrave.sj.8350037. Department of Sociology, City University, London, U.K.

Wakefield, A. & Gill, M. When security fails: The impact of human factors on the deployment of retail security personnel. *Security Journal.* ISSN: 0955-1662. Retrieved from http://www.palgrave-journals.com/sj/journal/v20/n1/full/8350037a.html.

WBDG Safe Committee (2007). Provide security for building occupants and assets. Retrieved December 2007 from: http://www.wbdg.org/design/provide_security.php.

Weizman, E. (April–May 2002). The politics of verticality (2)—an eleven-part series. *OpenDemocracy.* Retrieved July 2008 from http://www.opendemocracy.net.

Weizman, E. (September 2003). Ariel Sharon and the geometry of occupation (2)—a three-part series. *OpenDemocracy.* Retrieved from http://www.opendemocracy.net.

Wilson, J.Q. & Kelling, G.E. (1982). Broken windows: The police and neighborhood safety. *Atlantic Monthly*, March 1982, 29–37.

CHAPTER 8

Associated Press. (November 20, 2006). Gunman wounds 8 in German school attack. Retrieved on June 22, 2007 from http://www.msnbc.msn.com/id/15812606/.

CBC. (2006). School shooting at Dawson College, Montreal, Canada. Retrieved July 10, 2007 from http://www.cbc.ca/canada/story/2006/09/14/gunman-shooting.html.

Child Care Lounge. (2007). Retrieved July 7, 2007 from http://www.childcarelounge.com/Parents/questions.

Columbine Report. (2000). Retrieved on February 7, 2006 from http://www.cnn.com/SPECIALS/2000/columbine.cd/frameset.exclude.html.

Cornell, D.G. (1999). House Judiciary Committee/Oversight Hearing to Examine Youth Culture and Violence and Psychology of School Shootings. School of Education. University of Virginia May 13, 1999.

Crime prevention through environmental design program. (1994). Pepperdine University, Malibu, CA: National School Safety Center.

Crowe, T.D. (Fall 1990). Designing safer schools. *School Safety,* pp. 9–13. Encino, CA: National School Safety Center.

Day-care centers increasingly concerned with security. Retrieved July 18, 2007 from http://www.sun-sentinel.com/news/local/broward/sflflbdaycarenbaug.

Dinkes, R., Cataldi, E.F., Kena, G., & Baum, K. (2006). *Indicators of school crime and safety: 2006* (NCES 2007–003/NCJ 214262). Washington, DC: U.S. Departments of Education and Justice.

Dwyer, K.P., et al. (1998). *Early warning, timely response: A guide to safe schools.* Washington, DC: United States Department of Education.

Elliott, D.S., Hamburg, B.A.,& Williams, K. R. (1998). Violence in American schools: An overview. In D.S. Elliott, B.A. Hamburg, and K.R. Williams (Eds.), *Violence in American schools,* 3–28. New York, NY: Cambridge University Press.

Gaustad, J., et al. (November 1999). Building security into schools/fundamentals of school security. *ERIC Digest* 132—1999.

Hamby, J.V. (1999). *Developing a comprehensive violence prevention plan: A practical guide.* Clemson, South Carolina: National Dropout Prevention Center.

Henry, S. (2000). What is school violence? An integrated definition. *Annals of the American Academy of Political and Social Science*, 567, 16–29.

Kinercky, E., (2007). SecuritySystems.com Care centers look to security. Retrieved on July 8, 2008 from http://securitysolutions.com/news/day-care-security/.

Lackney, J. (2001). Classrooms of the future: thinking out of the box. Retrieved July 12, 2007 from ERIC.

Lowry, R. (March 1995). *Educational Psychology Review*, Vol. 7, (1), 12–18.

Nadel, B. (March 1998). Security has become a top priority in building design. *Building Design Magazine*, 1998, 28–29.

National Center for Education Statistics. (March 1998). *Violence and discipline problems in U.S public schools: 1996–97.* Retrieved June 7, 2007 from http://www.nssc1.org.

National Crime and Justice Reference Service. Accessed July 14, 2007 from http://www.ncjrs.gov/spotlight/school_safety/Summary.html12.

National School Safety Center. (1990). *School safety check book: School climate and discipline, school attendance, personal safety, school security model programs.* Malibu, CA: Pepperdine University.

Schneider, T., Walker, H.M., & Sprague, J.R. (2000). *Safe school design: A handbook for educational leaders applying the principles of crime prevention through environmental design.* Eugene, OR: University of Oregon, ERIC Clearinghouse on Educational Management.

Suttell, R. (February 2006). Security: A Blueprint for Reducing Risk. *Buildings.* Retrieved on February 3, 2007 from http://www.buildings.com/articles/details.aspx?contentID=2945.

Trump, K.S. (May–June 1999). Scared or prepared? Reducing risk with school security assessments. *The High School Magazine* 6(7), pp. 18–23.

U.S. Department of Education, National Center for Education Statistics. (2006). *Digest of education statistics, 2005* (NCES 2006-030). Washington, DC: U.S. Government Printing Office.

CHAPTER 9

AIA Best Practices. (2003). Information management: Security of building plans. The American Institute of Architects. *Best Practices Bulletin* 13.02.01.

Aluminum extruders council (AEC). (2005). High-rise building the "green" way is transforming Chicago's skyline. *AEC showcase.* Retrieved March 2006 from http://www.aec.org/assets/pdfs/GreenBuilding Showcase8.pdf.

Design Center for CPTED. Vancouver, BC. Accessed regularly since 2005 from http://www.designcentreforcpted.org/Pages/Principles.html.

DTI. (July 2006). *The energy challenge.* Accessed August 2006 from http://www.berr.gov.uk/files/file25079.pdf.

Hecht, P. & Wener, R. (January 10, 1994). Environment-behavior issues in festival & event planning. NIC Research in Brief.

International CPTED Association ICA. Accessed regularly since 2003 from http://www.CPTED.net.

Janega, J. (December 20, 2006). Artworks stand alone as cameras lose perch. *Chicago Tribune.* Retrieved July 2008 from http://www.chicagotribune.com/.

Jordan Wu, Senior in Landscape Architecture, University of Idaho; Master Plan for the University of Idaho Sandpoint Campus, Senior Studio: LArc 456. Stephen Drown, Professor.

Lester, A. (2001). Crime Reduction through Product Design. *Trends and Issues in Crime and Criminal Justice*. (No. 206). Canberra: Australian Institute of Criminology. Retrieved September, 2007 from http://www.aic.gov.au/publications/tandi/tandi206.html.

Lewis, R. (July 19, 2007). Expert opinion into security. (Personal interview). Coeur d'Alene, Idaho.

Lorenz, B. (January 2007). High rises: The next generation debuts. High-profile high-rises show the influence of 9/11—and the growing shift to sustainability. Building Operating Management, Facilities net. Retrieved September 2007 from http://www.facilitiesnet.com/bom/article.asp?id=5898&keywords=high%20rise%20design.

Novitski, B.J. (2007). Building as teaching tool—Intimate and flexible learning environments within a larger footprint encourage creativity and collaboration, among both teachers and students. *Schools of the 21st Century—Architectural Record* The McGraw-Hill companies. Retrieved January 2008 from http://archrecord.construction.com/schools/071213-SCH_FOS.asp.

Russell, J., Bershad, D., Felicella, E., Kelly, M., & Kennedy, E. March 2002 *Designing for security: Using art and design to improve security.* New York: Design Trust for Public Space and the Art Commission of the City of New York. Retrieved October 2007 from http://www.designtrust.org/publications/publication_97security.html.

Sawyer, T. Architects seek security guidance. (enr.com 11/7/01). *Business News. McGraw Hill Construction.Com* Retrieved March 2006 from http://www.construction.com/NewsCenter/Headlines/ENR/20011113b.asp.

UK Government Office for Science, Department for Innovation, Universities and Skills (DIUS). (2007). Foresight sustainable energy management and the built environment project: Report of scoping workshops. *The Energy Challenge*. Retrieved February 20, 2007 from http://www.foresight.gov.uk/Energy/Reports/Scoping_Workshop/Index.html.

UK Government Office for Science, Department for Innovation, Universities and Skills (DIUS). (October 2006–present). Sustainable energy management and the built environment. Retrieved February 20, 2007 from http://www.foresight.gov.uk/Energy/Energy.html.

Walonick, D. General systems theory. Retrieved September 30, 2007 from http://www.survey-software-solutions.com/walonick/systems-theory.htm.

Wu, J. & Drown, S. (2007). *Master Plan for the University of Idaho Sandpoint Campus, Landscape Architecture Senior Studio Service Learning and Outreach Project.* University of Idaho.

410729 65 83

CREDITS

CHAPTER 1

1.1 AP Photo
1.2a © Robert Reis/Alamy
1.2b © Lynsey Addario/Corbis
1.3 Courtesy of Rula Awwad-Rafferty
1.5 Courtesy of Rula Awwad-Rafferty
1.7a © isifa Image Service s.r.o./Alamy
1.8 © Bernard O'Kane/Alamy
1.11 AFP/Getty Images

CHAPTER 2

2.2 © david sanger photography/Alamy
2.3 Courtesy of Fairchild Publications, Inc.
2.5 Courtesy of Fairchild Publications, Inc.
2.8 Courtesy of Haymills
2.9 © Kevin Foy/Alamy
2.10 Courtesy of Ken Worpole

CHAPTER 3

3.1 AFP/Getty Images
3.2 AP Photo
3.3 Courtesy of Fairchild Publications, Inc.
3.4 © Shannon Stapleton/Reuters
3.5 Courtesy of Fairchild Publications, Inc.
3.7 Courtesy of Fairchild Publications, Inc.
3.10 Courtesy of Fairchild Publications, Inc.
3.11 Courtesy of Fairchild Publications, Inc.
3.12 Courtesy of Fairchild Publications, Inc.
3.13 © Tim Parker
3.14 © Stock Connection Blue/Alamy

CHAPTER 4

4.1 © Mike Baldwin/Cornered
4.2 Tim Boyle/Getty Images
4.5 © Aardvark/Alamy
4.6 Courtesy of Fairchild Publications, Inc.
4.7 AP Photo
4.8a © Jim Havey/Alamy
4.9 © Andrew Holt/Alamy

CHAPTER 5

5.1 Courtesy of Fairchild Publications, Inc.
5.2 Courtesy of Fairchild Publications, Inc.
5.3 © Ilene MacDonald/Alamy
5.4 Courtesy of ABMC
5.5 © JUPITERIMAGES/Thinkstock/Alamy
5.6 AP Photo
5.7 Spencer Platt/Getty Images
5.9 Courtesy of NCPC
5.10 AP Photo

CHAPTER 6

6.1a © Eastland Photo/Alamy
6.3a Courtesy of Fairchild Publications, Inc.
6.3c © Corbis Super RF/Alamy
6.5a © Stock Connection Distribution/Alamy
6.5b © Robert Stainforth/Alamy
6.5c © Mira/Alamy
6.6 © 2008 RTKL.com/David Whitcomb
6.8 Courtesy of Loyola University Medical Center Ronald McDonald Children's Hospital
6.10 © ER Productions/CORBIS
6.11 Courtesy of the St. Charles Medical Center

CHAPTER 7

7.1 © Frank Vetere/Alamy
7.3 © Anthony Dunn/Alamy
7.4 © Roger Ressmeyer/CORBIS
7.5 Courtesy of Hanna Persson, Bioregional Planning and Community Design graduate student, University of Idaho, in partnership with Stites community members
7.6 © Brendan McDermid/Reuters
7.7 AP Photo
7.8a © Paul Souders/Corbis
7.8b © Paul Gadd/Corbis
7.9 AP Photo
7.10 Photographer's Choice/Getty Images

CHAPTER 8

8.1a Cliff Grassmick/Getty Images
8.1b Kevin Moloney/Getty Images
8.2a © JUPITERIMAGES/BananaStock/Alamy
8.2b Courtesy of Fairchild Publications, Inc.
8.3 Courtesy of Fairchild Publications, Inc.
8.5 Courtesy of Fairchild Publications, Inc.
8.7 AP Photo
8.9 Blend Images/Getty Images
8.10 Corbis
8.11 © James Steinkamp/Steinkamp-James Ballogg Photography
8.12 © James Steinkamp/Steinkamp-James Ballogg Photography
8.13 © James Steinkamp/Steinkamp-James Ballogg Photography

CHAPTER 9

9.1 © Patrick Chappatte/The International Herald Tribune
9.2 Courtesy of Rula Awwad-Rafferty
9.3a National Geographic/Getty Images
9.7 Courtesy of Rula Awwad-Rafferty

COLOR INSERT

Page 1
(*clockwise from top left*) © 2008 RTKL.com/David Whitcomb; Courtesy of Fairchild Publications, Inc.; Courtesy of Loyola University Medical Center Ronald McDonald Children's Hospital; Courtesy of Fairchild Publications, Inc.; Courtesy of Fairchild Publications, Inc.

Page 2
(*top*) © James Steinkamp/Steinkamp-James Ballogg Photography

Page 3
Courtesy of Fairchild Publications, Inc.

Page 4
(*top*) Courtesy of Fairchild Publications, Inc.; (*bottom*) Courtesy of Fairchild Publications, Inc.

Page 5
Courtesy of Fairchild Publications, Inc.

Page 6
(*top*) Courtesy of Fairchild Publications, Inc.; (*bottom*) Courtesy of Fairchild Publications, Inc.

Page 7
Courtesy of Fairchild Publications, Inc.

Page 8
(*top*) Courtesy of Loyola University Medical Center Ronald McDonald Children's Hospital; (*middle*) © 2008 RTKL.com/David Whitcomb; (*bottom*) © 2008 RTKL.com/David Whitcomb

1072965583

INDEX